THE MONEY PLOT

ALSO BY FREDERICK KAUFMAN

Bet the Farm: How Food Stopped Being Food

A Short History of the American Stomach

THE MONEY PLOT

A History of Currency's Power to Enchant,
Control, and Manipulate

FREDERICK KAUFMAN

Other Press ▪▪ New York

Billie Eilish epigraph from "everything I wanted," by Billie Eilish
O'Connell and Finneas Baird O'Connell. Lyrics copyright © 2019 by
Kobalt Music Publishing Ltd, Universal Music Publishing Group.

Production editor: Yvonne E. Cárdenas
Text designer: Julie Fry
This book was set in Freight Text with Alternate Gothic
 by Alpha Design & Composition of Pittsfield, NH.

10 9 8 7 6 5 4 3 2 1

Library of Congress Cataloging-in-Publication Data
Names: Kaufman, Frederick, 1961– author.
Title: The money plot : a history of currency's power to enchant,
     control, and manipulate / Frederick Kaufman.
Description: New York : Other Press, 2020. | Includes bibliographical
     references.
Identifiers: LCCN 2020010462 (print) | LCCN 2020010463 (ebook) |
     ISBN 9781590517185 (hardcover) | ISBN 9781590517192 (ebook)
Subjects: LCSH: Money — History. | Banks and banking — History. |
     Commerce — History. | Precious metals. | Bitcoin.
Classification: LCC HG221 .K2925 2020 (print) | LCC HG221 (ebook) |
     DDC 332.4/9 — dc23
LC record available at https://lccn.loc.gov/2020010462
LC ebook record available at https://lccn.loc.gov/2020010463

for

Patty Laxton

Money is a kind of poetry.

— WALLACE STEVENS

I had a dream
I got everything I wanted.

— BILLIE EILISH

contents

I / SMALL MONEY

BEHIND THE CURTAIN

THIS BOOK TRACES the history of two activities we generally consider to be different—exchanging money and telling stories—to show how they are the same. Chapters follow parallels in the growth and development of each. Thus we have the money plot, at the core of which resides the most compelling symbol ever created.

This book does not ask whether we should love or hate or even need money. The question is: What drives our belief in this thing called money? The answer has to do with the nature of symbols, and why humans thirst for them.

When economist John Maynard Keynes declared in his 1924 *Tract on Monetary Reform* that money based upon gold was a "barbarous relic," he was arguing that gold was simply one possible manifestation of a substance that required no specific shape. Gold was a symbol, and as such could be replaced by a variety of other symbols. The form that money assumed was accidental. Money not made of gold was still money.

The symbolic nature of money—that is, the fact that money can inhabit any number of material configurations and remain money—was itself not part of the Keynesian theory. But without Keynes' embrace of money as a symbol there could have been no theory, much less Keynesian practices such as deficit spending, whereby a sovereign state may pay for anything it wants or needs with money it prints, money that symbolizes no more and no less than its own sovereign power. A dollar, for example, embodies nothing but the "full faith and credit" of the United States. Thus is a dollar symbolic.

When it comes to money, symbols are useful. That is why Keynes was not alone among economists. If they had ever met, Adam Smith and Karl Marx would have soon discovered that when it came to theories of prices, costs, wages, and profits, they disagreed. But, along with Keynes, both would have readily consented to the fact that even as money possessed an extraordinarily practical capacity to influence a wide variety of very real, nonmetaphorical things, money itself was metaphorical. Money's influence and the effects of its dominion may have been disputed, but there was no debating the fact that a dollar or a pound or a mark were placeholders, symbolic building blocks for what the great economists believed to be much larger concerns. Those larger concerns became the business of illustrious economic schools of thought that arose in the wake of Smith's ideas about free markets and Marx's ideas about class struggle and proletarian revolution.

Of course, it is perfectly understandable that the economists who came up with the most enduring and influential theories were not always as interested in studying the symbolic core of their systems as they were in its pervasive effects. Perhaps because so many economic subjects have been so bitterly disputed, the artifice that lies at the bottom of them all has been lost in the shuffle. The following pages turn the tables. Instead of surveying the far-reaching implications of this or that school of economic thought, this book will prioritize the symbolic bedrock.

Which is most definitely not to say that this book emerged without the influence of economic thought. The approach deployed throughout is in many ways indebted to the cultural insights of the Hungarian economic historian Karl Polanyi, who in 1944 — the year the Bretton Woods Agreement made the United States dollar the world's preeminent currency—published a book called *The Great Transformation*, followed thirteen years later by *Trade and Market in the Early Empires*, written with a group of colleagues and followers. In these books, Polanyi drew on cross-cultural anthropology to investigate the history of economies that had thrived before there were markets as we have come to know them, finding that something very much like money had existed long before coin and bill.

What we call money, what we consider finance, and whatever theory we propose about the economic system as a whole—all of these reflect our moment in time. Which is another way of saying that money conforms to the fictions of the age, whether those fictions go by the name myth, religion, historical narrative, literary masterpiece, or digital meme. For an economic philosophy, just like a social, political, or religious philosophy, can hold sway only as long as we believe the story it tells. A dollar without full faith and credit is a failed dollar. Another way of putting it is that the history of money, while closely related to the history of economics, is not the same thing. The history of money is a history of symbols, while the history of economics is a history of what we can do and have done with those symbols.

A symbol lies behind economics. But what lies behind the symbol? Since the moment someone declared that a bead was part of a story about something more than a bead, and the bead subsequently transformed in the listener's imagination from dross material to an amulet imbued with spirit and value, it has been the person who created, explained, and promulgated the symbol—that is, the storyteller—who has directed the show. The man who defines the meaning of the symbol is the man behind the curtain. Today, that curtain may be a digital firewall behind which lie the untold opulence of Amazon and Facebook, it may be the unbreakable code of a cryptocurrency, or the hopelessly baroque protocols of an index fund behind which reside retirement funds worth trillions. It may be the closed-door ruminations of the Federal Open Market Committee of the Federal Reserve as central bankers decide interest rates on billions of United States Treasury bills, or how to inject trillions into an economic system in need of support. The goal of this book is to pull back the curtain, crack open the doors, decrypt the encryptions, and lay bare the bones of the stories and storytellers that lie at the foundation of the symbol system known as money.

Over the past several millennia a great deal of human desire has been embedded within money—be the currency an armband fashioned from polished shells, an overflowing silo of wheat, a herd of goats, a bevy of concubines, an electronic hoard of Bitcoin, or the United States dollar. And just as striking as the extraordinary mutability of money has been the fact that certain basic human desires abide no matter what social, political, religious, or economic system may prevail. And human desire, which the American poet Wallace Stevens once called "the motive for metaphor," knows no economic school.

{1} THE SHELL GAME

To determine what a five-franc piece is worth one must therefore know:
(1) that it can be exchanged for a fixed quantity of a different thing,
e.g. bread; and (2) that it can be compared with a similar value of the
same system, e.g. a one-franc piece, or with coins of another system
(a dollar, etc.). In the same way a word can be exchanged for something
dissimilar, an idea; besides, it can be compared with something of the
same nature, another word.

— FERDINAND DE SAUSSURE

Capital is not a scandal to be denounced ... but a challenge to take up
according to symbolic law.

— JEAN BAUDRILLARD

WORDS ARE WHAT THEY AREN'T. The word "tree," for example, has virtually nothing in common with that massive amalgamation of roots, branches, and leaves. Words don't reflect reality so much as they reduce it to a more manageable, human scale. They give us a measure of control, and on this fundamental level the motive for turning the world into words coincides with the motive for turning the world into money.

About 65,000 years ago, *Homo sapiens* created the bead. The earliest were excavated in the 1980s along the coastal hinterlands of Kenya. Each measured half the circumference of a penny, and the parallel lines, dots, and hash marks that adorned them led archeologists to suspect they must have communicated an important message. They conjecture that the cave dwellers who made and marked them believed the beads possessed secret powers, so that those who wore them next to their bodies might not only gain status among their peers, but might decrease their exposure to risk and increase their good fortune.

The technical word used to describe such beads is *apotropaic*, which indicates a magic figure or incantation meant to avert evil. The word descends from the Greek word for turning toward or away from something else — *trópos* — which is also the root of the word *trophy* and for figures of speech such as *metaphor*, which in their own way turn one thing into another. That is why metaphors are also known as *tropes*.

Money averts evil. It decreases our exposure to risk. It keeps us clothed, sheltered, and safe. Not only does money deliver rank and standing, it is a way to guarantee that our hard-earned status will continue into the future. This is why anthropologists concluded that those first beads were elements of a much more complicated story than ornamentation. They were a form of risk aversion, an early model of insurance.

The epicenter of the first great financial crisis of the twenty-first century was a failure of much more modern risk aversion mechanisms. The crisis had bubbled up not from panic in the stock market nor a loss of faith in bonds, not from an insolvent bank nor surging gold nor tanking oil nor amber waves of rotting grain. The crisis had emerged from a maze of wagers and counter-wagers about the future, bets bundled within a multinational Goliath — an insurance company. It was the imminent collapse of AIG that sparked global waves of fear and dread about everybody's money.

Money has long been synonymous with anxieties about the future, and insurance has been a traditional way to manage the angst. Before there was the Dow and NASDAQ, before there were silver groats and bronze denarii, before there was a bustling slave trade and an active foreign exchange market in the ports of Benin, before the itinerant merchants of medieval Europe set up shop in one Champagne fair after another, and before there was canoe trade up and down the Rhine, the Thames, and the thousand islands of Melanesia—that is, back in the epic old days of archaic prehistory when it was man versus everything else in the world—there was insurance, and it could be strung around your neck.

Unlike modern insurance products, bead insurance was perhaps more spiritual than statistical. The world was never a safe place, and amulets and ornaments such as armbands and collars suggest narratives in which charmed objects protect and strengthen those they adorned. Such emblems and tokens were typical trappings of mythical figures as they floated across oceans and dueled on battlefields, from the impregnable armor of Achilles to the mail shirt of Beowulf. Caps of invisibility are common accoutrements, alongside a variety of musical instruments, from the lyre of Orpheus to Gabriel's horn. Merlin and Prospero had their staffs, Hercules and Thor their clubs, Eros his bow, Aphrodite her girdle. Such items come in handy when heroes traverse the land of shadows and other fraught landscapes—be the physical form of the talisman a ring, a flaming sword, the tooth of an ancestor, a relic of the true cross, gold coins struck with the profile of a river god, an electronic code that secures a proprietary pathway through the internet, or a necklace strung with beads.

All of which is to say that even if the prehistoric beads from the coastal hinterlands of Kenya possessed many key attributes of money, they did not conform in every way to the modern definition.

They were not stores of value, media of exchange, or units of account in the way we think about such things. They were not the same sort of money as the money that populates classical economics. They were more deeply embedded in our imaginations and psyches than that.

The most famous classical economist is the Scottish philosopher Adam Smith. In 1776 he published his masterpiece, *The Wealth of Nations*. As the American colonists were declaring their independence from England and trying to figure out how their new country might create currency from scratch, Smith suggested an origin story for all money—a distinctly non-magical, non-metaphorical, non-spiritual, and non-literary story. He did not declare that pounds and francs had been anchored in beads or rings endowed with the power to ward off evil. Instead, he supposed that the first money emerged as a shortcut to truck, barter, and exchange—"the principle which gives occasion to the division of labor," and consequently drives mankind.

According to Smith, before the revolutionary conveniences of coin and credit, a primitive potato farmer might have had to lug twenty sacks of fingerlings and russets around town in order to trade his sole unit of value and medium of exchange for the cooking oil, firewood, and cast iron pan required to make himself a batch of home fries. Smith speculated that such extreme inconvenience led to the creation of the ingenious, beneficial, time- and labor-saving device known as money. To the late eighteenth-century mind swimming in a rising tide of manufacturing, markets, and self-interested shopkeepers, Smith's theory made a great deal of sense, and over the years the idea that money evolved from barter gained wide popular acceptance. Unfortunately, Smith's theory has never been bolstered by a shred of evidence, as no example of a pre-currency barter economy has ever been discovered anywhere on earth.

Quite the opposite, in fact. The late nineteenth-century anthropologists and ethnographers who left the research university behind in order to conduct field studies among what were then perceived to be the "primitive tribes" of Africa, Asia, Australia, and Oceania reported at length about the role that symbolic media played in a wide and complex variety of rites, rituals, ordeals, and ceremonial sequences such as exorcisms, gift giving, inheritances, marriages, oath-taking, punishments, ransoms, rewards, entry fees for secret societies, and as payments for corpses on their journey to the land of the dead. If the first anthropologists who set foot on the shores of New Guinea thought they were going to discover bilateral exchanges of, say, candle wax for cassava or a dog for ten pairs of slippers, they were likely surprised to discover an economy of bones, seeds, shells, skins, and polished rocks that appeared to possess symbolic value akin to crowns, pesos, and shekels. Money—or something that acted very much like it—had been around long before markets.

This prehistoric presence of money may help explain why barter economies have only been found in post-currency environments, in which the concept of symbolic equivalencies and exchange has already been well established. Barter economies are economies not of first but of last resort, such as wartime economies in which currencies have become virtually worthless and scarcity of food and basic supplies become the rule, or prison economies with their highly constricted trade in candy, cigarettes, drugs, and weapons.

Truck, barter, and exchange could not elucidate the non-market money systems that late nineteenth- and early twentieth-century European ethnographers and anthropologists discovered among non-European indigenous groups. Nor could it explain why the hunter-gatherers of neolithic Kenya created those first beads etched with perplexing signs and symbols that predate written alphabets by tens of thousands of years.

One clue about the meaning and origin of those beads emerged from a chemical analysis, which revealed that their mineralogical makeup—almost entirely calcium carbonate—was identical to that of the shells of the largest birds on earth, the black-necked African ostrich. Before they were beads, the beads had been ostrich eggs! Which presented yet another mystery: Why expend so much time and energy sanding, drilling, and polishing the shattered fragments of an ostrich egg? No doubt, ostrich meat, ostrich leather, and ostrich feathers were more valuable than the shells. Why were these broken chips of calcium chosen among all other materials to ward off evil and promote good fortune? How did their shape (a small circle with a hole in the middle) come to be replicated around the world, from the first copper coins of Asia to the wampum of the Americas?

Archeological evidence further indicated that beads were not the only thing these neolithic people were making out of their ostrich eggs. If kept intact, each enormous egg could hold more than a quart and a half of liquid, as the hard, non-reactive calcium carbonate crusts had an average thickness of two millimeters. Before they were fashioned into beads, the ostrich eggs had been used as containers. That which could hold something valuable—rainwater, nuts, berries, or whatever else someone might have kept in an empty ostrich egg—had been transformed into something valuable in and of itself. The material which could serve as an insurance policy against hunger and thirst—the storage container—had been fragmented into an amulet that could mitigate all perils and hazards. That which could contain water or berries in order to alleviate the specific risks of thirst or hunger had transformed into a symbolic remedy for risk in general.

Karl Marx famously defined money as "the general equivalent," and on this point the capitalists agree. Traders, financiers, and other adepts of monetary mutability can transform their money into any currency they wish, not to mention a commodity like grain or heating oil, which can in turn translate back into money. Moreover, money can compensate for a wide variety of damages and protect from all manner of liability. Money is so generally able to replace one thing by another and change one thing into another that *change* is another word for money.

By the end of the twentieth century, some of the most technically advanced quantitative adepts of mathematical finance had taken money's shape-shifting ability to an extreme. They realized that they could use the tools of calculus and statistics to capture shifting *feelings* about money. Like ostrich eggs that could contain grain or water, the formulae of the so-called mathematical "quants" captured emotional states that could drive a market up or down, as investors either bought with confidence or sold out of fear. And, much like beads, these mathematical measures of confidence and panic would eventually be priced and traded themselves.

Still, a basic question about those ostrich eggs remained unexamined: What was the process whereby the *container* of material value could assume the value of the material it contained? How did an ostrich egg, which could hold food and drink, become modern money, which can hold just about anything? In short, how was money born?

The answer goes to the heart of *Homo sapiens'* essential nature, for in its uncanny ability to turn a physical into a mental construct and transform specifics into generalities, money mimics language.

The idea that money and language might somehow inform and define one another is hardly new. The great Roman *grammaticus* Quintilian instructed his students to "treat language as currency minted with the public stamp," while the French language emphasizes the monetary-linguistic bond in that there is no difference between the words for *treasury* and *thesaurus* — the hoard of money and the hoard of words. The eighteenth-century economist Anne Robert Jacques Turgot asserted that money "is a type of language," while his contemporary, the German philosopher Johann Hamann, suggested more deeply philosophical sympathies: "The theory of one explains the theory of the other." When scholars singled out the study of signs as an independent science known as semiotics, they appropriated the ancient Greek word *seme*, which means both "word" and "coin."

Bankers and economists are well aware that money possesses the power to transfer its form into any shape, but they are reluctant to follow this to its logical conclusion: In order to understand how anything and everything receives its universal equivalency — that is, its price — they must understand the nature of metaphor.

No doubt, this is because bankers and economists, along with many others, think of metaphors as literary flights of fancy: "my love is like a red, red, rose," or "all the world's a stage." But as the twentieth century has limped into the twenty-first, the issue of money's latent artificiality — its status as a symbol, or, as English professors say, an "imaginary" — has begun to draw attention to itself as never before, and not necessarily for the best reasons.

The global value of counterfeit goods and currencies surpasses three trillion dollars while the value of sovereign debt is three hundred times as much (although both numbers change so fast it's a crapshoot to specify). International currency manipulation has become common practice from Norway to Singapore. Repeated cycles of monetary doomsday visit the eurozone, Peru, and Venezuela. And the astonishing rise of the hedge fund in the first decade of this century has made it impossible to avoid the conclusion that the profits of the financial sector are increasingly unattached to any real value added to the economy.

The Wall Street debacle of 1987, the East Asian crisis of 1994, the flash crash of 2010, the commodity bubbles and economic recessions of 2008 and 2011, and the monumental market swings that marked the pandemic panic of 2020 have magnified the perception of money's propensity towards dissolution. Suspicion has mounted alongside global outbreaks of crypto-viral extortion, the obliteration of corporate firewalls, wholesale data theft, inundations of phishing scams, malware, ransomware, the toxic assets of zombie banks, and the so-called global scam economy. Trillions of dollars can be made to appear by an act of Congress, despite the fact that for years previous American economists, politicians, and media periodically reminded us that the cost of social programs, disaster relief, and the defense budget would surely break the bank. In the wake of the coronavirus contagion, proto-Nazi conspiracy theories of international banking cabals resurfaced on Facebook and Instagram, asserting that the infectious agent that can replicate within a host organism was not only a protein with malignant RNA, but money itself.

Add to this the growing popularity of the once unthinkable idea that a policy of free money for all might constitute not only good government, but also responsible fiscal policy—to the extent that from the outset of the economic turmoil of 2020, the greatest capitalists of all, the purveyors of private equity, were pleading for their share of the $377 billion small-business loan bailout that formed part of the Coronavirus Aid, Relief, and Economic Security Act. A series of trillion-dollar emissions from the Federal Reserve have served as an exclamation point for the first two decades of the twenty-first century, which witnessed an abiding and widespread re-evaluation of the value, if not the essential nature, of money. Yet another glaring example has been the rise of private currencies, artisanal currencies, and more than two thousand digital currencies, which now range from CannabisCoin (for pot) to Dentacoin (for dentists) to Whoppercoin (for buying Burger King in Russia), to Bitcoin, Ethereum, and Ripple, which possess a combined market capitalization that exceeds a quarter of a trillion dollars. And that's just the beginning. New currencies will soon be launched by industry behemoths Facebook, Google, Bank of America, and hosts of others, while the Treasury Department ponders plans to release a next-wave "digital dollar."

Not only does money possess the power to transform everything on earth into a price, but money itself is in the midst of a massive transformation. And that is why an understanding of the processes that facilitated the transfiguration of shattered eggshell fragments into prehistoric money has become more relevant than ever. One might go so far as to say that the future of money depends upon our understanding of its past.

Consider this series of observations about "primitive" shell money, made by Alfred Kroeber, who received the first doctorate in anthropology awarded by Columbia University in 1901. After graduation, Kroeber went on to publish more than five hundred articles and books, including a thousand-page *Handbook of the Indians of California*, which first appeared in print in 1925. This was a particularly impressive and thorough doorstop of a tome, with chapters on the ceremonies, customs, languages, and geographical spread of hundreds of indigenous groups — from the Mojave desert people of the south who planted crops in the floodplain of the Colorado River to the redwood forest people of the north, who pitched their tents in the frigid foothills of Mount Shasta.

Among the populations Kroeber studied were the Yurok, who lived near the Pacific coast in wood plank houses and exchanged as their currency the tusk-shaped shells of the scaphopod mollusk. These shellfish, which conceal themselves within the muddy bed of the salmon-rich Klamath river, could be unearthed from their hiding spots in the silt and fashioned into money the Yurok called *terk-term*, and which Kroeber referred to as *dentalia*. The currency had excellent exchange value, as a single 27-inch strand could purchase a dugout canoe. According to Kroeber, the Yurok

> are firmly convinced that persistent thinking about money will bring it... As a man climbs the hill to gather sweat-house wood...he puts his mind on dentalia. He makes himself see them along the trail or hanging from fir trees eating the leaves... In the sweat-house he looks until he sees more money-shells perhaps peering at him through the door. When he goes down to the river he stares into it and at last may discern a shell as large as a salmon... Saying a thing with sufficient intensity and frequency was a means towards bringing it about. A man often kept calling "I want to be rich" or "I wish dentalia" perhaps weeping at the same time... The practical efficacy of the custom is unquestionable.

To conjure money by thinking about money, to will yourself to see it hanging from the trees and floating in the river, to summon it by repeating its name, to deploy for dentalia's sake the ardent protocols of prayer and devotion, to remain in a constant state of concentration all for the sake of shells — such apparently baffling actions are commonplace to the modern banker, who as a general rule subscribes to a philosophy articulated by the twentieth-century German historian, Oswald Spengler: "Thinking in money generates money." Acquiring dentalia by thinking about dentalia was to the Yurok the obvious way to wealth. And even Alfred Kroeber had to conclude: "The practical efficacy of the custom is unquestionable."

Like the purveyors of Bitcoin and other next-wave alt-assets, the Yurok were thoroughly convinced that one's store of dentalia could increase and multiply as the result of a mental sequence, a set of concentrated and repeated algorithms. But unlike those who worship at the altar of cryptocurrency, the algorithm of the Yurok was not mathematical. It consisted of spoken words in the form of incantation and invocation — all for the sake of projecting one's desire onto the world in order to make it real. The result of this near-maniacal imagination of money was that everywhere he looked, the Yurok would eventually see dentalia staring back at him. This practice, too, is more commonplace than it might appear: To the real estate agent, an apartment looks like its rent and commission. To the mining magnate, a mountain looks like its copper or its gold. To the farmer, the field of wheat is cash. To the economist, everything in the world is yoked to price. Which is to say that money humanizes the non-human world.

The ancestors of our treasury secretaries and finance ministers were not abacus-toting accountants, but storytellers and spiritualists. They were poets who cast their words, spells, and songs into the spirit of a rock, a piece of wood, an eggshell, a seashell. The objects they possessed might thenceforward act as insurance, warding off evil and guaranteeing good fortune. The objects became metaphors for human desire. That was the first money.

When we project our aspiration for money onto the world and nature, the world mirrors money back at us. As previously noted, miners and farmers are familiar with this process, but so are the writers, poets, and other specialists in the forms and techniques of metaphor. The process of giving an animal or an object a voice, face, or other human attribute is known as personification, a word that descends from the classical Greek rhetorical term, *prosopopoeia*. Homer's epithet for the morning, "rosy-fingered Dawn," may be the most famous example of this ancient figure of speech, as the break of day has neither hand nor fingers.

The study of personification—that is, the study of the humanization of the non-human world—forms a part of the larger study of metaphor, which in turn forms a part of the larger study of rhetoric, which is one of the oldest continuing academic disciplines. The inventor of the field was an orator and vegetarian named Empedocles, who lived on Sicily's southwest shore in the fifth century BC. Empedocles' approach to language influenced his only pupil whose name has withstood the passage of time, a diplomat named Gorgias.

As luck would have it, Gorgias' work as head of a foreign embassy in Sicily led him to ancient Athens, which was at that point one of the best spots on earth to promote new branches of learning. In Athens, it soon became evident that given any topic whatsoever, Gorgias could convince anyone of anything. The men of the agora were impressed with him, and asked the diplomat to instruct them in his art of twisting our impressions of reality by means of words that laced one idea after another based on nothing but their internal logic and order. Perhaps they were also intrigued by the fact that unlike many of his ancient contemporaries, Gorgias did not bother to espouse virtue. Instead, he preached what he called "the totalizing power of language," the power of rhetoric to transform anything into anything else. Gorgias became so wealthy he commissioned a statue of himself made of gold. His followers were legion. They were known as the Sophists.

Perhaps it is no coincidence that the first rigorous and technical analysis of metaphor became popular in the ancient Peloponnese right around the time of the first appearance of what would become the most widespread and powerful metaphor of all time, namely precious metal coinage. No doubt, personification, one of the many subspecies of metaphor Gorgias taught, is crucial to understanding not only coins, with their "heads" and "tails," but a great deal of the apparent weirdness of so-called primitive money.

Money personifies the non-human world. The *kris* iron axe money of Borneo may be possessed by a human spirit to the extent that during a wedding it can stand in for the groom. Indonesian folktales recount how the two-foot tall jar money of certain tribes can run, sing, speak, marry humans, and produce baby jars. Franz Boas, the father of American anthropology, observed that each piece of Kwakiutl copper money from the Pacific Northwest possessed both a face and a name. He described one coin called *Maxtsolem*, which, roughly translated, means "all other coppers are ashamed to look at it." The most literal, if gruesome, example may be the skulls once exchanged as currency in New Guinea, Borneo, and the Philippines.

The reverberations of metal gong money once common throughout Melanesia, Tibet, and Vietnam were believed to be the voices of approving gods and spirits, and the bells and cymbals were deemed valuable according to their sonic strength and tenor. What might be called the "moneyness" of money was a human attribute projected onto these bells, cymbals, and gongs, their "voices" belatedly ascribed to the gods (who were themselves, arguably, yet another personification). Before money was embodied by grain, livestock, crude oil, gold, or paper, money possessed that most disembodied of human attributes: a voice.

This particular personification of money — that it could speak — would endure, not only in the cliché "money talks," but also in a short-lived literary genre popular in the eighteenth century, in which people wrote stories from the point of view of currencies, from shillings to rupees. The genre included such works as *Chrysal; or, The Adventures of a Guinea*, published in 1760, and *The Adventures of a Bank-Note*, which appeared in print ten years later, along with scores of other currency confessionals. The most famous example may be Laurence Oliphant's *The Autobiography of a Joint-Stock*

Company which appeared in an 1876 edition of *Blackwood's Edinburgh Magazine*. "In a few days my brief and stormy career will finally close," rued the equity.

> It was not my own fault that, like those who first hatched me, I was conceived in sin and shapen in iniquity, and became almost immediately the means of demoralising every one who came into contact with me, of deceiving those who trusted in me, and of crushing those who opposed me, until my own turn came and I fizzled out in a gutter of fraud.

Oliphant had personified money for the sake of social criticism. Likewise had sixteenth-century Dutch paintings depicted the money queen *Regina Pecunia*, and her chariot pulled by figures representing danger, fear, robbery, foolishness, envy, lust, and theft. In Germany, money was personified by the figure *Fräulein Geld*, and "Lady Credit" was a common figure in eighteenth-century British periodicals, famously portrayed by the novelist Daniel Defoe as a "coy virgin," a "strumpet," and a whore. But there was nothing metaphorical about the consequences of such metaphors. When Queen Victoria died, coins stamped with her profile were referred to by many English merchants as "dead money," and refused as currency.

If modern Americans believe they are beyond the "primitive" hocus-pocus of personification, why do we embrace currency with the faces of Benjamin Franklin, Ulysses S. Grant, Alexander Hamilton, Thomas Jefferson, Abraham Lincoln, Franklin D. Roosevelt, and George Washington, but have second thoughts about printing bills that feature Harriet Tubman? Why, when given the opportunity to circulate Susan B. Anthony dollars (almost 900 million of which were struck between 1979 and 1980) and Sacagewea dollars (more than 500 million of which were struck between 2000 and 2001), did we relegate them to collectors' curiosities, effectively negating their cash value? Clearly, money's voice—and gender—remains essential to its worth.

And while the greatest classical economist of them all, Adam Smith, may have been wrong about the origins of money in truck and barter, he was right when it came to metaphor. He invented what may be the most enduring of money's personifications: the invisible hand. Like bell, bone, tooth, and skull money, Adam Smith's imaginary hand is disembodied flesh haunted by a spirit. Yet the invisible hand has held a place of honor in the staid and sober science of economics for more than two hundred years, providing yet another illustration of the fact that bankers are just as poetic as the poets, so enamored are they with their metaphors. Like cash-drunk acolytes of Dionysus, the magnates of hedge funds and private equity have convinced themselves of the truth of their fiction. They ardently profess faith as all-encompassing as the Yurok's self-fulfilling prophecies of dentalia, namely their belief in a living, breathing, independent, homeostatic market. Not only do they believe the invisible hand is real, they devote their lives and livelihoods to Smith's two-hundred-fifty-year-old fiction.

The English professors, on the other hand, know a metaphor when they see one. From their perspective, the invisible hand of the market is equally as fanciful as an ostrich egg bead possessed by a supernatural contagion of containment. Moreover, they know that hands and invisibility both possess distinguished symbolic pedigrees. Invisibility is one of the oldest and most traditional of tropes, often alluding to the invisibility of the future, which the ancient Roman philosopher Lucretius noted consists of "forces hidden from our sight." Of course, forces hidden from our sight are precisely the forces economic forecasters are paid to see, and insurance is supposed to cover.

The tragedians of ancient Greece would have recognized the invisible hand as an appendage of the Moirai, the three sisters of fate who assign everyone their share of the future—the so-called *moiety*, a word that would itself eventually become crucial in the legal language of inheritance, property rights, and corporate shareholding. Invisibility, it turns out, is one of the enduring and essential characteristics of money, for less than 10 percent of the world's money exists in visible form, namely cash. The rest is nowhere to be found, except as a number that may occasionally flash on a screen then disappear into the void, a metaphor that requires no physical counterpart.

The invisibility of money is not confined to the digital universe. In ancient days, money's invisibility was even more obvious: gold and silver were hidden beneath the earth. But without an understanding of the metaphorical processes that underpin the substance, money can be invisible even when one stares it in the face.

For decades, economic historians did not know what to make of the most common and simple forms of "primitive" money, none of which was more widespread than the cowrie. These snail shells, technically known as *Cypraea moneta*, were plentiful as the sands and good as gold from Micronesia to ancient California. In Polynesia, they were called *tabu*—a word that in English came to mean a substance brimming with hidden and holy meanings. Yet to the European observer, they appeared worthless. They could not see the moneyness of the money. Nor did they recognize that the occlusion of sight they were experiencing—the fact that money's immaterial nature had been quite literally contained within a shell, and thus concealed—was itself a sign of something intrinsic to money.

Circular, punctured in the center, polished to a glossy smoothness, the shells were often mistaken for glass beads. Discovered among the ruins of settlements near the Red Sea and the Nile Valley, they may have been used as currency as far back as ancient Egypt. Some specimens discovered by archeologists date back even farther, all the way to the Stone Age, suggesting that people were considering the world in what some might consider proto-economic terms thousands of years before the first seed was planted, the first cow milked, the first ziggurat constructed, the first coin minted, the first paper money printed, or the first public offering of shares in a stock or debt in a bond.

The bankers of Bengal built storage houses for their cowries, which they stuffed into enormous palm leaf bags, each with a capacity of 12,000. In Nigeria and the Maldives, the shells were arbitraged by the million for precious metal. As recently as 1896 in Togoland, four thousand snail shells were equivalent to a German gold mark.

The polished snail shell was arguably the world's first global reserve currency, and if the nineteenth-century anthropologists were dumbfounded, they were also intrigued. They brought so many different examples home from the field that "ethno-conchology" emerged as a stand-alone field of academic inquiry, inspiring monographs and treatises. Among the wealth of observations, the Oxford anthropologist Rodney Needham noted that in Uganda, Bantu wise men held cowrie shells in their left hands while prophesying the future. Other reports indicated that throughout Micronesia the cowries were deployed in games of chance in much the same way as poker chips — that is, they were the central figures in primitive asset allocation rituals designed to divine whether or not the future would conform to prediction.

As arbiters of fate, as early artifacts of actuarial science, and as shimmering aggregates that could be stored for future needs and expenditures, the cowries had cash value. Yet the shells caused endless confusion among western ethnographers, as the primitive gambling chips and forecasting tools undermined a great deal of received wisdom about the nature of money—namely, that money is logical, sober, scientific, and above all, that money has nothing whatsoever to do with primeval superstition, pagan idolatry, magic spells, and a half-naked tribe's fantastic fables about fate.

What may be the most famous case of money blindness dates back to the first decades of the twentieth century, when a European philosopher and anthropologist named Bronisław Malinowski traveled to Melanesia to investigate what he called the "imponderabilia of actual life." The professor pitched a tent among the thatch huts of a group who called themselves Boyowas. He toiled alongside them as they constructed clumsy canoes destined to carry the bravest and strongest of their sailors on a perilous journey to the blue silhouettes that marked the ends of the earth. Those were the islands on the eastern border of New Guinea, where the Boyowas planned to conduct a ritual they called *kula* with the Motuans and Papuans. Dr. Malinowski was fascinated, as he was led to believe that the rites and observances of kula would reveal the Melanesian "magic of plenty." Malinowski, who had come from Europe on the brink of World War I, could not wait to witness kula.

The Boyowas, like hundreds of other groups across the boundless expanses of Oceania, were capable of sailing their rafts and outriggers thousands of miles over the open sea. They traveled from New Guinea to Indonesia, the Philippines, Borneo, Fiji, Vietnam, Samoa, Taiwan, the Celebes, the Bismarcks, Timor, Tonga, Sumatra, the Malay peninsula, the Solomon archipelago, and the thousand other atolls, islands, and islets inhabited by tribes and tribelets too numerous to name. Their incessant movement over the ocean gave the island people a chance to exchange material technologies such as pottery, weapons, and canoe design, in addition to consumable commodities such as vegetables, pigs, and dogs.

The so-called magic of plenty emerged as a product of travel and trade among the islands. Sometimes the argonauts of the South Pacific rowed their outriggers in great swaths of clockwise motion, at other times counterclockwise, and a full kula ring could take up to ten years to complete. The story Malinowski watched unfold was as epic as Homer's *Odyssey*. It was, perhaps, the most complex set of ritual transactions ever observed. And yet there was no truck, no barter, no bargaining, no haggling, and no market in the way we understand such things.

Kula, as Malinowski observed, concerned the exchange of red shell necklaces for white shell armbands on one island, which were in turn exchanged for another collection of red shell necklaces on another island, which were subsequently exchanged for an altogether different collection of white shell armbands on yet another island, after which came the long trek home. It was a complicated sequence, and when Malinowski witnessed the end of the story, he was struck by the circularity of the red-for-white-for-red-for-white-shell exchange. Why, he asked, "would men risk life and limb to travel across huge expanses of dangerous ocean to give away what appear to be worthless trinkets?"

In Melanesia, Malinowski had discovered a system that revolved around objects that looked like they might be money and acted as if they could have been money, yet like other ethnologists who recorded the strange uses of the snail shell, the clam shell, and the mussel, Malinowski could not see their value. The polished ovals appeared to be economic except for the fact that no one lost or gained anything other than sets of virtually identical polished ovals.

Malinowski's confusion only increased as it dawned on him that every necklace, armband, and nose ring could have been pieced together on the island native to the Boyowas, thereby precluding

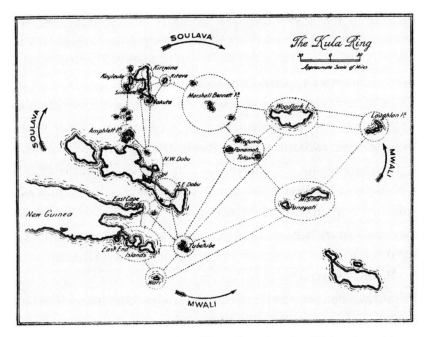

The kula ring. Bronisław Malinowski could map the trajectories of Melanesian outriggers, but he could not see the money.

the need to fell massive trees, hollow out graceless canoes, cast convoluted magic spells, invoke the ghosts of ancestors, row until exhaustion, and risk being inundated by the merciless waves of the South Pacific. Such extraordinary exertions, Malinowski was told time and again, advanced and enhanced kula.

What appeared to the anthropologists and ethnologists to be interchangeable trinkets appeared to the kula trader as something entirely different. They were proof of his good management of a malign universe. They were his return on investment, his cash under the mattress, the payoff on his bet. They demonstrated that within a sea of risk, he had successfully allocated his assets. Modern money has its roots in such symbolic assurances. Today's banker may feel this more deeply than anyone else, as his own professional fate cannot be extricated from the fate of his money. His year-end bonus, like shiny shell necklaces and armbands brought home from across the treacherous sea, personifies his powers.

In both its early form as cowrie shells and its modern form as (for example) an over-the-counter interest rate swap, money works to secure the insecurities of the future. Thus did the Micronesian sailor return from the unknown, his arms wrapped in beads. Which is to say that Bronisław Malinowski had traveled as far as possible from modern banking and finance only to come face-to-face with an essential feature of banking and finance. He couldn't see it, because it did not occur to Malinowski that all money was a shell game.

He had been trained in philosophy, in chemistry, and in economics, but had not devoted himself to the study of metaphor. If he had it might have occurred to him that sleight of hand—that is, substituting one thing for another—had long been the purview of poetry and literature, to the extent that English professors had a well-worn name for that which Malinowski could not fathom. The kula ring was an allegory.

In allegorical fictions, every element of a story corresponds to something other than itself, and it is up to the reader to break the code and translate the meaning. The most common form is the fable. When the fox, protagonist of "The Fox and the Grapes," comes to the conclusion that he "doesn't need any sour grapes," the statement is not really about grapes, but about those things we may want but cannot attain, and consequently disparage. In the fable, the grapes are not really grapes and the fox is not really a fox. The grapes correspond to unattainable desires. The fox corresponds to human nature. The characters are like ostrich eggshells, except that instead of food and water, they contain motivations common to all people.

The most highly rendered and fully realized allegories are epic poems from hundreds of years ago. In John Gower's Middle English *Confessio Amantis*, characters named Danger and Genius battle alongside rogues such as Covetousness, Usury, Simony, Perjury, Larceny, Ingratitude, Robbery, and Sacrilege. In the course of Edmund Spenser's sixteenth-century *The Faerie Queene*, which consists of seven books and more than 18,000 lines of iambic verse, a hero named Red Cross Knight fights a dragon named Error and meets a hermit named Despair, who, rather unsurprisingly, tries to drive the knight to suicide. The thirteenth-century French poem *The Romance of the Rose* presents a cast of allegorical characters based on a fairly complete set of the human motivations that drive plots—from Hatred, Misery, and Senility to Openness, Pleasure, and Reason.

In the centuries following the Middle Ages, allegory lost a great deal of its status. But it did experience a momentary renaissance in a series of volumes published in twenty-five parts from 1832 to 1834 entitled *Illustrations of Political Economy*, written by Harriet Martineau. *The Illustrations* illustrated concepts such as Production, Distribution, Exchange, and Consumption as elements of domestic economy—that is, as parts of a money system that centered around women. Monthly book sales reached ten thousand copies—far exceeding the competition, including *Oliver Twist*—and Martineau went on to publish thousands of newspaper and magazine articles. Her intellectual circle included an extraordinary assemblage of nineteenth-century luminaries, from Florence Nightingale to James Madison and Charles Darwin. Unfortunately, as an anonymous critic in London's *Saturday Review* noted in 1885, her writing emitted "a certain hard and indigestible quality." Today, her work is largely ignored.

By the twentieth century, allegory was no longer the most esteemed and hardly the most popular style of literary expression.

In this sixteenth-century Dutch allegorical engraving, Regina Pecunia, *the personification of money, sits in a chariot harnessed to Peril and Fear. Her right hand blesses the cold-blooded* Latrocinium, *who stabs a human heart. Allegorical figures of Foolishness, Envy, and Thievery follow in her wake.*

Compared to modernist poetry and naturalist novels, allegory was considered a simplistic and old-fashioned form, which may be another reason why the anthropologists, the ethno-conchologists, and Bronisław Malinowski could not recognize kula for what it was. But in 1970, an English professor named Angus Fletcher published a four-hundred-page volume, aptly entitled *Allegory*, which transformed perceptions of the genre.

In this deeply learned, much-reprinted classic of literary criticism, Fletcher argued that allegories not only express fundamental emotional and cognitive drives, but also mirror the ideas of society at large. The approach was expansive, arguing that since its late medieval heyday the genre had not gone away, but had quietly become an essential component of modern politics, business, media, art, and advertising. But he never did get around to addressing the fact that the most widely believed fiction of all — that is, money — was allegorical.

Fletcher argued that the characters in allegory appear to the modern reader as pared down and simplistic only because their role is to exhibit highly specified emotional states and psychological conditions — like the personifications of fear, foolishness, envy, and lust who accompany the chariot of *Regina Pecunia*. Angus Fletcher called such characters *kosmoi*. In *The Faerie Queene*, the character named Despair was a *kosmoi*, as were Error and Genius in *Confessio Amantis*. The motivations that drive these characters as they wend their way through the story are their *daimons*, a word closely related to "demon." In short, the demons are the invisible souls and spirits that animate the physical shells that are the characters.

Angus Fletcher had seen that allegories are ghost stories. And money, too, is a ghost story. Just as an author imbues his characters with life, possessing and controlling their thought and action, so, too, is money possessed. Slips of paper are otherwise nothing but slips of paper, not to mention the banana seeds, iron bars, bat bones, beetle legs, coconuts, feathers, salt, string, tobacco, woodpecker scalps, and all the other shells that money may possess.

The confusion the ethnographers and anthropologists faced with the beads, cloth, gongs, shells, and skulls of primitive money stemmed from the fact that they could not read the allegory. If they could, they would have seen that money was not one particular thing but a motivation that could possess all sorts of things. The polished snail shells strung into armbands — these were *kosmoi*. The good fortune and general wherewithal required to overcome the dangers, risks, and fears of the voyage — these were the spirits that possessed those *kosmoi*, and anointed them with their "magic of plenty." Like the neolithic ostrich eggshell beads, the seashells were containers, and what they contained — much like a modern insurance policy — was the desire to overcome risks, and the assurance of risks overcome.

Examine a United States dollar long enough and you may begin to suspect that the watermarks, profiles, eagles, seals, stars, letters, numbers, meanders, filigree, and signatures of the various secretaries of the treasury all point to spirits and meanings beyond the borders of the bill. Numismatists refer to these inscriptions with a literary term. They call them the *legend*. The eternally watchful eye of god and the geometrical, spiritual, and astrological mysteries represented by the Egyptian pyramid suggest unseen forces concealed within the ancient symbols. Scholars of the distant future — from a time when the dollar will be but an artifact of a long-lost money culture — may still be able to unlock the ideas of faith and security encrypted within these symbols, even if they will be challenged to define what was meant by the Federal Reserve or a secretary of the treasury.

The symbols engraved upon the dollar, like the symbols engraved upon the sixteenth-century rendering of *Regina Pecunia*'s chariot, are allegorical. For not only is allegory germane to the earliest forms of money, but to the nature of modern finance. And the same can be said for its plot.

The plot of an allegory is unlike the plot of detective fiction or murder mystery, in which the story drives toward a solution. Nor is the plot like a love story, in which individuals face obstacles along the way to romantic and erotic satisfaction. The plot of a mystery, a romance, or a tragedy might be envisioned as linear, starting at some point A, and leading to a resolution — call it point B. Put another way, no tragedy ends happily. The financier would love the plot of his money to work the same way — he would love to know the ending before it ends. But the money plot resists such confinement.

For example, a canoe engaged in a kula ring does not float in a straight line toward a solution to a crime, a betrothal, or a death, but moves in an apparently random zigzag pattern, divagating, digressing, doubling back, pulled by tides into strange harbors, waylaid by unforeseen forces. The canoe floats across an ocean flecked with a thousand ports of call, each presenting different customs and conditions. The course kula takes is neither linear nor circular but diffuse, like the ceaseless wanderings of Odysseus, who even after coming home to Ithaca, would once again depart.

The quantitative analysts employed by hedge funds and investment banks have a name for this type of journey. They call it a "random walk." The term was introduced by the English biostatistician Karl Pearson in 1905, and ever since has been found applicable to a wide variety of fields, from ecology to epidemiology, chemistry, computer science, and physics.

Plotted as a course, the random walk looks like the path of a foraging animal, a molecule traveling through a liquid or a gas, or the jagged ups and downs of the Dow Jones Industrial Average. The random appearance of the path doesn't suggest any particular goal—and that's because (unlike detective fiction or romance) it doesn't have any. Every step is independent of both the previous step and the next step. Every step is a new beginning.

Just about seven decades after Karl Pearson proposed his random walk theory, a Princeton economist named Burton Malkiel published a book about investing techniques called *A Random Walk Down Wall Street*, in which he popularized the idea of the market as an allegorical universe in which an investor embarks upon a journey, the contours of which can change at any moment.

The book went through twelve editions and sold more than 1.5 million copies.

Like the booms and busts that mark a day on Wall Street, the plot of allegory consists of the push and pull of a variety of emotional and psychological motivations, in which the resolutions to the conflicts are not final and definitive, but ongoing and continuous. For the fox's decision that the grapes must be sour tells us nothing about the true taste of the grapes, nor about the ultimate fate of the fox. The story simply presents an emotional state that emerges from the push and pull of competing desires.

Angus Fletcher saw that the plot of medieval allegory consisted of a random walk through a fictional universe inhabited by conflicting forces. In order to translate what he meant into usable literary terminology, he borrowed a term from the title of one of the earliest allegories, a Latin poem from the fifth century written by a Roman Christian named Prudentius. The thousand or so surviving lines describe a battle within an individual's psyche, in which Lust attacks Chastity, Anger attacks Patience, and Greed attacks Love. The battle is continuous. And as in the great public exchanges of the modern era, at any point one of the forces may take the upper hand. The name of the poem was *Psychomachia*.

Marketplaces like the Chicago Mercantile Exchange and the New York Stock Exchange represent the psychomachia of conflicting forces Adam Smith once imagined, an allegorical space inhabited by troves of warring personifications. Here, risk battles security and rationality battles instinct. Fear and greed and anger and patience confront one another in the ever-changing guises of equities, commodities, and currencies.

The stubborn lack of resolution to the plot has defined the challenge posed by modern money. It has long tempted merchants, traders, and bankers to anticipate and forecast, to act before anyone else, to predict the reversal no one else saw coming, to calculate the outcome of the conflict before anyone else, to unmask the forces behind the characters and see what no one else can see. What was once the purview of the seer, the soothsayer, and the storyteller has been appropriated by the derivatives trader, the financial analyst, and the economist.

{2} THE TROPHY WIFE

In a certain sense, people are in the same situation as commodities...

— KARL MARX

By the time the enslaved were emancipated, they comprised the largest single asset in America: $3 billion in 1860 dollars, more than all the other assets in the country combined.

— TA-NEHISI COATES

IN ONE OF THE MOST extraordinary alliances ever forged, money merged with plot, character, and metaphor to establish the customs, edicts, and mandates of marriage. Every wedding is a fairy tale to the extent that it magically transforms secular exchange into holy matrimony.

A recurring character in South Indian mythology is Manu. Sometimes he appears in the role of the first human being on earth, the subcontinent's Adam; other times he crops up like Noah, sole survivor of the flood. In some versions of the Vedas he becomes the first king of India, in others he makes the first sacrifice. Yet there is also evidence that Manu was an historical figure, a lowly shepherd who by virtue of his quick wit and incisive judgment became the most famous legal mind of his day. His opinions, memorialized in Sanskrit treatises called Dharmashastras, addressed the most complex, confusing, and fraught issues of his day. That is to say, Manu wrote the ancient rules of marriage and divorce, paying special attention to the disposition of the money.

The myths of Manu are allegorical. They appear to be about one thing, but are in fact about another. Such is the case in one oft-repeated tale, commonly referred to as "The Cucumber Problem."

A cucumber has sprouted in one man's garden, though the roots of the plant can be traced to another's. The end of a long, hot summer has arrived, and the cucumber is now ripe. It is ready to be plucked, peeled, and sliced into a refreshing cucumber salad. At this point a dispute arises: To whom does the cucumber rightfully belong? To the man in whose garden the fruit has ripened, or to the man in whose garden the cucumber took root?

Of course, the cucumber problem is not really a problem about cucumbers. The story is about metaphorical roots and fruits — that is, the story is about the nature of property and ownership. The man in whose garden the fruit has ripened might argue that by any objective measurement of distance, the cucumber had grown fat in closest proximity to him, and was thus his rightful property. The man in whose garden the cucumber took root might grant that while the cucumber in its present state was no doubt in closest physical proximity to his neighbor, the cucumber was in most *intimate* proximity to its roots, and thus the fruit should rightfully belong to him.

The use of proximity to resolve questions of property is telling, since both parties aspiring to consume the cucumber present legitimate reasoning. Such is the case because proximity not only underlies ancient legal arguments relating to ownership, but ancient literary methods that illustrate the idea of possession. In fact, proximity drives an entire subspecies of metaphor that illustrates a number of money's elemental and enduring features.

As Gorgias taught the Sophists who gathered around him in the ancient agora, there are many different types of metaphor. Just as ancient as personification is the subspecies of metaphor known as metonymy, the metaphor of proximity. Much like the idea of spiritual possession that lies behind personification, metonymy comes from an imaginary force anthropologists call sympathetic magic. The primitive superstition that lies behind sympathetic magic is that some invisible substance or contagion can creep from one material body to another and bind them together. That includes, of course, human bodies.

A familiar example of sympathetic magic is the voodoo doll adorned with a lock of a target subject's hair. The hair had been in close proximity to the target, and as a result that hair has supposedly been infused with the spirit of that person. Because of this magical sympathy, the hair connects the target individual to the figure of the doll. The result is that a pin stuck in the doll's heart affects the heart of the adversary.

An example of metonymy more specific to the nature of money is the use of a term such as "the crown." A king can be referred to as "the crown," because the king's authority seeps from his person to that which sits atop his head. The crown has been *invested* with the power of a king, and can return the favor, and invest a king with its own proprietary properties — such as shining brilliance. This same sympathy or contagion plays out in language, so that the wholly distinct king and crown become metaphorically one and the same, to the extent that instead of paying taxes to the king, one may be ordered to pay taxes "to the crown."

Larry Page's famous PageRank algorithm, which he and Sergey Brin developed at Stanford in 1996, relies on metonymy. The formula measures each web page as a function of its similarity and overlap with material from other web pages. The level of that contiguity creates the sympathetic magic that ranks each search result. Metonymy underlies the lion's share of Google's income. It is not worth billions of dollars. It is worth hundreds of billions.

The identification between metonymy and money is so strong that a "crown," imbued with the authority of the sovereign state, to this day remains the unit of value and media of exchange in Greenland, Iceland, Norway, Sweden, and the Czech Republic. The English "crown" (first minted under the authority of Henry VIII in 1526) was a metonymic coin, as opposed to personified coins like the French "Louis" (first minted in 1640) or the "Napoleon" (first minted in 1803).

An ancient grammarian named Tryphon of Alexandria was one of the first to define metonymy in his treatise *On Tropes*, published in 100 BC. Tryphon explained that this type of metaphor arises when the "thing that is contained" is called by the name of the thing that contains it—like asking a bartender for "another bottle" when what you are really after is not the bottle but the alcoholic beverage within. Metonymy brokered the transfer that turned ostrich eggs that contained food and water in neolithic Kenya into tokens of those commodities. The bead shape that resulted would become the first globally recognized feature of money, epitomized in strung cowries that would eventually act as the world's first reserve currency—and configure a price to contain anything. That is to say, cash value has been a long-standing and widespread feature of metonymy.

Metonymy clarifies why both Aristotle and the Roman rhetorician Cicero described metaphor as a form of clothing. Consider the phrase: "Nothing but suits in that room." The crown is close to the king just as the suit is close to the businessman, and their proximity enables the sympathetic contagions of metonymy to kick in. No surprise, then, that nineteenth-century anthropologists observed a relationship among clothing, ornament, and price.

The Swahili and Chikunda slave traders on the east coast of Africa predated their western counterparts of the transatlantic slave trade by more than seven hundred years and were more often than not themselves slaves — which may explain why they understood and presented their trade in concubines with a complexity beyond most other slavers. Perhaps to distinguish the slave from the slave of the slave, they encircled the waists of their captives with beaded belts and girdles. Contiguous to the flesh of their merchandise, this form of clothing indicated the price.

A seller of slaves might have had to explain to an ignorant buyer that the belt around his captive was different from other belts; that just as a container contains water, beans, and berries, the belt — itself a container — contains the wants, needs, and desires it encircles. What the seller of the slave woman did not have to explain was that a woman is herself a container, that her body can enclose the male phallus, hold the male seed, and that her womb may carry the couple's precious progeny.

All of which may help explain how and why women themselves became currency, their bodies twisted and figured into metaphors of price — first by means of beaded belts, later, with more modern equivalents. In seventeenth-century England, a husband might harness his wife in a collar, yoke, or halter around the arms, neck, or waist before publicly auctioning her off to the highest bidder. Thomas Hardy's nineteenth-century novel *The Mayor of Caster-bridge* begins as a grain merchant sells his wife and daughter to a passing sailor for five pounds. The practice remains popular. In October of 2019, BBC News Arabic uncovered a booming black market in female domestic workers advertised on Instagram, available for a few thousand dollars each. The following year, when the king of Thailand retreated to a hotel in the German Alps to escape the coronavirus, his entourage included a harem of twenty women.

Indeed, there is a high end for such luxury goods, as the most desired slaves and courtesans became the property of the ancient world's 1 percent, and the mothers of emperors. They were the first trophy wives. For if the crown's contiguity to the king transforms the royal hat into money, imagine what that might mean for the cash value of a queen.

The logic of metonymy explains how the female-as-ornament, the consort contiguous to the man, enhances male status and power. The ancient Greeks called such beautiful and sophisticated ornaments *hetaira*, in contrast to *pornai*, who as mere prostitutes were discarded after purchase and use. For the best of all trophies do not simply sit on the shelf, gathering dust. They are active and accrue wealth. Thus did one ancient Greek marriage song of praise — known as *hymenae* — compare the would-be bride to a fig and the bridegroom to the harvester of said fig. The fig nourishes the man, the fig harvest indicates the man's wealth — likewise, the wife.

Evidence uncovered in the ruins of an eleven-thousand-year-old settlement in Jericho indicate that the fig was the first fruit to be domesticated, its reproductive capacity brought under control. Moreover, it is reasonable to assume that eleven thousand years ago a man's wealth was defined not only by the volume and quality of his fig harvest, but also by all the other commodities on his orchard or farm he had made conform to his desires, first and foremost his wives.

The characters and metaphors of *hymenae* join other wedding rituals to underscore the point. When partners dress in metaphorical clothing, wear metaphorical jewelry, walk in metaphorical processions, and stand in proximity to each other and recite vows that join them in god-sanctioned unions, the betrothal can look like an exercise in metonymy, and brides like commodities.

Money of this sort reached a zenith of power and popularity in the last quarter of the twentieth century, a period known among scholars of economic behavior as "the long 1980s." Capitalist culture, bolstered by the policies of Ronald Reagan and Margaret Thatcher, more sure of itself than ever after the fall of the Berlin Wall, was expanding money's sympathetic magic to the ends of the earth. Its gospel resounded from the scriptures of pre-internet financial print culture, fictions ranging from Tom Wolfe's *The Bonfire of the Vanities* to Brett Easton Ellis' *American Psycho* to the weekly stockpiles of journalism churned out by *Barron's*, *Financial Times*, *Fortune*, *Forbes*, *Business Week*, *Money*, *Manhattan, inc.*, and countless other magazines, all delivering the same metonymic message: The man with the most toys wins.

Among the toys were women's bodies. In 1994, an article dedicated to this subject appeared in print, written by William Safire, an ex-speechwriter for Richard Nixon who had a Sunday column *The New York Times* called "On Language." On May 1, Safire's discourse was devoted to a character who to his mind summed up the money culture—namely, the trophy wife. Safire evaluated the taxonomy, dividing the species among gold diggers, supermodels, handbags, and bimbos. He noted that the first use of the now-ubiquitous term had appeared five years earlier, in a cover story for *Fortune* magazine. "Powerful men are beginning to demand trophy wives," wrote senior editor Julie Connelly. "The more money men make, the argument goes, the more self-assured they become, and the easier it is for them to think: I deserve a queen."

Perhaps the most infamous example of this would-be queen was a stripper turned Playboy Playmate named Anna Nicole Smith. A mere seven weeks after Safire's column appeared, the twenty-six-year-old cashed in her sexual capital by marrying the wheelchair-bound eighty-nine-year-old Texas oil billionaire, J. Howard Marshall, who died fourteen months later. It should come as no surprise that Smith did not appear in Marshall's will. Who leaves property to property?

Smith hired lawyers, for much like Manu's cucumber problem, the case of the trophy wife's ownership rights has always been open to interpretation. Unfortunately, the decision that eventually came down from the Supreme Court didn't make that much of a difference to Smith, who died shortly thereafter of an accidental drug overdose in a hotel room in Hollywood, Florida, surrounded by bottles of Ativan, Benadryl, Klonopin, and Valium. The sum total of her personal property at the time of her death was valued at ten thousand dollars.

The word trophy comes from the Greek word for the tokens of victory in battle, a battle in which Anna Nicole Smith was a clear casualty. The original trophies were the flags, weapons, and arms abandoned by the enemy after they had turned and fled the field. It was that verb "to turn" — *trópos* — that turned into trophy. Most everything left behind after the battle could be *troped* into an allegorical figure of triumph, including the wives of vanquished warriors — such as Hecuba and the Trojan women — who became the concubines of those who killed their husbands.

In preclassical Greece, currency in women circulated as the result of war, for a trophy, like a trophy wife, is a token of victory. And much like slave belts and business suits and bejeweled crowns and Google searches, the currency of concubines gains its strength and power from proximity. All of which brings us back to the cucumber problem.

After careful consideration, Manu the Wise ruled that the cucumber belonged to the owner of the garden in which it flowered, not to the owner of the garden in which the fruit had taken root. Unfortunately for Manu, this ruling appeared to everyone to be the wrong decision. As a result of this uncharacteristic error, the sage banished himself from Burma, renounced the world, became an ascetic, and after wandering from one corner of planet earth to the other, ascended to heaven.

Here, in the firmament of immortality, Manu discovered a set of immutable truths engraved upon the edges of the solar system, which with no further ado he brought back to earth. Collected in the Dharmashastras, these became the celebrated Laws of Manu. They describe in detail anything anyone ever might want to know about the provenance of property, with special emphasis on marriage, children, and inheritance. The protagonists of these stories are husbands, wives, and the money.

The allegorical nature of Manu's cucumber problem now became clear. The plot expressed a pared-down version of what may have been the first of all economic conundrums: What to do when human beings increase and multiply, simultaneously scaling up both the demand for resources (more mouths to feed) and the power to bolster the supply of those resources (more hands to hunt and gather)? To rephrase the question in monetary terms: What is the most effective way to generate wealth, and what is the most equitable way to share it?

That question has yet to be answered for everyone in a perfectly satisfactory manner, but the capitalists did eventually come up with what they believed to be a particularly effective solution: The most powerful way to generate wealth is through incorporation, and the most equitable way to share it is through equity. The word corporation comes from the Latin verb *corporare* — to combine separate bodies into a single larger body. The idea of such magical conflations (two or more elements becoming a single element) can be traced to ancient ideas about economy, as Aristotle himself argued that the oldest economic model of all was the *oikos*, which can be understood as a combination of three related but distinct concepts: the family, the family's property, and the physical structure of the house.

In so-called primitive economies, the closest equivalent to such modern financial ideas as growth, profit, and return on investment is the product of the family, a product that depends in no small part upon the reproductive wherewithal of women. This is yet another reason why wives and children became tokens of wealth. Before the advent of market-based economies, to be rich was to possess multiple spouses and manifold offspring, the management of which required a diverse cast of characters who could assume a wide variety of supporting and leading roles. The rules and regulations governing the complicated behaviors of all such stakeholders produced one of the earliest attempts to resolve what would become one of the most pressing inquiries of nineteenth-century economics: Who should own the means of production? One way to answer this question pitted capital against labor. An earlier version pitted the husband's family against the wife's.

When the son of one family and the daughter of another come together as a single corporation, there are obvious opportunities for profit and growth, but there is also a clear and present danger that instead of consolidation, the merger will result in a diffusion of resources. In order to avoid such wasting, scattering, profligacy, and chaos, the wisest of philosophers — people like Manu — sought to balance the opposing forces by prescribing plotlines for all the characters involved. In order to ensure prosperity and equity, marriage became an exercise in monetary allegory, with husband, wife, and family playing roles in a psychomachia of shared and contrary motivations.

Love is a relatively new criteria for lifelong partnership. The decision to marry, like the decision to invest money, was far more often an unromantic best bet about the future, a wager made in order to mitigate risk and cultivate security. As a result, the goal of marriage was not only to define characters, but also to anticipate plots. The aim was to forecast all possibilities of fate and fortune, which may help explain why Manu's laws of marriage defined rules for everything from infant betrothal to the mortgage value of descendants.

Anthropologists describe the redistribution of property as a result of marriage by articulating distinct "actor categories"; that is, by defining the different roles played and different fates enacted within the drama. The Laws of Manu specified characters called mother and stepmother, father and stepfather, son and daughter, sister and brother, maternal kin, paternal kin, widow, orphan, cousin, aunt, uncle, sons- and daughters-in-law, and specified all their associated appurtenances, clothing, cattle, and land. The Laws provided further guidelines for adjudicating the property status of children born out of wedlock, for the designation of full heirs, semi-heirs, and residual heirs, along with sets of sub-rules for a near endless variation of subplots featuring every imaginable kinship relation, each playing a role in symbolic and not-so-symbolic exchanges, all of this down to obsessive if not absolutely absurd levels of detail, such as the rights through marriage of a sister's son to the clothing of his maternal uncle.

At the center of it all was a character who went by the names "bride," "wife," and eventually "mother." That said, Manu's rules not only defined the so-called primary wife, but delineated in great detail how that primary wife differed from secondary wives, secondary wives from concubines, concubines from slave wives, not to mention each and every possible future consumer and producer of family resources — that is, the succeeding generations of sons and daughters who might be the result of evermore marital and reproductive mergers and acquisitions.

Such prepackaged plotlines for commodity characters are by no means unique to Manu and the Indian subcontinent. Among the Lobedu of South Africa, a sister of the groom can demand that a son of her brother's be her daughter's husband, as they are "born for" each other. Konkomba women of Ghana and Togo are mortgaged as infants. In Malabar, the marriage ritual begins with a down payment known as *kanam*, which is the same word used to refer to the sum a tenant farmer advances to his landlord as an initial interest payment. Such intersections of claims and interests worked to establish marriage as a form of insurance and security.

The Laws of Manu, inscribed in ethereal script upon the adamantine vaults of heaven, support the hypothesis that the first thing bought or sold was not a cucumber, but a woman. I would argue one step further: The first form of money was not the carefully carved shell of an ostrich egg or a polished cowrie, but a woman's body.

Bodies played an important role in Stone Age economies. Anthropologists have noted that "primitive" Congolese actuaries computed compensation for the accidental death of an innocent person from a neighboring group as ten iron hoes, an ox, and one girl. The girl did not serve as payment in and of herself, as she was delivered to her lessees (so to speak) on a provisional basis for the sole purpose of giving birth to a child (replacement cost). Once the female body had successfully executed the process of producing another body, its status as a medium of transfer and as a token of value was redeemed, the risk of social discord mitigated, the transaction balanced and settled. Released from the chains of price, she became, in every respect of the word, *free*.

The story of such a girl-payment may appear "savage" to us, but this is only because we have come to believe so ardently in the fiction of metonymy, the fantasy that two people may, as a result of spoken vows, ritual dress, gifts, and shared consumption of food, be joined together as one in sacred bonds of holy matrimony. This highly rendered plot, the stock characters, and the endless stream of metaphors have blinded us to what is really going on. And while the buying and selling of bodies still shocks us, we are hardly surprised to learn that anthropologists and ethnographers who observed marriages in a wide variety of cultures found that money — or something that appears to act a great deal like money — does not fail to congregate around the custom.

Alison Quiggin's 1949 *A Survey of Primitive Money* gathered ethnological evidence from hundreds of previous field studies. Among the anecdotes, Quiggin reported that in nineteenth-century Congo, a young man from the Batetela group who approached the girl he wanted to marry said, "I love you." If the girl agreed to the proposal, she assented by saying the following three words: "Bring the money."

In marriage, "the money" is only one of many metaphors that will be deployed to obscure the fact that a body is the real currency. No wonder the bride is swiftly subsumed by a new name, not to mention all the other material and symbolic harnesses that will envelop and adorn her body, such as thirty-pound copper collars, ceremonial dresses, garter belts, and rings. Such wedding vestments echo the etymological origin of the word, investment, which means *to clothe*. Just as Aristotle, Cicero, and the ancient rhetoricians understood metaphor as a form of clothing, bridal ornaments and textiles are cloaks, the vestments that make the woman's body — that is, the money — invisible.

The ritual wedding ensues, with its gifts, theatrical processions, and symbolically ornamented characters in costume, reciting scripts. Extravagant regalia accompany the bride as she enters into an exchange that modern futures and options traders might call a "forward contract." In fact, the traditional contract was explicit. The "bride's fee," known in the Dharmasthastras as *sulka*, acted as compensation for the drama's completion. In the Dharmashastras, the bride's fee could consist of buffalo, copper, cows, household utensils, jewelry, land, servants, and slaves. These remained the bride's property after the marriage, along with her combs, mirrors, perfumes, powders, and soaps.

Sulka was hardly unique to lands that felt the influence of Manu the Lawgiver. Bride price was well known throughout ancient Assyria, Babylonia, China, Japan, Mesopotamia, and Polynesia. The ancient Hebrews had their *ketubah*, the marriage contract. Among the LoWiili, the payment is 350 cowries, to be followed by three cows, one goat, and 20,000 cowries during the lifetime of the marriage, returnable upon divorce. As recently as 1970, bride price in northern Ghana was 20,000 cowries.

Price was so intrinsic to marriage that not even the immortals were immune. In ancient Greek myth, when Hephaestus, the god of blacksmiths, metallurgy, and fire, caught Aphrodite, his sex goddess wife, in bed with Ares, the god of war, he snared the pair in an invisible net and dragged them naked before all the other gods, who found the spectacle hilarious. But public shame did not satisfy Hephaestus. He demanded material damages. He had paid a good price for his trophy, he argued, so upon divorce his father-in-law Zeus should reimburse the money.

The elaborate metaphors of marriage conceal the underlying transformation of human bodies into units of account, stores of value, and media of exchange. To return to South Indian tradition, the *tali* is the marriage necklace that is said to indicate the eternal devotion of the bride to the groom. The *tali* must be carried in procession by a woman of the *Koviyar* servant class, the traditional class of herdsmen. On the wedding day, the *Koviyar* herds the bride to the groom and after the *tali* has harnessed the bride, the bejeweled bridle is encircled by a golden pendant known as the *mangalsutra*, which will secure the future good fortune of the husband. That pendant of good fortune will be tied around the bride's neck, where it will stay for the rest of her life.

As unremarkable as a wedding procession may appear to be, the bride's ritual walk down the aisle to be transferred from her father to her groom enacts the transfer of property and ownership. In Burma, the procession is from one house to another, as the groom, accompanied by friends and relations, appears with armchairs, boxes, bundles of mats and mattresses, pillows, and a feast for his bride. Anthropologists have cataloged many versions of the marriage procession, each direction and pathway of the journey indicating different provenances of property and ownership. Marriage may involve the movement of the groom to the bride's house ("uxorilocal marriage"), the bride to the groom's house ("virilocal marriage"), not to mention an extraordinary diversity of patrilocal, avunculocal, matrilocal, duoloal, or ambilocal marriages, each banking on proximity as an indicator of ownership.

The laws Manu brought down from heaven introduced strategies to resolve the confusions of incorporation, growth, and consumption. From then on, the conflicts of proximity and ownership were brokered by two kinds of rights — those that belonged to a class of shareholders called *agnates,* and those that belonged to another class of shareholders known as *affines.* Agnates are those who share a common male ancestor, like the roots of the cucumber; affines, on the other hand, are those related by marriage, with property claims like those of the adjacent farmer. If the former traces a vertical line, the latter line traces horizontal. Much like the plot of allegory, the tensions of ownership and inheritance were thenceforth mapped between these axes of conflicting requirements and obligations.

Without a map of marriage made of the grammar, rhetoric, plots, characters, and metaphors of money, civilization would not have

A groom harnesses his bride with a jeweled tali.

reached the heights of five-karat diamond engagement rings, luxe honeymoons in the Maldives, and monumental divorce settlements. These days, lawyers may specify in advance the number, dates, and type of sex that must be performed each month, the amount to be reimbursed in case of adultery, the custody of children in case of divorce, a checklist of inheritance and alimony rights, and "sunset" clauses which indicate the number of years after which the contract lapses — and all bets are off. Nothing about the modern prenuptial agreement would have surprised Manu, as the contract is made to control — a banker might say, "to securitize" — the future.

Shakespeare's comedies invariably end in double and triple weddings, because the long-standing goal of marriage has been to order what might otherwise have proven to be a violent and disorderly future. The obverse is just as true: When the marriage exchange is perceived to lack the proper balance, chaos ensues. One example comes from the medieval Gaelic saga *Táin Bó Cúalnge*. The story begins as the king and queen lie next to each other in bed, bragging about who possesses more property.

> "It still remains," Medb said, "that my fortune is greater than yours."
>
> "You amaze me," Ailill said. "No one has more property or jewels or precious things than I have, and I know it."

Medb and Ailill subsequently enumerate their exquisite objects, their servants, the number of soldiers under their command, their siblings, their land, their clothes, their chariots, the number of their iron pots, sheep, horses, and pigs — and all comes up even except for one thing the queen lacks: a white-horned bull named Finnbennach, property of the king and king alone.

Infuriated by the inferior status indicated by this lack of equity in the royal corporation, the queen vows to acquire for herself the greatest bull in all of Ireland — the brown bull of Cooley. A war march across the country ensues, and countless bloody battles. The saga ends as the sharp-horned ancestor of the statue that stands near Wall Street — the bronze embodiment of bullish behavior — unleashes violence upon the first human currencies.

> Then turned the Brown of Cuailnge on the women and youths and children of the land of Cuailnge, and with the greatness of his fury and rage he effected a great slaughter amongst them.

Mayhem and death engulfed the land.

The substitution of actor categories — costumed, choreographed, garter-belted, golden-ringed, and scripted — for the flagrant trade in human bodies had been meant to forestall such devastation. On a certain hour of a certain day there would be a glorious ceremony marked by metaphors that allegorized the exchange. And, perhaps to a surprising degree, the transformation of men and women into grooms and brides proved capable of producing public order. Manu's metonymies of marriage would eventually scale beyond agnates and affines, mature into the laws of property, and extend its narrative structure to the organization of city-states, nations, and global markets. Such were the perils and profundities of Anna Nicole Smith and her long-defunct sisters. Without the trope of trophies, money would not be money.

{3} ACTS OF VIOLENCE
AND OTHER WORDS

Making the earth say beans instead of grass — that was my daily work.

— HENRY DAVID THOREAU

The person who experiences greatness must have a feeling for the myth he is in.

— FRANK HERBERT

TO THE ANCIENT MIND, the subjugation of nature to human will was the result of divine interventions. Who but a god could have shepherded the transfiguration of wild grasses into wheat and savage animals into beasts of burden? Today we downgrade these archaic narratives of supernatural intercession. We call them myths. But to the citizens of the first city-states, such plots and characters created a new language of money — a language of worship and domination.

The most dominating language of all belonged to the ruler of the city-state. His call for tribute came straight from god, and applied to everyone. Thus this chapter's epigraph from Frank Herbert: The great one himself, he who merits the consecration of revenue, must have a "feeling for the myth he is in."

The quote is from one of the world's best-selling science fiction novels, *Dune*, published in 1965. The novel describes an imaginary planet where the main economic activity consists of harvesting and selling a rare and addictive drug that gives those who take it the power every Wall Street banker craves: the ability to predict the future.

When multibillionaire Craig Wright was growing up in Australia, *Dune* was his favorite book. Obsessed by alternate worlds, mythology, and fortune-telling, he eventually wrote his dissertation at United Theological College on the "Gnarled Roots of a Creation Mythos." "If you ever need to know of Dionysus, Vesta, Minerva, Ceres (Roman Goddess of the corn, earth, harvest) or other mythological characters — I am your man," Wright boasted some years later on the social network LinkedIn. "I could even hold a conversation on Eileithyia, the Greek Goddess of childbirth and her Roman rebirth as Lucina."

In June of 2017, an in-depth 35,000-word profile of Craig Wright appeared in the *London Review of Books*, not because of the subject's love of science fiction, nor because of his self-declared knowledge of creation myths, but because Wright claimed that under the pseudonym Satoshi Nakamoto he had created a new form of money called Bitcoin.

More than a decade after the debut of Bitcoin on January 3, 2009, many dismiss the digital currency as a speculative figment, a boom waiting to bust — in short, a myth. Others assert it is nothing special, an element unearthed from the depths of the internet by a souped-up computer's high-speed mathematical wizardry, the modern equivalent of mining. Still others take a more expansive view, arguing that Bitcoin's most enduring significance will not be as a currency, but as a decentralized inventory technology that can keep track not only of money, but of everything from medical supplies to rental cars to music royalties. Most people admit they don't understand it. But the plainest truth about Bitcoin lies on the surface, in its name.

There is no way to take the *coin* out of Bitcoin. And if a digital coin appears exotic and strange, so did precious metal coins when they first surfaced throughout the Peloponnese in the fifth century BC. Today we naturally associate coins with money, but thousands of years ago, coin's advent presented the world with a new sort of symbol—one that would eventually eclipse shells, cattle, and fig harvests, if not wives.

Just as there is nothing inherent within Bitcoin that makes it money, there is nothing inherent within a coin that makes it money, particularly not the metal. The history of numismatics is rife with pounds and marks and dollars composed of wildly divergent percentages of gold and silver ores and alloys. When the emperor Nero changed the silver content of the Roman denarius, nothing much happened—except that Domitian eventually changed it back. Fifteenth-century Ottoman sultans made it a habit of reducing the weight of their silver *akçe*, while nineteenth-century Germany switched coinage from silver to gold and kept the name the same.

In the United States, the melt value of one hundred pre-1982 pennies (mostly made of copper) hovers around $2.20, while the melt value of one hundred post-1982 pennies (mostly made of zinc), is closer to sixty cents. Yet we accept as fact that each is "worth" the same one-hundredth of a dollar. The only possible explanation for such egregiously bad math is that the value of a coin does not depend upon the substance of the coin, but the metaphor.

The power of the word *penny* can make two entirely different elements mean the same. Words possess an uncanny ability to turn our attention away from what is, a potential most commonly exploited by the use of pseudonyms, the fake or *pseudo* names common throughout our culture, from Clark Kent and Peter Parker to catfishing on dating sites to phishing scams meant to defraud or exact revenge. Which brings us back to Craig Wright's pseudonym, Satoshi Nakamoto.

A Bitcoin is commonly known as a Satoshi. And just as the word *penny* gives us confidence in a coin of questionable metallic value, so does the name *Satoshi* deliver a sense of history and meaning to Bitcoin even if an actual flesh-and-blood person named Satoshi Nakamoto has never existed. Grammarians from Aristotle to Tryphon of Alexandria were fascinated by this particular ability of names to divert our attention away from the things being named, and concluded that the nature of pseudonyms extended to the nature of language itself, that all names do two opposite things at the same time: reveal and conceal.

In the last chapter, we noted a number of ritual actions taken by brides during weddings that effectively conceal the exchange of human currency at the heart of the ritual, but glossed over the fact that the word *bride* is itself a pseudonym, a mask created to conceal an old identity and reveal a new one. The word *bride* is as much of a harness as the bejeweled *tali* used to herd the South Asian woman to her groom, confining her, by the bridle of bridehood, to specific and preordained paths of social behavior, wifely duty, and biological reproduction.

The concept that the word *bride* bridles a woman into wife-currency is just as applicable to copper ovals and polished snail shells. The spirit of money can be imposed on a wide variety of substances, and the imposition does not indicate a deep-seated truth about women or metal or seashells so much as a truth about the nature of language. English professors call that quality *catachresis*, a word that descends from a brilliantly simple contrivance that first appeared on earth around 10,000 BC and has remained in just about the same form ever since. That technology is known as a yoke—or a halter, rein, restraint, or in the case of racehorses, a martingale. Ten thousand years ago, it was the bridle that harnessed and domesticated certain animals, reducing them from wild to tame, transforming them into a revolutionary kind of money, and baptizing them with new sets of names. Thus do the words "cattle," "chattel," and "capital" share semantic genealogies.

Archeologists have noted the connection between the birth of agriculture, the birth of accounting, and the birth of writing. But to the English professor, the so-called revolution of the plow—the yoking of large quadrupeds, forcing them to move in straight lines back and forth across a plot of land—means something entirely different, something basic to the nature of language. To name anything is to harness it to words. To the English professor, catachresis means "violent naming."

An example: the *legs* of a table. Does a table really have a leg the same way a human or a dog has a leg? No, but at the same time there is no better word to describe the thing that keeps the table upright. Another example: the act of reducing the sublime vault of heaven to the word *sky*; or of erasing the individuality of every member of a gender to the word *women* or *men*. Catachresis is common practice among branding gurus who most likely have never heard the term but understand the cash value of turning all facial tissues into Kleenex, all copies into a Xerox. Look behind a trademark and you will find catachresis.

The same power of violent naming holds true in economics: From the genetic sequence of a chicken to an acre-foot of fresh water to Kim Kardashian's Instagram feed to the history of your Google searches, everything on earth has been harnessed to a price. Some believe that the bridle of money has turned modern *Homo sapiens* into *Homo economicus*, the narrowly self-interested character for whom all decisions have been reduced to rational expectations of optimal returns, the "maximizing animal" who became a model for twentieth-century behavioral economic theory.

Strange as it may seem, the animal bridle, the language bridle, and the overarching bridling effect of money all emerged around the same moment in human history. All were connected by the great transformation that occurred about ten thousand years ago, when the wild auroch became a cow, the wild boar a pig, and the wild tarpan of Eurasia a horse. In each case, the animal had to be harnessed in order to become a beast of burden whose capacities were thenceforth confined, limited, tamed, and reduced. The name of the creature changed as it made the switch from "wild" to "domestic" and its body became money.

Without a collar around an animal's neck there would have been no pre-machine industrial power — no turning of wheels, no grinding of grains, no crushing of sugar, no pressing of oil. The collared animal provided war power, and through its manure, fuel for more agriculture. Without the domestication of plants and animals there would have been no city states, no development of bureaucratic government, no priestly, no legal, no royal, and no leisure class. Without the yoke and bridle, without catachresis, there would have been no economy as we know it.

Today, if most of us even bother to glance out the car window at a herd of cows or sheep or a field of corn or soy, we have long lost our sense of awe. But try to imagine the shock felt by a nomadic tribe of hunter-gatherers when they caught sight of the first farms, whose inhabitants had decided to stay in one place and program life for themselves. It was as if they were printing a new kind of money, more powerful than any ever before. Thus were the mythical creators of grain and livestock — Neper and Hathor of ancient

Egypt — the distant ancestors of Satoshi Nakamoto, pseudonymous creator of the Bitcoin.

Nor only did the yoke and bridle create new names, but new fates. For the farmer's bridle blinders the beast, limiting the path of future options to a set of binaries: left or right, forward or back, much like the pared down options a bride faces when she walks down that narrow aisle in lockstep to the strains of Lohengrin, or the highly constrained choices any character faces at a fateful moment in a plot.

In order to domesticate a plant or an animal, the domesticator had to make countless choices — who should live and who should die, which lineage would continue and which would end. The choices were fatal, as countless varieties had to be left behind for the sake of the chosen seed whose descendants would increase and multiply like the stars in heaven. A hero would be selected, be he or she the sweetest apple or the oiliest olive. The rest would share the fate of weeds. It was an annual *Sophie's Choice*, and there was a lot riding on the bet.

More fraught than the life or death of a plant species was the life-or-death choice for animals. One brother would be elevated to protected status, the other consigned to wander the earth as a vagabond and a fugitive, and perhaps be lost forever. The transfer of traits from one character to the next is the farmer's stock-in-trade, and the driving force behind the transfer is the farmer's belief that the chicken, the pig, the cow, and the earth itself should be characters in his story, harnessed to the fate he foresaw. Once yoked, the animal can be led through a narrative from birth to death. The plot was no longer a random matter but of something more closely resembling certainty.

In ancient days, such connections between domestication and fate were obvious to everyone. A king concerned about the ramifications of a fateful choice would call in his haruspex, a counselor who could read the future by examining the patterns written on the entrails of sacrificed sheep. The oomancer could see the future through eggs; the aleuromancer through scattered flour.

The ancient farmer was once on a par with the soothsayer, as he possessed the power — to quote Thoreau — of "making the earth say beans." The farmer seized control of the future, beginning with the offspring of his animals. Undesirable or superfluous males were castrated and either sent to the field to work or slaughtered for their flesh; others were forced to stud. Females, who could also be milked or compelled to calve, were more valuable: money machines that could quite literally bear interest.

Without that collar around an animal's neck there could have been no domestication of livestock — and as a consequence no milk, no cheese, no eggs, no steady supply of protein, and no plowing of the land to produce grain harvests beyond imagination, harvests that could translate into immense stores of flour, enough to feed a class of people who did not need to work the fields. Today, the products of domesticated plants and animals remain the underlying values of massive wagers placed on futures and options contracts. Betting on the prices of commodities such as flour, eggs, milk, and the flesh of cows and pigs laid the foundations for the modern derivatives market. And branding, perhaps the most literal form of violent naming, is an essential feature of both cattle and modern marketing. Thus did the yokes and bridles of domestication translate into the various guises of money.

Well into the twentieth century, ethnographers reported that buffalo were being utilized as a general unit of value in parts of Vietnam, as members of the Annamite tribe paid their taxes with the animals. The tradition continued with paper money, as numismatists wryly observed that in nineteenth-century Wales the one pound note showed one sheep; the two pound note, two, while the lamb note—the baby sheep—was only worth ten shillings. And much like those first farmers, modern businessmen continue to bank on the plot of seedlines. It's just that today, these bets have less and less to do with food.

In 2013 Shuanghui International of China bought Smithfield Foods, the world's largest hog farmer and pork processor. It was the biggest takeover of an American company by a Chinese concern up until then, but the goal was not to own the bacon-making protocols, the food storage technologies, or the marinade recipes, but the rights to the underlying DNA of Smithfield pigs—that is, the plotline for all future pork. This biological code was calculated by quantitative analysts in lower Manhattan to be worth something along the lines of $5 billion, and thus were the patents on porcine intellectual property sold. Based on their brokerage of the sale of that seed, the share price of Goldman Sachs, which owns just over 5 percent of Shuanghui, spiked. Here was a pile of stories on top of stories, and at the bottom of all the stories was the harness that first touched the neck of a wild boar.

From the start, harnessing the energy of a wild animal specifically aligned with the history of reading and writing. Perhaps the most obvious example is the ancient custom of reading in a back-and-forth motion, known as boustrophedon. Instead of being read right to left, like Hebrew or Arabic, or left to right, like Italian or English, boustrophedon follows the oxen, *bous*, then takes the turn of the plow, the *strophe*. In boustrophedon, one line is read right-to-left, the next line left-to-right. It is a common form of stone inscription in ancient Etruscan and Greek. To follow the oxen was to follow the money, and to follow the oxen was to read.

The earliest reading and writing was invented ten thousand years ago in Mesopotamia by administrators and bookkeepers faced with the task of accounting for enormous stores of capital. The first

Ancient Greek boustrophedon, discovered in southern Crete, describing the laws of personal property rights, marriage, and divorce.

bureaucrats kept track of the royal supply of grain and vast herds of cows, sheep, goats, pigs, slaves, and wives by means of tokens and amulets. The first writing was born when, for the sake of not having to make a new figurine for every property, someone discovered that if you pressed one of them into wet clay, it left an imprint. In what is called proto-cuneiform, the impression of a small bucket stood for milk, a beveled-rim bowl for cereal products, and schematic representations of animal heads for pigs and sheep. The marks on clay transformed the ledger of possessions from three dimensions to two, at which point the art and science of grammar, rhetoric, plot, character, and metaphor was only a matter of time. On the first spreadsheet—that is, a clay tablet—the domesticated beast was born into a new universe. The outline of an ox's face still stares out from the first Greek capital letter, Alpha.

A was for money.

In 1842, French archeologists began to excavate the ancient city of Nineveh in northern Iraq. Among the artifacts unearthed beneath the ruins of what had once been the largest city in the world, the explorers exhumed thousands of clay tablets covered with hash marks, curlicues, pictograms and other inscrutable scores and marks that looked as though they would be right at home along the borders of a dollar bill. The bishop of Zealand, Friedrich Münter, was the first to notice that the same design element appeared before each block of what everyone was certain were examples of primitive text, even if no one could read it. The Bishop conjectured that those scratches meant *king*, at which point the great nineteenth-century scientists of language plunged into translation, confident they would soon be reading Sumerian creation myths, Sumerian history, and epic tales of the splendid Sumerian sovereign, Ashurbanipal.

Years later, when the philologists were finally able to translate those scratches on clay, they found that among all those thousands of tablets, the king was just about the only character. The remainder of the story, if one could call it such, was a laundry list of everything the king owned — the grain, goats, pigs, slaves, and wives. The first writing had nothing whatsoever to do with telling a story the way we think about a story. There was neither narrator nor chronology. The first writing had no plot.

Eventually, more than 150,000 such tablets were discovered. And just as the study of ancient snail shells became ethnochoncology, so did the study of ancient property lists earn its own designation among nineteenth-century German philologists, who called it *Listeneissenschaft*.

The first writing of our species soon progressed from bushels of wheat and containers of milk to deeds of sale, deeds of purchase, and endless lists of tributes, rations, rentals, loans, taxes, and the prices of commodities. Some enumerate the number of fattened young goats sacrificed to the great gods Enlil, Enki, and Utu. Others note the same for sheep, ewes, and lambs. The first writing was accounting. The first words were all about the money.

It is possible that to the Babylonians and Assyrians, the lists sang out like the dithyrambs of Euripedes, that the message was as profound as the theology of Christ. Perhaps the people who created the lists were held in as high esteem as the visionaries and prodigies of BuzzFeed, who turned the science of list-making into "The 50 Cutest Things That Ever Happened" and "25 Signs You Drink Too Much Wine," seven billion monthly views, revenue in excess of $100 million, and a 2015 valuation of $1.5 billion.

Bitcoin, too, is powered by lists: secured by the so-called distributed ledger technology of the blockchain, every Bitcoin possesses within itself a chronology of all its previous owners and transactions, verified across thousands of far-flung individual computers. Like a token pressed into the wet clay of a Mesopotamian tablet, the record of sale of the first Satoshi endures within the hard drive of Craig Wright's computer:

12c6DSiU4Rq3P4ZxziKxzrL5LmMBrzjrJX.

If Bitcoin is a language, that was its first word, the latest in a long line of pseudonyms for money, as impossible to pronounce as the code is impossible to break. Its name reveals absolutely nothing about its substance. And that's the prerequisite for both money and language.

That's why it doesn't matter who created Bitcoin, and perhaps better for everyone if nobody knows what identity, if any, lies behind the mask. Even if people doubt that Craig Wright is Satoshi Nakamoto, no one doubts that Wright is rich. He has harvested more than a million of his invisible coins, which brings his net worth within shouting distance of $10 billion.

Yet for all its apparent newness, the first cryptocurrency has a great deal in common with primitive money. Like the Yurok's dentalia, Bitcoin will remain concealed until unleashed by sustained focus and concentration. Like the Boyowas' magic of plenty, Bitcoin will emerge as the outcome of a journey only a few are equipped to undertake. Craig Wright could conjure currency from the electronic ether because he realized that the wired world we presently inhabit is not so different from the archaic world that banked on invocation and incantation.

Long ago, the prophet, the soothsayer, and the storyteller made money out of myth, and coaxed the cosmos into allegorical figures for human fears and desires. Before the truck and barter of market economies, currency was a matter of personification and metonymy — money that had a face, money that could be worn, money that could sing, speak, and swear. The first great city-states of Mesopotamia cemented the enduring power of the priest and bureaucrat, for the organization and maximization of sovereign assets depended upon the ability to harness nature through the increasingly technical science of accounting for domesticated grains, yoked animals, bridled brides, and endless other commodities listed in thousands of crumbling cuneiform tablets. Over the millennia, such lists have grown to encompass everything on earth, from where we live to the air we breathe to the DNA within our cells.

Catachresis proved essential to the development of modern riches, which are less linked to real things like barley, goats, and royal tribute, and more dependent upon ethereal concepts like collateralized bond obligations, consequently requiring currency flexible enough to support credit default swaps, baskets of options and indices, and public offerings of corporations the size and span of which eclipse the greatest of Mesopotamia's long-lost city-states, from Babylon to Ur.

That broad flexibility of currency — required for more abstract and expansive transactions than ever before — became both a terrible burden and a source of endless fascination for a new generation of priests and bureaucrats who had been mesmerized by the radical story of a revolutionary character with an uncanny sense of parable and metaphor, a human yet divine intercessor more intimate, approachable, and accessible than the indifferent deities of the archaic city-states.

For what could be more evocative of eternal profit and irredeemable loss than the word made flesh?

{4} THE SOUL OF MONEY

*To what purpose is the multitude of your sacrifices unto me? saith the
LORD: I am full of the burnt offerings of rams, and the fat of fed beasts;
and I delight not in the blood of bullocks, or of lambs, or of he goats.*

— ISAIAH 1:11

CITY-STATES EXPANDED into empires, a political construct that proved
particularly congenial to coinage. Masters of the mint could embed
extraordinary depths of plot, character, and metaphor within these
glittering microcosms. Coins could communicate puissance and
power to the farthest reaches of a realm, but they could also point to
the pathos of downfall and defeat, mirroring the emotional mix that
forged one of the most stunning innovations in the history of storytelling: the birth of tragedy.

The ancient trade route between southern, central, and western Asia was known as the Grand Trunk Road. The city of Kandahar lies in the middle of this route, and two thousand years ago was
known for its ten varieties of apricots, its tender pale pink grapes,
the strongest strains of *Cannabis indica,* and an abundant supply of
white quartz crystals shot through with veins of gold. The kingdom
was rich and the king was learned, wise, and holy. One day, he read a
prophecy that shocked him.

The stars told him of a monarch much greater, mightier, wiser,
more spiritual, and many times as rich as he, a ruler whose wealth

would stagger the accounts of the greatest cotton and musk merchants from Chittagong to Kabul. So, being a pragmatic king, he ordered up a caravan, filled it with the gold of Kandahar, and headed west. Along the way he ran into two other kings who had deciphered the same message in the sky and packed their own caravans with two of the other great luxury commodities of ancient times: perfume to anoint royalty and oil to embalm the dead.

It is no coincidence that the king of Kandahar's name was Casper, descended from the ancient Chaldean word for *treasurer*. He was the oldest of the wise men, so had the honor of being the first to kneel before the newborn in the manger and the first to leave an offering. The gift was gold — because of gold's purity, its power, and its perfection. Most likely, the Vatican still has it somewhere.

Ever since the Middle Ages, the three kings' visit to Bethlehem has been commemorated by the feast of the Epiphany, a sacred meal featuring a cake within which has been baked a trinket of some sort, traditionally a coin. The ritual meal is called king cake, and the prize within promises good luck, great fortune, and a share of equity in salvation.

The story of redemption promised by that coin came to a head in the time of Pontius Pilate. Every spring, more than two million Jews made the pilgrimage to Jerusalem to reenact through prayer, sacrifice, and ritual meals the Exodus from slavery unto Pharaoh in Egypt. Some modern historians estimate that each pilgrim spent the equivalent of three to four thousand dollars in today's money during their journey, so that Passover in ancient Jerusalem generated revenues worth hundreds of millions of dollars.

One source of this revenue was the sale of sacrificial animals. Blood had marked the doors of the Hebrews as they escaped from ancient Egypt, so in order to celebrate one's own symbolic Exodus, each devotee was required to ransom himself all over again through the blood of an animal. The pilgrims had to purchase a lamb that not only was alive, but certified kosher by the temple priests — that is, a beast perfect enough to be chosen then slaughtered. Which is to say that the priests in the temple of Jerusalem had cornered the market on Pesach.

When Jesus rode his donkey through the gates of the holy city on the first day of Passover two thousand years ago, Jerusalem was a Roman province, ruled by Roman coin. The silver denarius — the Roman reserve currency — was legal tender from London to Damascus. Despite the prevalence of the denarius, archeologists and numismatists have unearthed more than forty-five thousand different coins within the holy vicinity, from Greek *assarions* to Syrian *staters*, solid-gold Egyptian *oktadrachms*, unstamped copper, lead blanks, and numerous counterfeit molds. Which is no doubt why the priests had to carefully weigh, assay, and measure every shape, alloy, and denomination presented for exchange, as all the different incarnations of value had to be reduced to one sort of incarnation, the only kind that could purchase the blood of redemption, and that was the temple shekel. On temple grounds only temple money counted, not money melted and minted by Ethiopians, Iranians, Moabites, or any other apostate or *apikoros*.

A rabbi himself, Jesus was well versed in the temple tradition of exchanging precious metal for precious blood. He observed the pilgrims as they changed their native coins into temple coins, temple coins to temple animals, temple animals into holy blood, holy blood into a share of redemption. But there was something about the scene that set him off.

> He overturned the tables of the moneychangers and the stools of those who sold pigeons, and said to them, "It is written in the Scriptures that God said, 'My Temple will be called a house of prayer.'"

In a jealous rage, he lashed out against the only fiction that might prove to be as pervasive and powerful as he. Henceforth, Jesus decreed, the payment that mattered would not be made in denarii, *oktadrachms*, lamb's blood, or temple shekels. The only currency that could recoup original sin, redeem our souls, ransom our captivity to gross materiality, and repossess the long-lost property in Eden would be his own blood.

The parallel between the life of Christ and the life of money was fully expressed in 1925, when an advertising executive named Bruce Barton published one of the best-selling books of the early twentieth century, *The Man Nobody Knows*. The book was a guide to success in money and business in which the model capitalist was Jesus.

Barton began his professional life as a magazine journalist before hearing the call of advertising, a business in which the evidence of his success has endured. Not only did Barton create Betty Crocker, he came up with company names for both General Electric and General Motors, which indicated consistency of his branding philosophy, if nothing else. Barton's brand eventually made it all the way to the nation's capital, where he served in the United States Congress representing the silk stocking district of Manhattan's Upper East Side. But advertising and politics were mere preludes to his literary accomplishment, which articulated how the story of Jesus and the story of money were one and the same.

The titular *Man Nobody Knows* was Jesus — but not baby Jesus or Christ on the cross or the vengeful crusader on Judgment Day. *The Man Nobody Knows* was the redeemer as a public relations guru, brilliant copywriter, super salesman, hobnobber, and flesh pumper par excellence. *The Man Nobody Knows* understood how to get people's attention and how to hold it. He was the prodigy who brought together twelve strangers, inspired them by invoking the powers of personal motivation and sacrifice for the sake of the team, and created the greatest corporation of all time. He oozed charisma and leadership capability, but kept his eternally watchful eye on inventory and sales. He was a man's man, he was the son of god, and he never lost sight of the fact that his kingdom was valuable real estate. He was Jesus the chief executive, and he knew his gospel had cash value.

While Barton may have been the most accomplished articulator of Jesus the capitalist, he was not the first. The knot of Christianity and commercial culture formed the bedrock of one of the most enduring American philosophical movements, summed up by the title of Andrew Carnegie's 1889 essay, "The Gospel of Wealth," which spearheaded the popular worship of the Protestant work ethic. The American Baptist minister Russell Conwell summed it up best in a speech he delivered more than six thousand times, in which he promised that a life of Christian virtue would bring "acres of diamonds." "I say that you ought to get rich," the reverend famously declared. *"It is your duty to get rich."*

In a 1905 speech at the University of Chicago, John D. Rockefeller proved himself an acolyte. "I believe the power to make money is a gift from God," he said. "I believe it is my duty to make money — and still more money." The idea appeared to make a great deal of sense to vast numbers of people.

"By a fortunate dispensation, the virtues enjoined on Christians — diligence, moderation, sobriety, thrift — are the very qualities most conducive to commercial success." That quote is from a magazine article that ran in *The New Republic* in the spring of 1924, expressing the sentiments of a generation to whom it had become apparent that a godly life would be compensated on earth as in heaven, that poverty was one step away from sin, and that the businessman's credo of hard work and self-deprivation was an imitation of Christ. "People are entitled to the rewards of their industry," wrote President

Calvin Coolidge. "What they earn is theirs, no matter how small or how great. But the possession of property carries the obligation to use it in a larger service."

This new religion was called "prosperity theology," and it would be taken to extremes not only by businessmen and politicians but by preachers such as Oral Roberts, who donned Italian silk suits, flaunted diamond rings and gold bracelets, and threatened suicide if his television ministry failed to raise the millions he demanded. Roberts's example inspired future generations of televangelists, and brought to American living rooms the gospel according to Billy Graham, Jimmy Swaggart, Joel Osteen, and Pat Robertson—whose holy ministry netted him more than $100 million. These men understood that the plots of spiritual redemption and pecuniary redemption were virtually identical, give or take a few technical terms, which may explain why the initial coin offering of a cryptocurrency known as "Jesus Coin," despite being a hoax, attracted significant investment.

One reason why the gospel of wealth was believed by so many was that money was godly long before He rewarded the Pentecostal preacher Kenneth Copeland with a personal net worth of $760 million, long before Trinity Church's real estate holdings in Manhattan surpassed $2 billion, and long before King Casper left a pot of gold for baby Jesus. Prosperity theology and "abundant life" theology are as old as ostrich egg beads, trophy wives, and kula.

In *Works and Days*, the ancient poet Hesiod introduced a long line of precious metal gods. Gold was the child of Zeus, tin the offspring of Jupiter, copper of Venus, iron of Mars, and lead of Saturn. Silver was the white goddess, ruled by the moon. Human history began when those "immortals who dwell in Olympian homes brought into being the golden race of mortal men...who lived like gods without any care in their hearts, free and apart from labor and misery." The golden race lived in the Golden Age, and after those Edenic days had come and gone, the gods of silver, bronze, and iron took turns ruling their own increasingly bleak epochs, all of which ended badly, culminating in what was, according to Hesiod, "evil war and terrible battle."

Jesus descended from a long genealogy of heavy metal gods whose precious blood ran with copper, silver, bronze, and gold. Such gods, as a general rule, were tragic. In Nigeria, the metal myth centers around Ogun, the Yoruba god of iron, who kills himself with his own sword. Ogun's iron body disintegrates and diffuses beneath the earth, but his soul lives on as the sacred guardian of metalsmiths. Another tragic tale recounts the sad fate of the Greek god Hephaestus, flung down from the heights of Olympus, consigned for all eternity to forge armor and weapons of bronze and steel, only to hear secondhand about the frolics and flirtations of his unfaithful wife. Chief among the ancient chthonic deities was Pluto, not only the wealthiest of all the gods, but also the most tragically confined to darkness.

In the myths, each metal character possesses his or her own *telos*, the Greek word for both fate and payment. This fate-payment-telos was as a general rule gruesome, for the precious metal gods were each in turn overthrown, and more often than not, ripped to shreds. Like the protagonists of classical tragedy, the metal gods weren't just murdered. They were pulverized and flung to the far-thest reaches — where they found refuge in lodes and veins buried deep within the mountains or hidden within the silt of riverbeds. In ancient Greek drama, the ritual of ripping apart and scattering the corpse of a sacrificial figure was such a common plot point that it had its own name: *sparagmos*, the most famous example of which occurs in Euripides' drama *The Bacchae*. In this tragedy, Dionysus and his followers, the raving Maenads, exact revenge on the hero, King Pentheus of Thebes, by tearing his body into pieces.

Precious metal coinage appeared for the first time in the Peloponnese in the middle of the fifth century BC, simultaneous with the birth of tragedy. The coincidence has engendered an erudite debate among classicists as to why these two transformative innovations evolved in the same place at the same time. In retrospect, prosperity theology provided a clue: The reincorporation of a tragically dismembered hero produces acres of diamonds.

Not long before Pentheus met his barbaric fate, the bodies of the metal gods were broken, fragmented, and dispersed. *Sparagmos* was enacted and reenacted over and over again throughout the ancient world, typically in animal sacrifice, as the bleeding bodies of countless rams, lambs, and goats could attest. The roasted dividends of sacrificial rituals would then be distributed among initiates who most likely believed that their consumption of the shares turned them into members of a single corporate body — much like the eucharist, which endures as a ritual communion in honor of that other broken god.

The earliest metallurgists — a combination of priest, magician, shaman, and scientist — learned to collect the shattered remnants of lost gods. They knew how to incorporate the remains into slurries, and bless them with salts, solvents, heat, and pressure. They understood that the fragments would then purify, repair themselves, and galvanize into miraculously reincarnated wholes, and that the spirit of a vanquished god could be recovered and transformed into material prosperity. They were betting that the empire of the metals would rise again to hold sway over grain money, livestock money, and even polished snail shells.

Coins presented a subtly different surface than the cowries of Micronesia, the wampum of North America, or the "ghost face" copper and tin *pinyin* of China. The major design innovation was that they did not have holes drilled through the middle, which meant that they could not be worn as adornments like wedding rings, beaded belts, anklets, or necklaces. In place of the hole there was now an image, be it of a ruler, a river, a city, or a god.

But the most striking thing about coins is that they are indistinguishable from their replicants — all are stamped with the same signs and symbols, as if they are a phalanx of soldiers or identical offspring of some far-flung family. Their numbers are validated by the phrase that appears on most United States currency: *e pluribus unum* — of many, one. The coin implies the larger system that has brought the coin into being, a system that can produce more and more coins. The individual points to the group.

Bankers are particularly attuned to such relationships. A typical investment bank, private equity firm, or hedge fund has a so-called credit desk devoted to the cause of replication. It's where money multiplies faster than grain or livestock ever could. It's where dollars are harvested any time of year and delivered from the womb with far less fuss than cows or pigs. So readily do coins beget more coins that financiers no longer require mints to stamp out their supplies. Instead, the arbitrageurs utilize a metaphor they call "leverage."

The phrase "leveraged buyout" became infamous when two reporters from *The Wall Street Journal* memorialized a $31 billion deal to acquire RJR Nabisco in a best-selling book that epitomized the money culture of the 1980s, *Barbarians at the Gate*. The largest leveraged buyout in history came around two decades after the Nabisco debacle, wrought by the frenzied *sparagmos* and byzantine reassembly of a coal and nuclear power giant called Energy Future Holdings. That deal generated so much debt it delivered a rare $900 million loss to the iconic American investor Warren Buffet.

And just as allegory, personification, psychomachia, metonymy, and catachresis are ancient tactics of symbol making and storytelling familiar to writers and poets, so is leverage. And like most other rhetorical strategies, it has its own name: synecdoche.

Synecdoche is the metaphor in which a part — such as a single coin — can stand for a whole, such as a multitude of coins not present. Likewise, in the study of fiction, is a character often declared to be a "type," which means that the character can stand for more than one person — say a class or a gender. Typology is nothing new to anyone who has ever made his or her way through late medieval allegories such as *The Pilgrim's Progress*, *Piers Plowman*, or (most obviously) *Everyman*, each of which presents a protagonist who stands for all of us. Jesus is another example of this type.

A more narrowly linguistic example of synecdoche is "the ABCs," a phrase that implies all twenty-six letters of the alphabet, although only the first three are present. Likewise, a metaphor such as "the hand of God" indicates all of god, as one part of the body — the hand — leverages the presence of the entire body. A visible part that stands for an invisible whole is a way of making absent things present to the imagination, an essential quality for bank loan officers, who as a matter of daily business make whole sums appear from fractions.

In *The Modern Corporation and Private Property*, often cited as the classic text of United States corporate law, authors Adolf Berle and Gardiner Means observed the odd accumulation of parts that comprise the modern corporation, and tried to make sense of it. They noted that while big business was formally owned by its corporate entity, shareholders possessed shares, and directors controlled activity. The result of this hodgepodge, argued Berle and Means, was that the fragmentation of the whole into an abundance of parts had, in their own words, "destroyed the unity that we commonly call property."

In the preface to the 1967 revised edition, Berle asked a most basic economic question: Why have stockholders? "Stockholders toil not, neither do they spin, to earn that reward. They are beneficiaries by position only. Justification for their inheritance must be sought outside classic economic reasoning."

In fact, the justification for the ownership of shares was not economic reasoning whatsoever. It was literary reasoning — most specifically, the logic of synecdoche, the literary rule of "part for whole." The idea of owning a portion of "stock" (itself a legal fiction) that could rise or fall in accordance with the fate of a corporate whole (yet another legal fiction) satisfied the rules of metaphor and the history of fragmented gods, even if it made little empirical sense. The public offering and valuation of stocks was as much a matter of myth as of math.

Bankers use synecdoche to power the *e pluribus unum* of coinage, to secure their leveraged buyouts, to offer imaginary slivers of ownership as companies "go public." In all of this, the bankers prove to be just as poetic as the poets. Their most magical act of all is using the logic of "part for whole" to generate profits through fractional banking.

Both retail and investment bankers loan out money that is not theirs, and do so in great multiples. The implied meaning of the bank — that it overflows with wealth, that it stores all of your money — is the opposite of its literal meaning, which is that it overflows with debt and stores a mere fraction of your money. The bank's irony, generally a well kept secret, only comes to our attention on tragic occasions such as failures, financial crises, and times of severe inflation. In these extreme cases, it becomes obvious that in no way, shape, or form do the fractional parts add up to the whole. And in such cases the remedy is as old as myth: the fragmenting of the body into its constituent parts and selling these off, as was the fate of the storied investment bank Solomon Brothers after the financial crisis of 2008.

As allegory made money out of cowries, metonymy made money out of wives, and catachresis made money out of livestock, the magical thinking that guides synecdoche also came to define a great deal of what we consider money. For epic as the revolutions of precious metal coinage, leveraged buyouts, stockholding, and fractional banking may have been, they barely skim the surface of synecdoche's role in finance. The idea of *e pluribus unum* goes to the heart of what may be the most perplexing question of all in the history of money, a question so logically impossible to answer that we have simply chosen to stop thinking about it: How can a trove of precious metal, securely locked in a vault, extend itself into the realm of paper currency? It is synecdoche that lies behind the idea that a state's reserve of bullion might somehow allow that sovereign entity to emit a virtually endless stream of bills and notes — and call them money.

There are those who say that paper money lies at the heart of all financial woe, and we will address the question in some depth in subsequent chapters. But returning to a gold or silver standard only raises an older and deeper question: How and why did precious metal, particularly gold, come to stand for money in the first place? How did minions of metal replicants, gathered from the mud and silt, ever come to surpass perfectly good metaphors such as shells, bells, and bulls?

They did so by proving themselves most perfectly adaptable to synecdoche. They did so by the way that bronze, copper, iron, silver, and gold fit into the tragic plot of *sparagmos*. They did so by delivering on the dream of making things whole again — that is, the dream of *incorporation* — that their fragmentation and dispersal long ago

Gold, locked behind the bars of an underground dungeon known as the United States Federal Reserve.

had augured. And they did so by conforming to the myth of the coldest, darkest, and richest immortal of them all.

In ancient Greek, *ploutos* meant the wealth of precious metal, but Pluto has also been translated as "the hidden one," a definition that has endured as sound advice. It's why pirates and thieves bury their coins and bullion. It's why Pluto lives underground, where no one can find him. It's why plutocrats conceal the nature and scale of their assets and debts.

The word "plutocracy" entered English in 1666, a mere seven years after a pair of London scriveners wrote by hand the first recognizably modern personal check, that is, a customized fragment of money, just for them. Words such as *plutolatry*, the worship of money, and *plutomania*, money madness, were introduced shortly thereafter. Recently, yet another related word has entered the language, coined in the title of a 2005 client report from Citigroup: "Plutonomy: Buying Luxury, Explaining Global Imbalances." The first sentence sums up the thesis: "The World is dividing into two blocs—the Plutonomy and the rest." The publication, noted the writers, "generated great interest from our clients." These clients had an average net worth of more than $100 million.

The Plutonomists' foundational myth may be instructive, but it is certainly not pretty. The story is as follows: After ten million years of darkness, Pluto mounted his golden chariot, burst above ground, and after his eyes adjusted to the light he spied a beautiful young maiden gathering wildflowers, whom he summarily tossed into the back seat. The earth yawned open, and Pluto's four black stallions rushed the god and his hostage back to his underground palace. Here, he hid her, raped her, and forced her into marriage—which would not have bothered any of the other gods except that the maiden, Persephone, was the daughter of the goddess Demeter.

After Demeter, who presided over the fertility of the earth, threatened that unless she got Persephone back she would send the planet into eternal winter, Zeus demanded that his older brother Pluto come to the bargaining table. Eventually, Pluto agreed to allow his queen to rise to the surface each spring, just in time for renewal feasts such as Easter, Passover, Persian New Years, the Babylonian barley festival, and the Bosnian bacchanalia of scrambled eggs. Come fall, Persephone must return to the underworld and her life as Pluto's bride. Their monstrous merger generated a son, Plutus, the "divine child," who is both lame and winged. Like money, he takes his time arriving but is gone before you know it.

After a long line of defeats, Pluto had notched a decisive victory for metal, and it came at the expense of the grain goddess herself. Pluto had pulled off a profitable merger and acquisition: Not only had he fractionalized his wife, he had leveraged spring, and the bargain led to an astounding run.

Archeologists have discovered that the first precious metal coins were neither gold nor silver, but a mixture of both called electrum, found in abundance in a river that flowed through an ancient kingdom called Lydia, presently a part of Turkey. The coins were struck with the image of a lion, its front paws flailing in the air. It is generally agreed among numismatists that this lion was the insignia of a king named Alyattes, who ruled from 620 BC to his death in 560.

Alyattes' son was Croesus, generally considered the richest man of the ancient world. He amused himself by guzzling wine from golden pitchers and devouring mutton with golden utensils until the Persian King Cyrus raised a cavalry of armored camels, marched across the plains of Babylonia, lit a bonfire, barbecued Croesus, and melted all his coins. After Cyrus came Darius, who melted all of Cyrus' coins and reminted them in order to broadcast his own epic story and declare his infinite power. Then Alexander of Macedon came along to burn, rape, and pillage the Persian empire, melt all of Darius' *darics*, and stamp coins with Macedonian faces.

The Romans tossed Alexander's coins into the same cauldron as the booty they had stolen from the Angles, Gauls, and Teutons, melting the old coins and fashioning new ones with the portraits of Caligula, Claudius, Diocletian, Hadrian, Marc Antony, Nero, Octavius, and each of the Twelve Caesars. Before mass media and social media, before Facebook and Twitter, these Roman emperors disseminated political propaganda through the one thing every citizen needed. Their coins did not advertise cities or gods, but themselves, their military victories, their great edicts, and eventually exposed their greatest fears. When Rome was sacked for the first time, the coins featured the Emperor Honorius, his eyes bugging open in abject terror.

The Empire's gold fell to the hordes of Hun, Ostrogoth, Vandal, Visigoth, and Byzantine rulers, who established their mints in Carthage, Constantinople, Ravenna, Rome, and Toulouse. In due course, the Ottomans confiscated what was left of the empire's eastern hordes of bezants, while the western coins met their fate as nobles and guldens stamped anew by medieval mints in Bavaria, England, Frisia, and Saxony. After deaths and rebirths too numerous to count, some of King Alyattes' gold likely endures within the ingots stacked in the basement of the United States Federal Reserve. Thus had the cycle of *sparagmos* and reincorporation as imagined in the myths of archaic metal gods foreshadowed more than two millennia of near-maniacal melting and minting.

Some say that the very first Lydian coin was enough to buy eleven sheep, including all rights and privileges to the hundred or so pounds of wool they produced each year. Others estimate the value at ten goats — and the hundred or so pounds of milk they might produce each day. Still others, perhaps most extravagantly, estimate three jugs of wine. An exact account of their value doesn't matter as much as the breadth of their circulation, as within a century of their birth millions of them had migrated across Europe, and Phoenician merchants on the southern coast of the Iberian Peninsula were exchanging coins with Carthaginians from North Africa three thousand miles from Lydia. They were a hit, even if the consequences of precious metal coinage would eventually prove dire. For there is a myth about that river that floated through ancient Lydia, brimming with glitter — that it was the river in which King Midas washed the golden touch off his hands. That mythical king, alongside Pluto, has long been an idol of the banking class.

There are many versions of the story, but as a general rule the mythographers agree that when the future ruler was a baby a colony of ants nested in his mouth, leaving behind bits of grain. In ancient cultures of the Mediterranean, dominated and defined by seed money, an infant with a mouth full of grain was an omen. It meant that one day, the child would be rich. But this particular story provides an early case of what English professors call dramatic irony, which is an essential element of tragic plots. For Midas, the richest of all kings, would die without a drachma. That's the part of the story the financiers forget.

The tragedy begins as the king, wandering through the forest, comes across a stinking drunk, potbellied, bald-headed, horse-eared god of sex, drugs, and the closest thing that passed for rock and roll at the time, which was lyric poetry. This gluttonous and grotesque old man was a well-known character. His name was Silenus, and ancient statuettes depict his appearance as hideous on the outside; but locked inside was a resplendent figure in the perfect shape of a god. Socrates called that inner form "divine, golden"—like the glittering surprise of a coin discerned within the dough of a king cake—which may explain why the image of Silenus made it to some of the world's first precious metal mintages, appearing on various silver tetradrachmas dating back to the fifth century BC.

Some say Midas took Silenus captive; others, that Midas guided the inebriated satyr to his castle and tucked him into bed to sober up. In either case, when it became clear that Silenus was no longer gallivanting naked through the forest, Dionysus went looking for his mentor and discovered that King Midas had kept him safe. As a way of saying thank you, Dionysus promised the king whatever his heart desired: the ability to make everything he touched turn to gold.

The first thing Midas transformed was a twig. Next, a stone. He pulled an apple off a tree and held a golden apple. He stuck his hand up to the wrist in a pile of stinking filthy mud and lifted up a clump of purest gold. The allegorical powers of organic nature—shells, seeds, skin, teeth, canoes hollowed out from sacred trees—all now bowed to precious metal. Unfortunately, everything meant everything. When Midas brushed his hand against his young daughter she, too, turned to gold. The Roman poet Ovid described the result:

> Dismayed by this strange misfortune, rich and unhappy, he tries
> to flee his riches, and hates what he wished for a moment ago.
> No abundance can relieve his famine: his throat is parched with
> burning thirst, and, justly, he is tortured by the hateful gold.

Midas, starving to death and sick with grief, fell on his face and begged the gods for mercy. In Aristotle's retelling there is none, and Midas dies. But the myth has an alternate ending in which the drunken hermaphrodite, Dionysus, pities the fool. From the Bullfinch version of 1855: "'Go,' said he, 'to the river Pactolus, trace the stream to its fountain-head, there plunge your head and body in and wash away your fault and its punishment.'" The river Pactolus was the same that flowed through the ancient kingdom of Lydia, its silt saturated with the electrum of the first precious metal coins.

Collecting, consolidating, and leveraging shares of scattered remnants—be they electrum from the silt of Pactolus or relics of the true cross—is a plot that endured from ancient myth to medieval Christianity, and eventually consumed early modern European thought, culture, and finance. Synecdoche not only propelled coinage into monumental iterations of credit and debt, but created the first recognizable examples of retail banks, investment banks, insurance companies, mortgage dealers, and multinational corporations.

{5} THE CRUSADE

Remember, that time is money.

— BENJAMIN FRANKLIN

Everything is already dead and risen in advance.

— JEAN BAUDRILLARD

THE DOMESTICATED PLANT, the harnessed animal, the wife, the bead, the shell, the coin — none of these intimated the infinitude that lay ahead for money. For that leap into the immeasurable, medieval monks deserve a great deal of credit. They were the ones who built stories on top of stories until every plot, character, and metaphor dissolved into doomsday, which was throughout the Middle Ages a financial term of art.

In 1085 William the Conqueror needed money. Taxes were the obvious solution, so he sent out dozens of royal commissioners to compile data for an inventory of every property and resource within England. Bound in boards of oak, the final account was voluminous. Its 888 pages of parchment described more than 13,000 districts and localities, mentioned by name more than a quarter of a million people, and included a financial reckoning of every church, castle, meadow, animal, fishpond, and acre of farmland. It was called *The Domesday Book*, and as it turned out, everything listed inside it added up to an astounding fortune for William the Conqueror. Translated into today's dollars, the young king learned he was worth something along the lines of $250 billion.

One hundred years after its publication, Richard FitzNeal, treasurer of Henry II, explained the origin of *The Domesday Book*'s name. "We have called the book 'the Book of Judgment'...because its decisions, like those of the Last Judgment, are unalterable." FitzNeal's concise explanation anticipated the kind of story money would become in the Middle Ages, and it possessed the same apocalyptic contours Marx and Engels would outline eight hundred years later. Although neither are works of fiction, *The Domesday Book* of 1086 and *The Communist Manifesto* of 1848 share a preoccupation with what is arguably the most important part of any story: The End.

The ancient Assyrians prophesied the final day and hour, which was scheduled to have been over and done with more than two thousand years ago. To the Norse, The End would come in the form of a titanic war between frost and fire, culminating in mud. Every Passover, Jews open their front door for Elijah, hoping for the conflagrations of redemption to sweep through the world, destroy their enemies, and bring about the Messianic Age. The ancient Egyptians and Sumerians, the Hindus, the Hopis, the Mayans, and the Inuit—all have written the last acts of the cosmic drama.

Not to be outdone, the Christians presented their own highly detailed, finely rendered, hair-raising story of The End. The dead would wake, zombies rise, the oceans freeze, the sky burn. Time would stop, Christ return, and the accounting would begin—to be followed in quick succession by the big either/or: a seat in the heavenly choir or a coal in the furnace of eternal damnation. The only particular left out of the Christian scenario was, as Jesus himself noted, the expiration date: "Of that day or that hour no one knows, not even the angels in heaven, nor the Son, but only the Father."

Despite the horrors of dictatorship, nuclear holocaust, climate change, genocide, pandemics, and currency collapse, the majority of twenty-first century *Homo sapiens* feel impelled to create at least a modicum of pragmatic goals for themselves. Not so for the monks and Christian theologians of the early Middle Ages, who did not conceive the story of their lives through narratives of career advancement, marriage, family, or the accrual of 529s and 401ks. The End, as foretold in the book of Revelations, framed the plot.

According to the church fathers, the first apocalyptic discontinuity in the steady stream of time had come with the fall of man, followed by the flood, the incarnation, and the resurrection. Judgment Day was up next, at which point the monks would cash in their Christian chips, and the ensuing redemption would more than make up for their celibate lives of solitude, work, study, poverty, prayer, and more work. The monks believed in the value of waiting. They believed that time would tell. So they scrutinized every sign and portent. They contemplated clues for years on end, for they believed they were playing an essential role. They were crusaders, engaged in a mental fight, bringing the day ever closer. One result was that the medieval mind grew accustomed to considering the world in reverse chronology, not from the beginning going forward, but from The End going back.

The monks' obsession with hastening The End of the cosmic plot would be neither the first nor the last effort to harness and domesticate the hours. In this long-standing endeavor to control and manipulate time, money would prove to be a valuable tool. The enterprise has endured, as a thousand years after the monks' apocalyptic obsessions Bitcoin also defined its end in the beginning. By regulating the rate at which the currency would be released and estimating demand, Satoshi Nakamoto was able to calculate that the last of his pseudonymous coins — twenty-one million in all — will be mined sometime between May and October, 2140. The date holds whether or not there is such a person as Satoshi Nakamoto.

Like a photograph or a diary, coins preserve the moment. In ancient Europe, a visit from a rich, famous, extremely learned, powerful, or holy person was a matter of such consequence that it often called for a series of commemorative coins. Stamping a profile on metal was a means to freeze time, or at least slow it down. Today, such coins are collectibles — to be safely preserved as opposed to circulated.

Classics scholars have noted the ancient Greek word for these freshly stamped, newly minted, time-petrifying precious metal advent coins. They were called *parousia*, which roughly translated means *arrival*. The word was related to the Greek for the sudden appearance of messengers on a theatrical stage, and to the spectacular and supernatural appearances known as epiphanies — such as the glorious manifestation Saul of Tarsus witnessed on the road to Damascus.

About two decades after this epiphany, Saul — now known as Paul the Apostle — visited the chief synagogue of Thessaloniki in northern Greece. (Coincidentally, this city would become home to one of the greatest mints in all ancient history, and produce thousands of the Byzantine Empire's most iconic coin, the golden bezant.) After Paul had preached the gospel for a few weeks, riots broke out. Fearing for his life, the apostle snuck out of the city in the middle of the night and a few months later found refuge in Corinth, where upon further reflection he decided he had a great deal more to tell his Greek converts about The End. He wrote down his words of wisdom and sent them off in a series of secret letters, the second of which can be found in the New Testament under the heading "2 Thessalonians." A great deal of this letter concerns the day the story stops, apocalypse descends, the hours grind to a halt, creditors take their profits, and debtors are either forgiven or rendered bankrupt—and summarily punished. It was the day, Paul explained, "when the Lord Jesus is revealed from heaven with his mighty angels in flaming fire."

In that sentence, Paul chose the word *parousia*—the word for commemorative coinage—to cite the Second Coming of Christ. This was only logical, as the "surprise" coin in the King's Cake consumed at the Feast of the Epiphany not only commemorated the arrival of baby Jesus, but also anticipated universal redemption. What metaphor was adequate to describe the birth and rebirth of god? Only money.

Despite the similarities of Christ and coin, denial endured. For many years, the standard history of money in Europe's Christian Middle Ages was that modern finance only began after the conflicts between churchmen and merchant adventurers had been resolved in such a way that the great English, Dutch, French, and Italian banking concerns were unshackled from the ancient proscriptions against usury and set free to fund the Renaissance, empower the Enlightenment, subsidize mercantilism, provide credit and equity for the Age of Conquest, and establish the basis for global capitalism.

The masterminds of modern finance—so this version of history goes—emerged victorious from their thousand-year dispute against the toothless and emaciated monks and church fathers, who harbored deep suspicions of the devilishly inspired plots, characters, and metaphors of any banking instrument remotely related to interest—including mortgages, loans, lines of credit, and exchange rates.

The twenty-second chapter of Exodus was hard to ignore: "If thou lend money to any of My people, even to the poor with thee, thou shalt not be to him as a creditor; neither shall ye lay upon him interest." But as the medievalist Raymond de Roover noted in a 1967 monograph, the scholarly monks "devoted so much space to this one subject and overrated one problem to the neglect of many others, that they created the impression of being devoid of a sense of balance." De Roover, who had turned his attention to the Middle Ages after graduating from Harvard Business School and earning a doctorate in economics from the University of Chicago, proposed that the church fathers' approach to money was not an impediment to but a precursor of modern economics.

The new perspective on medieval money was summed up in the title of Robert S. Lopez's much-reprinted 1971 treatise, *The Commercial Revolution of the Middle Ages.* Close readings of surviving texts and records showed that the abbeys and monasteries, relying on cheap labor, rent revenue, and credit financing secured through a variety of complex financial arrangements, were not anti-banking, but proto-capitalist. The conflict between the merchant and the monk, the battle royale of money against Lord God Jehova — no such thing had ever happened.

Today, few dispute that the story of money and the story of god remained as closely intertwined during the Middle Ages as they had been during the days of canoe trade and cowries, animal sacrifice, and Pluto's gold. The Lord was always entitled to a share of the medieval merchant's profits and liquidations, and even had his own account, listed by bookkeepers under the unsubtle heading, "To God."

The result was that the church found itself in the paradoxical position of celebrating poverty while accumulating massive economic power. It was this relationship between the worldly and the otherworldly that prompted the Scholastics — that long line of intellectuals and schoolmen from Ambrose to Ignatius — to scribble their volumes of tortuously twisted logic, leading to their unenviable reputation of having spent their lives calculating the number of angels that could dance on the head of a pin. In fact, the work they were engaged in was far from impractical. The not-quite-economic insights of the Scholastics transformed into religious edicts and decrees, to which the medieval merchants would conform. Together, they composed a new chapter of the money plot.

If Scholastic prose was tortuous, perhaps it was because the Scholastics were absorbed in a painstaking process of discovering something they weren't sure they wanted to know. They were searching for the words to describe how the character of money could, like the children of Israel, increase and multiply as a function of time. They found their answer within the prism of apocalyptic thought.

We may wonder at such an obsession with The End, but the reasons were obvious enough to anyone who lived back then. The life of an average early Christian was filled with dread and death. As savage commando units laced terror up and down the Danube, the only certainty was that the next mass bloodletting was only a matter of time. Tomorrow's batch of barbarians could be Avars, Bavarians, Berbers, Franks, Frisians, Ostrogoths, Saxons, Slavs, or Vandals. Walled towns, enclosed monasteries, the assurances of feudal lords, the patronage of petty rulers and princes — all were tenuous safeguards against annexation, disease, conscription, invasion, and the unpleasant but very real choice between servitude or being flayed alive.

In addition to locusts and drought, one of the hazards of medieval agriculture was plunder, which happened with such gruesome regularity that depredation eventually became as predictable as Persephone's return in the spring. Instead of wasting time, energy, sons, and daughters fending off raids, rape, and utter demolishment, the peasants accepted their sorry fate and attempted to pay off their pillagers with bushels of rotting wheat. But even when the half-starved Huns decided to leave the serfs alone, primitive farming techniques and overburdened land led to pitiful harvests and famine so severe it occasionally devolved into cannibalism. Prices were dropping, yields falling, and freshly minted coins increasingly rare. A good horse was worth more than a slave, and would likely last longer.

And that was hardly the worst of it. In 541, the first cases of bubonic plague were documented in and around the port of Suez, and within a year the Black Death had raged north from Egypt to Constantinople, leaving more than twenty-five million corpses in its wake. Those twenty-five million accounted for roughly 13 percent of all human beings on earth, annihilated in two years — the modern equivalent would be something along the lines of a thousand million people dead. When snow fell the following summer and a dense, dry, noxious fog descended over Europe, many believed it was a portent. Some thought the only explanation for such a run of calamity and chaos was that the Eastern Roman emperor, Justinian, was the devil come to earth, just as the Book of Revelations had predicted. No one doubted The End was near.

None of these horrors — not even the advent of Satan sitting on the imperial throne of the Great Palace in Constantinople — came as much of a surprise to the hermits and the monks, who were already counting the hours to Doomsday, when the coinage of Christ's *parousia* would be worth its weight in celestial gold. This consciousness of themselves as characters in a cosmic narrative allowed the monks to embrace their otherwise dismal moment, for their suffering underscored the truth of the one and only story that mattered to them. They perceived themselves as forces within the allegorical text, avatars of the apocalypse.

One of their greatest instructors in reading that text was a hermit named John Cassian. Born into money, provided with an excellent education, Cassian's youthful ambition was to purge himself of all desire for material wealth and polluted possessions, and to replace his carnal animality with a pure and visionary spirit. Such aspirations were perfectly reasonable, given that Alaric the Visigoth had recently breached the walls of Rome and sacked the capital. As the pagans gathered forces along the banks of the Sacco and the Tiber, John Cassian decided the time had come to find god in the Egyptian desert.

Not much is known about his time in Egypt, but traces of his biography pick up several years later, when the hermit emerged from the wilderness and appeared in Constantinople, where he was made archon-in-chief of accounting for all the treasures of the cathedral that was the home of Byzantine Christendom during construction of the Hagia Sophia. From Constantinople, Cassian traveled to Rome, where he became a full-fledged priest and disappeared for another decade or so, most likely lost in a labyrinth of papal politics. Smatterings of evidence indicate that he eventually wended his way back to the geographic center of violent conflict between Christian and barbarian.

In the coastal city now known as Marseilles, Cassian founded two abbeys, one for men and one for women, and began to write his *Institutes*, a didactic work of Latin literature that would become essential to the philosophy and worldview of the Benedictines, Cistercians, Dominicans, Trappists — and, bizarre as it may sound, essential to the philosophy and worldview of bankers, financiers, mathematical quants, and derivatives traders on Wall Street.

Late in life, John Cassian, now a venerable church father, lectured at a series of Christian conferences on the virtues of asceticism, fasting, prayer, and poring over scripture. During these lectures, Cassian at long last divulged the details of the rapture that had filled him with spiritual inspiration so many years before in the Egyptian desert. God, he revealed, had taught him a new way to read. To be specific, god had taught him to differentiate between three old ways of reading, and one new one.

Four altogether distinct ways of reading may sound like the kind of gratuitously complicated interpretive method that could only have been hatched by a hallucinating hermit who had read the Bible a dozen too many times, but Cassian's rubrics of reading persisted throughout Christian history, and eventually made their way into the tool kit of twentieth-century literary critics. They are:

1. Literal
2. Tropological
3. Allegorical
4. Anagogical

A literal interpretation of scripture answers the question: What happened? The response takes the form of a straightforward, unadorned chronological account. A literal reading is the journalist's who, what, where, and when. It is the ethnographer's and anthropologist's scribbled notebook of observations. What is lacking from this method of reading is the *why*, just as a bank statement explains nothing about the nature and origin of money.

In contrast, a tropological reading refers to the interpretation of a text by means of isolating and analyzing its metaphors and figures of speech. A tropological interpretation of the Bible unlocks the meaning of the various stories by translating their who, what, and where into lessons the stories are meant to impart: love thy neighbor, follow the commandments, turn the other cheek, relinquish the vanity of the world. While literal readings unveiled history to the early Christian, tropological readings provided the moral of the story.

When the numismatic anthropologist and ethno-conchologist Alison Quiggin noted the prevalence of ring-shaped money among a wide variety of primitive tribes, she was providing a literal reading of currency. When she wrote about the "feeling of enclosure and safe keeping about the ring form," she was reading primitive money tropologically. Likewise, in previous chapters, the figures of collars, yokes, and girdles suggested the idea that money was involved in tropes of harnessing and controlling future outcomes. These readings explained the meaning of money through its imagery, symbols, and metaphors.

We have previously used the adjective *allegorical* to refer to a form of one-to-one correspondence between character and meaning in fables such as "The Fox and The Grapes," and noted that the money plot was allegorical, in that money was an effective method of transferring meaning through its near infinite capacity for one-to-one correspondences. But in John Cassian's strictly Christian scheme of reading, the one-to-one correspondence of allegory was specific to the life of Jesus. To Cassian, the allegorical interpretation of the Bible meant that every story in the Old Testament corresponded to a specific element or episode in the life, death, resurrection, or return of the redeemer.

The meanings of kula, marriage ritual, livestock money, grain money, snail shell money, precious metal coinage, and any other language money speaks can be pried open by literal, tropological, and allegorical readings. But it was Cassian's fourth approach to reading — the anagogical — that had the greatest impact on the commercial revolution of the Middle Ages, as it reverberated as strongly among the church fathers as among the new breed of merchant.

John Cassian instructed the monks to read the plots, characters, and metaphors of the Old Testament as shadows cast by the plots, characters, and metaphors of Doomsday, thereby suggesting that the way for earthly beings to understand god's plan was by projecting the narrative to its settlement date then stopping and turning around. Anagogical readings revolve around counting — not from the beginning to the end, but from the end going backward to the present — which is in fact not so different from how we think about money: wages tallied at the end of the hour, taxes at the end of the year, corporate earning reports at the end of the quarter, and interest compounded at the end of every second. Just as Christ the Redeemer will appear at the appointed hour, anagogical money appears at the hour of its redemption.

In anagogy, the end always comes before the beginning. Which is to say that ideas about expiration dates, settlement dates, and due dates of agreements and contracts lie at the core of anagogical readings. For example, when a lender calculates the schedule of interest payments on a mortgage and tells you the date of the last payment you will have to make before you cut a check for the first, he has read your mortgage anagogically. Thus did the word "fynance" enter the English language at the height of the Middle Ages, its etymological origins from the Latin noun, *finis*, meaning The End. Thus did the word "mortgage" descend from the pledge of the *mort*, which is death, which more often than not indicates the end of a story. It was only fitting that the medieval narrative of finance, like god's narrative of the universe, would begin at The End.

No doubt, motivations such as status and power lay behind the accumulation of ostrich eggshell beads, polished snail shells, domesticated animals, and trophy wives. But insurance, security, and control over the future were just as salient, if somewhat less statistically quantifiable. After sixty thousand years of sustained effort to prophesy and predict, time remained opaque. But as had been revealed in the Egyptian desert to Saint John Cassian the Ascetic, and despite all visible evidence to the contrary, time itself could be reconceptualized as something like a mortgage: The final redemption started from the end and counted back to the present moment. For god had not fashioned his first and holiest creation piecemeal but in its fullness — alpha and omega at the same time, the end in the beginning.

Like a banker, Cassian believed that the only sure way of calculating profit or loss was to look at things from the perspective of expiration. Such an approach has been widely copied, perhaps most infamously by a Houston energy company called Enron. By using a form of accounting called "mark to market," Enron declared profits of $101 billion in 2000, and all was well until it came to light that this vast sum consisted of hypothetical *future* profits, which had been recorded as if The End had come to pass before the present. The resulting bankruptcy cost Enron shareholders more than $10 billion.

In the aftermath of the Enron scandal it was revealed that such accounting practices were fairly common among the wizards of finance. No doubt, such anagogical thinking would have made perfect sense to the monks, as it still does to most of us. Annuities, pension plans, IRAs, and 401ks are all plots that begin at The End.

The Europe that inspired John Cassian to exalt The End was one of the more backward spots on earth. The murderous politics practiced by the savage tribes of France and Germany could not approach the sophistication of civilizations in the great cultural centers of Egypt or Ethiopia. Yet by the end of the Christian Middle Ages, European art, architecture, and music were as imperial as the vast hoards of pounds, florins, doubloons, dinars, ducats, ecus, groats, and guldens that filled the coffers of the Alberti, the Albizzi, the Balbi, the Ziani, and the Medici — family banks as rich and splendid as the greatest sovereign states. The Europe of 500 prayed for Doomsday. The Europe of 1500 brought doom to anyone foolish enough to stand in its way. It was anagogy — the churchmen's obsessive desire to manage cosmic time translated into secular terms — that spurred the development of money systems the size and complexity of which the world had never witnessed.

Historians peg the last year of pagan Europe as 481. That was the year a Frankish king named Childeric died and was buried clutching the solid gold head of a bull, indicating that Childeric was an old-school, metal-hoarding, domestic-animal-worshipping monarch. Childeric's son, Clovis, followed his father's uncouth footsteps until he found himself losing a battle to a tribe of wolf-costumed Alemanni chieftains whose primitive huts lined the gold-flecked banks of the Rhine. Historians disagree as to the exact date of the Battle of Tolbiac — depending on whom you ask, it occurred in the early 480s, the late 490s, or in 506 — but all agree that the medieval German wolf warriors were slaughtering Clovis's best and brightest until the distraught king fell to his knees and invoked the new god his second wife, Clotilde, had recently begun to worship.

Unlike the ever-bleeding sacrificial bull-gods who were reincarnated as baby bull-gods not long after they were ritually slaughtered, this new god was an ever-bleeding sacrificial man-god who would be reincarnated at some point in the not-too-distant future. As his troops hemorrhaged and the savage Alemanni closed in, Clovis figured Jesus might be worth a try. The sublime poetry of his supplication to the savior was dutifully recorded by the historian Gregory of Tours, who was not there.

Clovis's prayer hinged upon a deal: If the Franks emerged victorious, the young king would be baptized a Christian. Whether or not by divine intervention, Clovis' soldiers staged an astonishing comeback; and so, on Christmas day a few years later, Clovis paid a visit to the lovely, champagne-soaked district of Riems, where he stepped into a marble bathtub wearing nothing but his crown to have his sins washed away by Bishop Remigius. This ceremonial dunk in Riems is generally considered the end of ancient Europe and the start of the Christian Middle Ages — and the birth of money culture. The sacrament of baptism symbolizes the believer's faith in the resurrection

King Clovis, born a gold-worshipping heathen, baptized into the corpus of Christ.

of the dead at the end of time, and Clovis' anagogical conviction duly welcomed a new form of money defined by time, structured by time, as unrelenting and unforgiving as time.

Now, with the crusading fury of Christ the Avenger, born-again Clovis sliced his way up and down the Somme and the Loire, conquering kingdom after kingdom. His empire soon expanded to almost two hundred thousand square miles, at which point the first king of what would be known as France realized that in order to govern, he would have to codify laws for all his subjects. To this end, Clovis appointed four advisers to create a coherent system from the hodgepodge of rules, regulations, and resolutions his empire had inherited from Frankish, Christian, and Roman tradition. The result was a set of sixty-five titles memorialized in Latin, which for the next two centuries ruled an astounding diversity of subjects, from Bavarians to Ostrogoths, Visigoths, and ill-behaved Parisians.

Back then, it was generally understood that retributive justice was a matter of payment, and the form of payment was a body. As the Bible put it, "life for life, eye for eye, tooth for tooth, hand for hand, foot for foot, burn for burn, wound for wound, bruise for bruise..." The old legal accounting systems were as violent as they were irrefutable. But Clovis's committee of wise men reached the conclusion that while the eye-for-an-eye and tooth-for-a-tooth model possessed its primitive charms, the equivalencies were not conducive to the growth of an empire. A gouged eyeball was not a particularly useful commodity to have in one's possession going forward. Mangled bodies lost asset value. They were not investible, nor did they accrue.

No medieval child of Christ dared doubt the sacred character of Jesus, their "pearl of great price," nor lacked faith in the denouement of his plot. Christ's incarnation had secured the end of the story in advance. The destruction of that material body had pre-paid all the debt. So, instead of ever more bodies being required to take the role of money, from henceforth in Clovis' kingdom, money appropriated the role of bodies. The emperor demanded that his wise men calculate and specify monetary equivalents for every drop of blood, for all the arms and legs, fingers, teeth, eyeballs, and miscellaneous body parts that could be broken, chopped, cracked, hewed, and shattered. Currency became the basis of legal recourse, ethical repair, and political reparation for every man, woman, hostage, lord, slave, pig, horse, and goat. The set of plots, characters, and metaphors previously deflected into bride price and wedding ritual was expanded to all matters of balance and settlement.

The levy of a fine — the word is itself a form of *fin*, as in the fee to be paid at *the end* — to replace physical punishment exacted upon a body was certainly a sign of civilization's advance from barbarity. Yet the replacement also highlighted an irony that became increasingly apparent as the commercial revolution gained momentum: The mortgages, rent revenues, and credit financing employed by the church operated on the theory that the more time passed, the more money would grow. Yet the more time passed for the body — in Salic law, money's equivalent — the more the body decayed. How could money wax as bodies waned? And this irony was a shadow of an even greater philosophical question, one that dealt with the nature of time itself. From the standpoint of a mortgage, time did not advance but *decay*. Why should money, left to its own devices, *accrue*?

The word comes from the Old French *acrewe*, meaning that which grows from the ground for the profit of an owner. In order for money to generate more money, it had to be animate; and in order for money to be animate, it had to possess or be possessed by some living character or spirit — the Indonesian jar money that sang, the gong money of Borneo that spoke, or Hesiod's personified metals. The idea that money was alive is as old as money: In ancient

Mesopotamia, the term used to refer to the interest on a loan was *mas*, the word for newborn beasts. In ancient Greece, the term was *tokos*, which also meant animal offspring. "Remember," wrote Benjamin Franklin, in his succinct "Advice to a Young Tradesman," "that money is of a *prolific, generating nature.*"

> Money can beget money, and its offspring can beget more, and so on. Five shillings turned is six, turned again is seven and threepence, and so on, till it becomes a hundred pounds. He that murders a crown, destroys all that it might have produced, even scores of pounds.

But once possessed by a living spirit (in Catholic terms, the *vitae spiritualis ianua*, as per the Council of Florence in 1314), what was there to keep money from acting like any other living organism? Too orthodox an embrace of this *vitae spiritualis* led to a number of grave Catholic misunderstandings. Twentieth-century ethnographers observed that instead of baptizing their children, some of the peasants who lived in the Cauca Valley of Colombia baptized their currency. Their reasoning was impeccable: Only after the Christian mystery could money possess spiritual life and consequently increase and multiply. The cost of the Cauca's transaction was truly Mephistophelian, in that the child deprived of his own baptism for the sake of a baptized bank account would, at the last syllable of recorded time, be shut out of his or her share of the corporate body of Christ, and consequently denied redemption.

Money was the opposite of decaying flesh; it was a living spirit. The apparent cross-purposes of the two led to one of the most perplexing and impenetrable questions faced by the medieval mind, a question that would linger at the center of endless debate among the brightest priestly lights of the Middle Ages: How did man-made money attain the same spiritual status as god-made man?

The only way to answer was to flee the question, because the fact of the matter was that despite repeated biblical injunctions against usury, the medieval church fathers understood that interest-bearing loans had become essential to the survival of their corporation. The Roman curia and all its subsidiary abbeys and monasteries would have gone bankrupt without credit financing and mortgages. The most profitable branch of all the Medici's banks was the one located in Rome, in closest proximity to the Vatican.

The logically impossible task of justifying interest while condemning interest landed in the lap of the most renowned economic thinker of the Middle Ages, a Franciscan missionary named Bernardino of Siena who had made a name for himself by delivering a series of hours-long sermons railing against mirrors, high heels, perfume, cards, dice, witches, Jews, and sodomites.

Capital, Bernardino assured the popes and prelates, could increase and multiply. Medievalists are in the habit of quoting the saint's dictum in the original Latin: *Quandam seminalem rationem*. Translated, it means that not only can money grow indefinitely, it is the only *rational* thing for money to do. Bernardino's argument was similar in approach to what became known in the twentieth century as econometrics, which analyzes economics by means of probability and statistics, confident in the belief that money acts in an efficient and consistent manner. And why should money act logically? Because money is logical. The tautology is often ignored today, so perhaps it should come as no surprise that Bernardino's book, *On Contracts and Usury*, was considered the last word on the subject in 1433.

Christened by San Bernardino as a *reasonable* being, and granted proprietary powers of procreation, money as an accrual measured by time's steady rate of diminution—that is, *the interest rate*—was ready to join other figures of money's allegorical universe, eventually to become one of the dignitaries of twentieth-century quantitative finance. Derivatives traders call the interest rate rho. They also have a name for time, theta. The redemptions of the former and the march of the latter were twinned from start to finish. But of all the characters in the money plot, theta has the most pathos, for it is measured by its decay.

The medieval laws of rho and theta were set in five massive gatherings held over the course of four centuries, when hermits, monks, and bishops traveled from the ends of Europe and the Middle East to convene at the Lateran Palace, the papal residence in southeast Rome. These so-called Lateran Councils generated thousands of decrees, edicts, and regulations. The voluminous and well-preserved records of the proceedings have long served as windows into the early Christian mind, which was just as preoccupied with credit and debt as with damnation and salvation.

A number of these Lateran rulings concern those who went on epic journeys to defend the Christian empire against the evil infidels. These knights — technically speaking, a Christian warrior sitting on a horse — managed the near-constant apocalyptic state of siege that marked the Middle Ages. Their journeys, called *peregrinatio*, came to be known as the Crusades, and were considered essential to god's plan. Moreover, they cost a lot of money, more than one and a half million lives, and two centuries of ever-decaying time.

After Lateran IV adjourned in 1215, the curia published a now obscure ruling, known as Constitution 71. It decreed that if "kings, dukes, princes, marquises, counts, barons" cannot themselves go on these Crusades, they must bear a portion of the cost of those who go in their place, and keep paying replacement cost for three years. "To those who refuse to render aid, if any should be found to be so ungrateful to God, the Apostolic See firmly protests that on the last day of the final judgment they will be held to render an account to us in the presence of a terrible Judge."

This was an extraordinary moment in the history of accounting. The greatest religious intellectuals of the day were suggesting that among the proceedings on the last day of history, during the final seconds of time, as rivers of blood overflowed their banks and the sky exploded into flames, there would be a formal presentation of evidence against those who had failed to provide funds for a knight or two to feed his horse on the way to Jerusalem and back in Anno Domini 1215. Such delinquent kings, dukes, princes, and barons would then be damned for all eternity.

Thirty years after Lateran IV the church fathers gathered again, this time in Lyons. "The unfathomable greed of usury has brought many churches to the verge of destruction," was the conclusion reached by the 250 bishops who gathered before Pope Innocent IV. Along with calling for a new Crusade against the Saracens in order to accomplish the speedy redemption of the Holy Land, and declaring that all cardinals must wear red hats, the assembly officially decried the fact that "some prelates are very negligent and remiss in paying off debts, especially those contracted by their predecessors, and are too much inclined to contract further debts, especially by mortgaging the properties of their churches."

Since maximizing returns for shareholders was the task of the corporate body of Christ on earth, and since the corporate body consisted of all the properties of the church, leasing out those properties was akin to mortgaging the body of Christ. If the mortgage payment could not be met, default became assault against the holiest body of them all. Pope Innocent compared such wicked fiscal behavior to one of the five wounds of Christ, implying that the outflow of His sacred blood and the outflow of the church's money were equivalent. This is one reason why Pope Innocent IV is often credited as one of the intellectual founders of corporate personhood, the notion that a corporation possesses a character of its own, with privileges on a par with people — such as freedom of speech for corporations, articulated in the form of political donations.

In the Middle Ages, corporate personhood went by the name *persona ficta*, and this form of alt- or crypto-character could travel to Granada or Jerusalem in place of an actual human being. One could replace the other, as the theory of corporate personhood made a corporate body's money the same as its flesh and blood. From there it was but a small step to accept the idea that money could reimburse or repair any injuries or liabilities pertaining to the corporation, including the sins of individual members. And as anagogical thinking became more and more commonplace, those liability payments would not only be made in order to hasten Doomsday's glories and horrors, but also to hasten an individual's ascent to heaven. By shrewd deployments of Christian charity — that is, by contributing money to the church — sinners could discount as much as 45,000 years in purgatory, and join the heavenly company that much sooner.

It is easy to condemn medieval Christians for their confusion as to where money ended and god began. In fact, the church had entwined itself with money not because the church was evil or the church was venal or the church was corrupt. The medieval church became inextricable from medieval money because on the allegorical level of plot, character, and metaphor, on the level of corporate bodies and *personae ficta*, the character of money and the character of Jesus could hardly be distinguished. And what would in the long run become degrading for religion would become innovative for capitalism, as the interchangeability of a corporation to a body and of a body to equity shares would revolutionize buying and selling.

The commercial logic of the Middle Ages was perhaps most evident when it came to defining in specific contractual terms the character of the slave, the kind of commodity that — unlike jar money and gong money and interest-bearing capital—actually could dance, speak, and procreate. More than one thousand years ago, one could mortgage oneself into lifelong servitude through spoken vows, as in the following eighth-century record of the words of a nameless woman from a part of the Merovingian empire known today as Germany:

> As it is well known to all that I have not the means to feed and clothe myself, I have begged your pity, and your will has granted it to me, to allow me to be delivered into and consigned to your protection…As long as I live, I shall owe you service and obedience…and for the rest of my days I shall not have the right to withdraw from your power or protection…

The slave was an ancient figure, but the person who contracted for his or her own servitude was new. It meant that becoming a *persona ficta*—a body that could be bought and sold—was an option for every *persona* non-*ficta*, too. The terms were convertible.

As a result of Clovis's financial legal codes, bodies came to serve as leverage for a wide variety of business agreements. One of the more famous instances occurred in 1259, when Baldwin II, the bankrupt last monarch of the Latin empire, delivered his son and heir, Philip of Courtenay, as security for a loan to two merchants from Venice. This was not a particularly shocking arrangement, as mortgaging people was simply imitating the character of Christ, whose body was generally understood to have taken on the structure of a loan, the final repayment of which was fast approaching. The model endured far beyond the Middle Ages: In order to raise money to build Monticello, Thomas Jefferson mortgaged 150 of his slaves.

The driving principle behind a mortgage was the expectation that one day both principle and interest would be settled. The inability to fulfill that obligation and reimburse the money that had been advanced indicated failure to mend the riven corporate body and make it whole again, which may help explain the brutal nature of the penalties the church inflicted as a result of default: anathemazation, excommunication, divine malediction, public proclamation of heresy, denial of church burial, and perhaps worst of all, the disinternment and scattering of one's bones so that, like Humpty Dumpty, the fragments could never be fitted back together. Just as bad as default was payment in counterfeit currency, as corrupt coins would become a part of the body only to pollute it. Thus did the Lateran Council of 1123 specify that the penalty for producing counterfeits would be expulsion from the body of Christ on Judgment Day.

Moreover, because the corporate body of the church was now a living, breathing, procreating character, the ticktock of the *persona ficta*'s life was impossible to ignore. As if to underscore this fact, huge time-telling machines began to inhabit the cathedrals of European cities. The world's first mechanical clock was built in 996 by the scientist priest Gerbert of Aurillac, who would later become the first French pope. Perhaps the greatest of all the monk clockmakers was Peter Lightfoot, a resident of Glastonbury Abbey, who constructed his astronomical clock for the Wells Cathedral in the West of England between 1386 and 1392. The dial features angels, stars, and the sun and moon revolving around the center of the universe: the earth, of course.

"I know well enough what it is," Saint Augustine said about the nature of time, "provided that nobody asks me." But in the thousand or so years between Augustine's *Confessions* and the apex of Christian clockmaking—Prague's astronomical clock of 1410 in which all twelve of Christ's long-dead apostles miraculously reappear at the top of every hour—what had once been an insubstantial rhythm, impossible to hold or grasp, now became a taskmaster, a drumbeat to which all must march in step. And in the Christian narrative, everyone meant everyone, including the dead.

On the one hand, the bones, hair, and fingernails of defunct saints hoarded in medieval church basements looked a lot like the bones, skulls, and teeth found in Nigerian and Micronesian hoards of so-called primitive money. The difference was the Christian belief that on the day of redemption and settlement the collected body parts of holy martyr and wicked sinner alike would piece themselves back together and zombie walk their way to reward or punishment. This was just a matter of time, and the ticktock had become impossible to ignore.

By the late Middle Ages, what had once been the fairly straightforward idea of "bride price" had turned into a schedule of payments with a complexity far beyond the most ornate ring, silk, girdle, jeweled tiara, or herd of oxen. For the first time, marriage became an *investible* asset in the modern sense — an investment that could accrue, and its accrual calculated in precise pecuniary terms. The best example of this is the *Monte delle Doti*, a public fund established in Florence in 1425. This was in the wake of the Black Death, the devastation of which had severely diminished the supply of grooms. Demand rose, the cost of betrothal boomed, and a marriage market was born in which brides' families were expected to offer as much cash as possible for the privilege of having someone marry their daughters. As a result, dowries inflated beyond the means of the average household.

In order to preserve itself and its people, the government decided that marriage had to be institutionalized not only culturally but as a form of asset management, and that the business of wife procurement would henceforth be a time-based investment measured in fractional units figured in reverse. A father could begin contributing to the *Monte delle Doti* fund when his daughter was five years old, and keep adding to the principle every year. His capital was guaranteed to accrue at an annual rate of 11 to 12 percent, the terms fixed either for seven-and-a-half or fifteen years, and the money could be redeemed by the family at the end of the allotted time period in the form of a dowry. The terms of consummating a marriage and consummating a loan had become the same, and neither churchmen nor merchants nor heads of state nor heads of family found the arrangement remarkable. What securitized the enterprise was an anagogical reading of the wedding, the predestined end.

By the late Middle Ages, the commercial revolution was in full swing. Commodities and credit flowed at an unprecedented pace up and down the Danube, the Volga, the Loire, the Rhine, and the Elbe, and fortunes were made and lost on ships packed with extraordinary miscellanies of linen, silk, cinnamon, nutmeg, salt, and pepper. Lucrative agricultural commodities such as beer, butter, preserved meat and fish, wine, and sugar were stowed in ever-larger holds alongside high-demand items such as mercury, wax, and glue, not to mention the secretions from the most precious glands of a male deer from Tibet, marketed as musk.

A 1341 letter from a Venetian merchant clarified the stakes: "If this journey goes well, I shall live comfortably the rest of my days; if it does not, I shall sell all I own." The fact that ever-larger sums of money could be extracted from ever more complex narratives of risk, fear, and time focused the minds of medieval merchants on the character of money as never before. Since potential fortunes could be extinguished in a shipwreck, a robbery, or any other sudden change of luck or twist of fate, and since such catastrophe would spell end and ruination, the merchants began to act like authors and weigh every possible denouement. "You ought to keep always with you a small notebook," Benedetto Cotrugli advised in his widely circulated book, *On Commerce and the Perfect Merchant*, "in which you shall note day by day and hour by hour and even the minute of your transactions."

The overall effect of medieval economic thought was that fate and fortune, once considered the purview of inscrutable, indifferent, vengeful, and violent gods, took a few more steps toward their modern incarnation as accountable, calculable, and manipulatable. A commercial system based on imagining stories that could branch into every possible twist and turn of plot had begun. The apocalypse — be it flood, fire, shipwreck, storm, or whirlwind — would from now on come under a schedule of reimbursement and expenditure, as each possible ending could now be assessed based on sets of prearranged benefits, collaterals, contingencies, dividends, and premiums.

In the face of new onslaughts of commercial activity, the key to avoid financial doomsday was the notebook. Before the birth of bookkeeping, the medieval merchant kept a record of all possible endings in narrative form, like the books of the merchant Francesco di Marco Datini, who committed so much of his business to writing in 1395 that he neglected sleeping and eating and ended up unable to get up out of bed. The gradual emergence of "double-entry" bookkeeping, a shorthand method to express what might be lost or gained in the case of all outcomes, gave the merchant a window into the future, memorializing outflow and inflow, anticipating profits while predefining the possible extent of loss. Like clocks and coins, the books were a way to wield control over time. Like prehistoric ostrich egg containers of nuts and berries stowed away for future use, they were a form of insurance against the vicissitudes of fate.

Increasingly exact bookkeeping practices also allowed for increasingly complex credit arrangements, the earliest of which appeared in the 900s. The *pactum* was a simple and straightforward floating credit instrument by which Venetian merchants could procure food and wine at stopping points on trade routes without having to open dozens of bank accounts along the way. In the bad old days, one might starve. Now, the only element required for a full stomach was the pactum.

We take the idea of floating credit for granted, but to an outside observer, unversed in the mores of banking, the idea would surely appear strange. The merchant began his voyage with an invisible asset and shepherded it through multiple manifestations as the magic of plenty transformed itself from one iteration to the next. His peregrinations ended with a final tally in increased or decreased numbers of the same thing with which he had begun—which was credit. The arrangement looked like nothing so much as a kula ring. Why, the nineteenth-century anthropologist Bronisław Malinowski had asked, "would men risk life and limb to travel across huge expanses of dangerous ocean to give away what appear to be worthless trinkets?"

Replace trinket with credit, and the same confusion ensues. For wherever the merchant sailed, his credit sailed along with him, an ineffable bounty beyond the gross embodiments of shekels and *shahrukhis*. Credit lay behind the far-flung trade in exotic luxury goods—the commercialized shadows, one might have imagined, of the glories to be found in paradise. Mid-ninth-century lists of imports from India included panthers, elephants, and coconuts. From Yemen came giraffes, gems, incense, and dyes. From Iran came pomegranates, figs, vinegar, and dancing girls. From northwest Africa came iron, lead, mercury, and eunuchs.

In the twelfth and thirteenth centuries, merchants converged four times a year in different towns of northern France for the famous Champagne fairs. They exhibited fractions of their materials, promising that bulk purchases would be made available on the basis of down payments, which were often brokered by a money changer. In this way, a merchant by the name of Francesco Balducci Pegolotti was able to sell more than 280 different items, from cardamom, cotton, camphor, and coral, to pepper, perfumes, potions, powders, and a popular form of pharmaceutical called electuaries, which were drugs whipped into batches of raw honey. Pitched on the basis of samples—that is, peddled as part for a whole—the financial structure of the deal was based on credit, which is to say, the promise of redemption upon payment. The money plot had grown complex, but the narrative was validated because the scenario was already so widely embraced. It was the cosmic narrative: Merchandise and remuneration would materialize upon expiration of the contract, just as the invisible spirits of the dead would materialize on Doomsday. As the books of prophecy promised Christ, so did the books of Balducci Pegoletti promise profit.

At the same time as anagogical reading had launched the global economy, it also opened new worlds of possibility for narrative. Appraisals of everything that could go wrong drove a plot that endures until today, a plot known to bankers and businessmen as protecting the downside. Those who became the best at making money were no longer the strongest or the wisest. The best at limiting liability were those who could contemplate the most complicated stories.

Such men realized that the real money lay in an idea about business that transcended the discipline of manufacturing, transporting, and peddling widgets. Like Michael Dell—who by selling an ever-changing variety of computer upgrade kits became the twentieth richest man on earth and a fixture on the syllabi of Harvard Business School—the most successful medieval merchants understood that the most valuable commercial attribute was the speed with which they could adapt to changing circumstances. One contract from 1264 made clear how fluid the expectations were for a successful merchant adventurer, who was free to travel "from Pisa to the kingdom of Sicily and to wherever else he may go or send for the good and advantage of his investment, without fraud, in whatever ship or vessel, at the risk of the sea…"

This monetary wanderer was a descendant of the primitive canoe trader. But the medieval plot required more than a camel or a cog, more than gold coins, and more than seashells. The journey had become intellectual. The project now required backers, letters of credit, and shareholders. And in order to procure buy-in from all such stakeholders, the merchant had to define the characters of rho and theta in advance, the time of return and the rate of returns. The medieval businessman did just that in the form of oaths, bonds, and assurances that articulated every detail of future redemptions, and memorialized the agreement by signing a *rogadia*, a contract named after the verb *rogare*, which meant *to pray*.

Like marriage, the *rogadia* made two real bodies into one fictional body. The contract consisted of a pledge that the first merchant would take money from the second merchant in order to make said money increase and multiply. While the second merchant could stay home and tend to domestic concerns, the first merchant would become the agent of the *persona ficta*, the newborn corporate body, at liberty to follow the money anywhere on earth that body saw fit. At expiration, one partner would return the money the other partner in prayer had invested—with a premium. By doing nothing but praying for success, the merchant who stayed at home could grow rich. The similarity to the dentalia of the Yurok is hard to ignore. Thinking in money made money.

The popularity of the *rogadia* inspired ever-larger groups of individuals to pool their resources and join together in ever more intricate corporate bodies that came to be known as *societas*. These partnerships were structured in such a way as to mitigate risk, manage fear, and demarcate time. Like demigods, these *personae* could define the duration of their own existence and the hour of their expiration, declaring when the fragments of their shares would be gathered, consolidated, and consumed for the profit of all. And so the medieval merchants and investors, like the early Christians, could declare themselves bonded as spiritual brothers and sisters, as in these vows from 1253:

> In the name of the Lord, amen. Orlando Paglia; Giovanni Puliti; Ranieri of Verona; Giacomo Migliorati; Consolino, son of the late Konrad, German; and Friedrich, German, acknowledge that they have jointly made among themselves a societas to last forever for the purpose of buying mines, furnaces, or veins for the production of silver in Sardinia or wherever God may guide them...And they are to share the expenses of said societas in food and drink and chartering of boats and renting of houses, both in sickness and in health...

A similar type of financial body was called the *campagnia*, in which an even wider variety of participants could purchase shares. *Campagnia*, cognate to *company* in English, comes from medieval Latin *cumpanis*, which means "one eating the same bread." A comparison to shares in the eucharist was hard to avoid, as were the somewhat more unsettling echoes of Noah's Ark in a version of a similar contract known as "everyone in the same boat." By 1486, when a popular book appeared in London describing how to hunt, fish, shine one's armor, and other necessary know-hows of the knightly class, the author included a section on a new quasi-religious sect of gentlemen, the "faith of *Merchandis*."

Alongside the new faith arose new high priests. These men arrived at the Champagne fairs and sat behind their portable benches — *banques* in Middle French, *bancos* in Old Italian, *banc* in Old High German. They were the first to make a stand-alone profession from the metaphor of money, and their challenge was to create order from the chaos the merchant adventurers had unleashed with their abundancies of credit and debt measured in deniers, dinars, drachmas, and ducats — and that was just the Ds. To do so, the moneyers invented their own scenario, known as *cambium et recambium*, or "exchange and re-exchange," which stipulated in advance both the rates of transferring one currency into another, and the rate for changing it back. Clearly, these were interest-bearing loans in disguise, and they were soon widely imitated.

Similar to the *cambium et recambium* was the *ricorsa*, a written agreement that guaranteed a group of investors who had advanced money to a merchant a favorable exchange rate when the merchant returned from a distant country accompanied by a boatload of foreign currency and floating credit. The *ricorsa* came in handy when the *personae ficta* made up of pilgrims, merchants, bankers, and itinerant dealers conducted business with the *personae ficta* made up of prelate and priest, as the church had become a multinational business with countless foreign offices. And since the curia's banking interests concerned near endless varieties of currencies, by the beginning of the fifteenth century the Scholastics had to redefine the rules of rho. From 1443 onward, interest would be a sin only in the context of a domestic bank loan, not as a matter of foreign currency exchange, which the schoolmen differentiated by creating yet another new term, *permutatio*. No less an apologist than San Bernardino of Siena opined that *permutatio* was "essential to the support of human life."

At its commercial height in the late Middle Ages, Florence boasted eighty banks, and its mints were producing 500,000 gold florins a year. But no matter how many ingot-bearing caravans arrived from

Senegal, the bankers' narrative ran far ahead of dross matter. The great merchant families of Italy—from the Alberti to the Ziani—did the only reasonable thing under the circumstances and became hoarders of material reality, depositing coins in heavily guarded vaults, and using these as reserves to leverage lending on paper.

Every medievalist who has crunched the numbers reaches the same conclusion: The amount of notional currency hurtling back and forth across the continent was far greater than the physical currency secured in hoards. The resulting universe of notes and promises was ruled by ratios: one material groat was good for twenty imaginary groat, and one material gold ducat traded at 240 imaginary ducats. The proliferation of interest bearing, self-generating, ever-expiring, ever-expanding credits and debts would eventually overwhelm physical reserves of gold, silver, and bronze. This scenario, glorious for the merchants and terrifying to the priests, was familiar to writers of allegory, who had learned long ago that their characters were not only prone to taking on lives of their own, but that those imaginary lives often overshadowed the lives of their authors. In the case of medieval commercial culture, those authors were bankers and the characters were money.

Despite the anagogical obsessions and narrative prolixity of the bankers, the denouement of the story that was their money could still prove surprising. It came as a shock when the Bardi and Peruzzi *campagnias* collapsed in 1343 and 1346, respectively. Their fatal mistake proved to be an advance of more than 1.5 million gold florins to King Edward III of England. The Florentine bankers could see that armed conflict between England and France was imminent, but their narrative imaginations had failed to grasp the possibility that the war would last one hundred years.

The greatest expansion of commercial culture the world had ever witnessed led to financial collapse on a scale never before envisaged. And as the Middle Ages drifted into early modernity, nowhere was medieval money's disintegration more insidious than in Spain. The Kingdom of Castile's economy had been strained by endless wars against the pagan emirate of Granada and the Sultanate of Morocco, not to mention centuries of incessant and costly battles against England, France, Genoa, Naples, and Portugal. With its financial back against the wall, the Spanish crown had funded the most famous merchant adventurer of them all. This was of course Columbus, who was soon followed across the Atlantic by hosts of killer knights. The precious metal mines of the New World initially appeared to be a gift from god, but unfortunately, the influx of Mexican and Peruvian gold and silver ended up sending the Spanish economy into death spirals of boom and bust.

It is likely no coincidence that Castile's economic collapse coincided with the innovations that marked the Golden Age of Spanish literature, out of which emerged the first bona fide school of economic criticism. The *arbitristas* were friars, canons, priests, and doctors of theology who published treatises on contracts and corporations, gold and banking, currency exchange, credit, and debt. They believed that the evisceration of their country's economy was due to the persistence of puerile plots and characters — specifically, the medieval obsessions with the end of time. They ridiculed their fellow Spanish citizens who, instead of engaging in productive work, gulled themselves into believing they were heroic *hidalgos*, above getting their hands dirty, convinced that their passive participation investing in shares of the national annuity, the *censos*, would as a matter of course bring about their salvation. The *arbitristas* concluded that their countrymen were insane.

As money collapsed and self-deception spread across the Iberian Peninsula, a new literary genre was born. It was called the novel, and the characters who inhabited the plots were no longer vanquished gods, epic warriors, crusading knights, tragic heroes, doomed kings, allegorical types, sacrificial redeemers, or suffering saints. Instead, *Lazarillo de Tormes* and *Guzmán de Alfarache* were proverbial street urchins. Their world was so hopeless and their poverty so abject that cheating, stealing, starvation, and servitude no longer evoked the transcendent emotions of tragedy, but the cruel laughter of the Spanish *burla*, the harsh and heartless joke.

From this vile, vulgar, and disillusioned world emerged the only writer Shakespeare ever took seriously as a rival. Miguel de Cervantes was employed by Spanish bankers as a purchasing agent, an accountant, and a tax collector. Balancing the bankrupt books of starving royals sporting silk sashes and ceremonial swords may have inspired him to conceive of *El Ingenioso Hidalgo Don Quixote de La Mancha*, the doddering old reader of romances deluded into thinking he was a knight in shining armor and that the local prostitute was his lady in waiting. The Quixotic imagination mistook metaphor for material, much like Spanish elites under the impression that the spirit of interest would guarantee their redemption, only to realize too late they had gone bankrupt.

Cervantes' epic spoof touched a nerve, and the book sold so well that a decade after its initial publication the author released Part II. Perhaps it is no coincidence that the word "fictitious" entered the English language that same year — not as a term of literary but of financial art, as a warning to beware of those "fictitious precious stones" a merchant might seek to pawn off as real. The art of fiction was fast maturing, as *Don Quixote*, Part II, inaugurated its own new twist. The now world-famous knight made it clear to his readers that crazy as he might have appeared to be, one thing he knew for sure: He was the hero of a book called *El Ingenioso Hidalgo Don Quixote de la Mancha*.

He knew this, because he'd read it.

Such a literary trick had never been pulled before. A character in a fiction who had been driven mad by reading about other characters in other fictions was stating flat out that he understood he was a *personae ficta* in someone else's book. The dizzying self-referentiality of it all opened up a world of renewed potential for plots, characters, and metaphors. In the twentieth century, literary scholars came up with a name for this knot of reality infused with fiction, and fiction entangled in reality. Cervantes's novel, they concluded, was not fiction but *metafiction*—the fiction about fiction that spurred the modern novel, modern drama, and a new universe of possibility for the greatest fiction of them all.

Don Quixote has never been considered a guide to finance, but it demonstrated that when allegorical figures become aware of themselves as allegorical and when stories take note of themselves as stories, characters begin to imagine the unimaginable: They can conceive of the expiration date of their bondage to the underlying plot, and they can declare their independence. Such pronouncements mark the moment a character emerges from the incarceration imposed by his or her creator. That's the day the person known as "wife" tells the person known as "husband" she will no longer be his possession, the day the person known as "slave" declares he will no longer be anyone's property.

Here, at last, was what the waiters had been waiting for. The medieval monks had sickened and died praying for the rapture, the popes had invested millions of ducats and florins in their effort to exterminate the infidel and prepare for the way of the Lord. The poets had composed the longest and most morally perfect allegories of noble Gawain, Galahad, and Red Cross Knight—but none had come close to the victory achieved by Quixote. The greatest crusader of the Middle Ages was a blessed lunatic from the wastelands of Extremadura.

Money's first metaphoric leap may have turned a shattered ostrich egg into a bead, but today's economists immerse themselves in models, regressions, and hosts of second- and third-order descriptive and diagnostic tools. Wall Street analysts worship their plots about plots, the metafictions that irradiate from their metaphor of metaphors. That was the gift of the epiphany first rendered by Cervantes and his knight-once-removed. After Quixote and his eponymous book, neither money nor story could exist as they had before.

II / BIG MONEY

THE SILVER OF COUNT
HIERONYMUS VON SCHLICK

LITTLE IS KNOWN about the prehistoric people who inhabited the dollar's native soil. No artifact bears a hint about why they decided to dig deep within the mountains that mark the present-day border between the Czech Republic and Germany. All we have are ancient Germanic folktales recounting legendary beings known as *nibelungs*, an ugly, outcast race who unearthed strange quarries from the depths of the massif now known as the Ore Mountain Range. No doubt they were intrigued by what they found: the remains of ancient magma injected between strata of sedimentary rock, then cooled into masses of igneous rock called "plutons," in honor of the wealthy rapist of the underworld. And somehow these mysterious people unfolded yet another mystery: Within the plutons lurked black crystals that could be smelted into a pure, soft, silvery substance that neither crumbled nor tarnished.

Today, geologists call those black crystals cassiterite, and that pure silvery substance that neither crumbles nor tarnishes is known as tin — a commodity that can be bought, sold, swapped, optioned, and otherwise traded on metal exchanges around the world, alongside aluminum, cobalt, copper, lead, nickel, silver, steel, and zinc.

It's a big business. The annual value of products traded on the London Metal Exchange alone generally exceeds $10 trillion.

Around 2500 BC, that four-hundred-square-mile area between the future kingdoms of Bohemia and Saxony became the earliest mining district in Europe, and the mountain people began to practice the dark art of metamorphosing minerals from one form to another. They discovered that a chemical element as fundamental as tin could be improved. If the metallurgists mixed it with copper the result was an alloy that was stronger than either metal on its own; stronger, in fact, than any metal known before. That alloy was bronze. The obvious next step was to make bronze weapons, and not just to make them, but to trade them for gold. Ancient wholesalers and retailers — the earliest ancestors of medieval merchants — packed up their bronze ax-heads, spearheads, and knives, and traveled along the Amber Road north to the Baltic and south to the Mediterranean Sea.

Around 600 BC — the time of King Alyattes, the birth of tragedy, and the first coinage of precious metal — a tribe of ancient Celts settled in the Ore Mountains. Here, the Druids grew rich. They killed their neighbors. Their settlements spread. Their rulers built castles and a tradition began: Each family would cultivate its own seam of the earth, dig its own pits, lift its own ore, and smelt its own metals.

By the tenth century AD, when Christianity had finally vanquished the last pagan taboos against clearing the forests and woodlands of central Germany, demand for a next generation of agricultural tools emerged, particularly the miraculous technology known as the iron hoe. Within two hundred years, thousands of newly constructed merchant sailing ships created a demand for iron anchors, and the metallurgy business boomed. Miners, smelters, and all manner of metalworkers migrated to the mountains of medieval Bohemia, and the ancient Celtic settlements began to resemble towns.

The most talented smiths left the fashioning of farm tools, pots, and pans to apprentices and devoted themselves to more difficult and remunerative projects, such as pikes and lances. Of course, anyone who purchased a pike would want a suit of armor, too, and the metallic accoutrements of feudalism grew to include metal wardrobes, from visor to greave, all made in Bohemia. When the word *bill* entered English around the year 1000 — the linguistic ancestor of half of *dollar bill* — it referred to a medieval weapon constructed out of a long pole tipped with a hooked blade. The bill possessed the stopping power of a spear and the cutting power of an ax.

By the sixteenth century, when European demand for coinage had reached historic heights, the citizens of one small Bohemian hamlet, Joachimsthal, had mastered metallurgic methods far more ambitious than the primitive recipe for bronze. They had become experts in locating, extracting, crushing, and washing great lodes of quartz, sulfur, salt, and clay. They had learned how to flux the slurry with liquid lead and roast the remains in blast furnaces. The result was a much more reflective and ductile metal than tin. The result was silver.

By then, the magic mountain that loomed above the village had become the property of the great Count Hieronymus von Schlick, and in 1516 his family began to mine and smelt and melt and mint coins in honor of themselves. It was the height of the Renaissance, and the silver coins from the von Schlick mines of Joachimsthal, known locally as *Schlickenthalers*, were as exact and perfect as the polychrome panels of a Brunelleschi cathedral. They were the product of thousands of years of geological study, innovation, and refinement, and soon became famous for their purity and beauty.

As they spread across Europe, *Schlickenthalers* became known as *Joachimsthalers*, in honor of their place of birth. But the word *Joachimsthaler* was unwieldy, so the bankers, merchants, and traders eventually shortened the nomenclature to *thaler*. Right around the time that the Italian explorer Giovanni da Verrazzano and a crew of fifty sailors anchored their small caravel near the southern tip of an unexplored island in the New World — less than a mile from what would one day be known as Wall Street — the first thaler landed in Amsterdam, where it became known as a *daler*. For the next fifty years, the daler flirted with English, appearing in print as a *daleir*, *dallor*, *dalder*, and *dolor* before taking its final form in 1601.

That's how the *dollar* got its name. Eventually, the name would be all that was left.

{6} MONEY WANTS TO BE FREE

Even apart from the instability due to speculation, there is the instability
due to the characteristic of human nature that a large proportion of
our positive activities depend on spontaneous optimism rather than
mathematical expectations, whether moral or hedonistic or economic.
Most, probably, of our decisions to do something positive . . . can only
be taken as the result of animal spirits . . .

— JOHN MAYNARD KEYNES

THE DECLARATIVE STATEMENT that serves as the title of this chapter—
money wants to be free—insinuates neither a political nor an economic agenda. The phrase is not meant to suggest that money
should be given to anyone, anywhere, anytime. The implications of
the phrase are strictly narrative.

Imagine money as the hero of a plot. Now imagine that the hero
has been locked in jail. Who wouldn't root for the hero's liberation,
even if the prison were made of gold?

The history of modern money is the narrative of that escape.

Many find it hard to imagine money's liberation. From shells and
beads to cattle and coin, money has assumed physical form. But bondage within material substance has not always worked to money's best

advantage. In fact, economists have struggled to explain why systems that depend on gold-backed currencies suffer through cycles of boom and bust. English professors, on the other hand, are familiar with this sort of thing. In *The Poetics*, Aristotle called the violent twists and turns of plot *peripety*, which means *reversal*. It is the basis of narrative momentum, the reason we keep reading.

The money plot is full of reversals. A typical example came after the Roman Senate declared war on the Egyptian Queen, Cleopatra, in the spring of 32 BC. When the queen was joined by her lover and ally, the Roman Triumvir Mark Antony, civil war engulfed the Republic.

The conflict ended when the Roman imperator Octavian's fleet sank five hundred rebel ships in the Battle of Actium, after which both Antony and Cleopatra retreated to Alexandria and committed suicide, as immortalized by Shakespeare. Still, Octavian decided to play it safe and murder his one remaining rival, the last heir to the Egyptian throne, a seventeen-year-old named Caesarion. Only after the murder did Octavian believe himself victorious, declare himself emperor, and change his name to Augustus. Then he paraded his trophies through the streets of Rome: Antony's three young children by Cleopatra, and all the gold of Egypt's royal hoard.

That was the best day ever. Gold — which has lingered for millennia as money's most enduring metaphor — meant food, drink, long afternoons at the spa, evenings at the orgy. Gold meant imported amber, ivory, musk, ostrich feathers, silk, truffles, and odd-toed ungulates from faraway lands. Gold meant wagonloads of iced oysters from Brittania and strange-hued fruits from even farther afield. Gold would double the empire's annual budget and unleash the flow of credit up and down Rome's Wall Street, the Via Sacra.

The Great Society had finally arrived, the empire's confidence soared, and the mints went into overdrive. Six hundred million bronze sesterces were used to purchase real estate for the veterans of foreign wars, and after that came money for aqueducts, public baths, and temples dedicated to the gods of sunlight, moonlight, death, sex, war, eternal spring, and Juno Moneta, queen goddess of metal coin, whose fortified temple stood atop Capitoline Hill. Her name, *Moneta*, likely derived from *monere*, the Latin word for a "warning."

Neither English professor nor economist, finding him or herself magically transported to ancient Rome, would have been surprised by the subsequent reversal of the plot. The price of British oysters, German amber, and Mongolian musk went through the roof. The scarcity resulting from increased demand was compounded when dockworkers went on strike and a rebellion broke out in northern Gaul. In a matter of decades, all the beautiful things a silver denarius could buy became too expensive for the average Roman citizen. The plebeians, who found themselves unable to afford their daily bread, took to the streets with torches and threatened to burn the senators alive.

Bankers tried to manage the fluctuations of the currency, but due to unfortunate investments in spice ships that sank in the Red Sea and Ethiopian caravan routes over which nothing of value ever materialized, the great investment house of Quintus, Maximus & Lucius Vibo went under. Soon, rumors began to circulate that a much larger firm, Pettius Brothers, had secretly taken a massive stake in Quintus, Maximus & Vibo, and as a result was now deep in the red. Another ominous portent came when a plutocrat named Publius Spinther redeemed thirty million sesterces for gold, which caused his bank to fold. The insolvency crisis swept up firms from Lyon to Byzantium, Carthage, and Corinth. In a matter of a few short years, the Roman economy had descended into one of the severest of all ancient economic crises, known along the Via Sacra as the Great Panic.

Bank credit exhausted, the value of ostrich feathers, silk robes, ivory toothpicks, and odd-toed ungulates tanked. The phrase most often encountered in the work of scholars who revisit this episode in Roman history: *panic engulfed the Capitoline.* Grand villas overlooking the Mediterranean, gorgeous thoroughbreds, and African elephants with stupendous ivory tusks were auctioned off for nothing.

At the height of the troubles, a delegation of senators visited the reclusive new *Pater Patriae*, Octavian's stepson Tiberius, whom they found in his usual state of despondency at one of his twelve villas in Capri. Informed of the turbulence engulfing his empire, he demanded the arrest of a Spanish magnate, Sextus Marius, who was summarily apprehended on a trumped-up charge of incest, hauled off to the capital, dragged to the top of the Tarpeian rock, and in full public view ceremoniously flung to his death.

Imperial Rome seized the oligarch's property, which not so coincidentally consisted of copper and gold mines. After a decent interval, Emperor Tiberius disbursed one million newly minted gold pieces into the financial system, and the Roman economy reversed direction once again, now lurching forward.

Call it boom-bust, twist of fate, or reversal of fortune. A constant state of change in the value of currencies, commodities, and equities has become a hallmark of money. Markets fluctuate, and at one time or another, everyone has been flucked. In order to postpone if not avoid the inevitable, bankers have long sought to bring the seemingly chaotic ebb and flow of exchange under their control. They dream of identifying, isolating, and harnessing plot reversals, so that instead of being at their mercy, they can use them to their advantage. Thus would a new character eventually join Theta and Rho on the allegorical battlefield of quantitative finance: volatility — *change incarnate* — henceforth to be known as Vega.

The nature of change is of course not only a financial but a long-standing writerly obsession, from the pre-Socratic philosophy of Heraclitus ("Everything flows and nothing abides; everything gives way and nothing stays fixed") to the sixteenth-century poetry of Edmund Spenser's "Mutabilitie Cantos" to Kafka's *Metamorphosis*. Literary Vega comes in many shapes and sizes. In the modern novel, for instance, transformation became an essential element of character development, and peripety the powerhouse of plot.

One of the earliest, most dramatic, and most enduring of plot reversals is the one that propels a character from captivity to escape, and in the long, protracted character development of money, the protagonist's most persistent captor has been gold. Yet, as medieval bankers and churchmen realized, money worked more efficiently and increased more rapidly the less it was locked to gold. Thus, from the birth of the global credit economy in the Christian Middle Ages, the impetus to shut money into a golden cage has consistently been met by a contrary impulse to let money escape all material confines, no matter how shiny, warm, and malleable.

Metal aversion became central to the history of the American dollar, a chronicle that has much in common with other classic American narratives that oppose bondage, from the high-blown rhetoric of Revolutionary polemics to the intimate prose of first-person slave narratives. Gold is the prison house that money still cannot entirely avoid, the enduring seat of the fantasy that money is a thing as opposed to an idea, the perennial stumbling block of money's struggle for liberation. The dollar has long aspired to escape the harness. From the perspective of economics, the idea is paradoxical: money wants to be free. From the perspective of literature, the idea is perfectly intelligible: The money plot is a captivity narrative.

The phrase "captivity narrative" is a term of art in English studies. It originally denoted the first international best-selling genre from early American literature: the nonfiction accounts of white Puritan women taken prisoner by Native Americans during the decades of war against the natives. More than one thousand colonists were carried away by indigenous groups during these conflicts. Similarly sensationalistic reports and diaries of sojourns through the American wilderness began to appear as early as the seventeenth century.

Much like epic and tragic narratives, captivity narratives often begin in medias res. The uncouth barbarians encircle a settlement, set it on fire, shoot arrows through the hearts of a few brave Connecticut frontiersmen, and drag a terrified white woman from her home. The Narragansetts, Pequots, or Wampanoags subsequently march their prisoner of war through snowy forests for weeks on end. The captive walks a hundred miles, repeating random verses of the bible to herself. Fed on scraps of horse gristle and bear fat, she suffers privation and hunger, but most of all she fears rape — although physical violations never do occur.

The concept that such seemingly rude brutes might in fact be governed by their own strict set of regulations regarding prisoners of war never occurs to anyone, and the stories end when, thanks to the grace of God, the white man negotiates a price with the brown man, and redeems his woman. In the case of Mary Rowlandson, who wrote the first and most famous of these narratives, the ransom came to twenty English pounds, paid at Redemption Rock in Princeton, Massachusetts, in the spring of 1676.

In its purest forms, the captivity narrative delivered genuine sagas of emancipation, such as the pre–Civil War first-person slave narratives of Harriet Jacobs, Frederick Douglass, Olaudah Equiano, and Henry Bibb. The plots of these best-selling accounts begin with either capture or birth into a life of servitude, and invariably end with escape and freedom. Perhaps the most excruciating example is the account of Henry Box Brown, who, in order to escape, had himself nailed into a wooden box three feet long, two feet wide, and two-and-a-half feet high, which was then mailed north. All things considered, Brown was luckier than most. Those who remained in chains never had the opportunity to write of their escape.

During the 1960s, captivity narratives expanded to embrace any kind of story in which a character escapes enslavement — be the bondage physical, mental, economic, or social. The genre came to include prison narratives, stories of sex addiction, drug addiction, food addiction, and other sundry commodity addictions of consumer culture, such as shopping and hoarding. By the late 1990s, reality television had thoroughly documented and exploited the plots of those obsessed by money in all its guises, such as real estate, fashion, and lifestyle brands — each ensnaring our focus and attention as thoroughly as dentalia gripped the Yurok mind.

Money has a way of shackling human thought and dominating human feeling, and at the historical center of this centuries-long captivity narrative was gold. It was gold that held Europe in thrall in 1492, when a group of Guanahani natives observed the outlines of a caravel appear from beneath the horizon. The indigenous ones watched as the pale foreigners waded ashore, planted a stick in the sand, and blabbered about something called the Crown of Castile, which was thereby and unto eternity taking possession of all the beachfront property in the Bahamas.

Then Columbus asked: *Where's the gold?*

The natives huddled together to develop a diplomatic response and came to a conclusion emulated across oceans and continents for centuries to come. They nodded their heads vigorously, pointed to the horizon, and waved goodbye as the visitors sailed away with six of their brothers and sisters in chains. To pay for their slaves, the sailors left behind a generous installment of smallpox and measles.

On his way around the world ten years later, Vasco de Gama dropped anchor in the East African coastal town of Kilwa. Here he noted a sixteen-domed mosque supported by an engineering marvel of arches and pillars, a palace with an octagonal swimming pool, a hundred perfumed rooms appointed with pearls and Chinese porcelains, and a massive hoard of gold imported from a mysterious land called Zimbabwe. Four years later the Portuguese fleet returned. Their goal: to commandeer what turned out to be four thousand mines of the inland empire, which were unearthing more than a million ounces of gold a year.

Not to be out-golded by Portugal, Hernán Cortés and his surly band were soon slogging through the jungles of Mesoamerica to the Aztec capital, where the conquistador asked the king: *Where's the gold?*

Montezuma presented Cortés with a bunch of tchotchkes suitable for melting and minting, which only made him want more. So he took the king hostage and demanded ransom — in gold.

Eventually, the colonizers must have realized that in Tenochtitlán, the generally accepted currency was the cacao bean. One hundred could buy a canoe. Did the conquistadors, in a flash of recognition, come to see that gold money was just as notional as chocolate money? They did not because they could not, and they could not because their minds were gold's vassals. For the conquistadors, it was gold or nothing. It was gold or death, and there was plenty of each.

Despite the protestations of the Peruvian natives, whose gold-tipped arrows bounced off Francisco Pizarro's armor, the Spaniards liquidated Incas by the thousand, gathered up their gold crowns, gold daggers, and other trophies strewn across the killing fields, and brought them to the cauldrons. Like Cortés, Pizarro took the king captive and demanded a ransom. He received just under three thousand cubic feet of gold, more than sixty billion dollars' worth. Then Pizarro killed the king.

And that was just to get things started. No doubt, the Yellow Brick Road lay somewhere in the Valley of the Essequibo, perhaps in the far reaches of the Orinoco, or high in the mountains of Bogotá. One beautiful morning, as dawn dropped her golden dew upon the Colorado River, the explorer García López de Cárdenas, hot on the trail of the Seven Cities of Gold, found himself standing on the precipice of the Grand Canyon, the first European to peer into the sublime expanse. History records that he was unimpressed. *Where was the gold?*

It would be an understatement to say that the miners and conquistadors did not lead examined lives. They did not consider the philosophical implications of gold holding everyone and everything captive, including themselves. Late in the nineteenth century an American historian named Alexander del Mar would publish a massive tome based on more than two decades of research, entitled *A History of the Precious Metals from the Earliest Times to the Present*. It is an extremely long and cumbersome piece of prose, and by the time Del Mar got to the end he was thoroughly disgusted:

> The slaves have perished, the temple is leveled to the dust; the religion which shared this ill-gotten wealth is obsolete; nothing remains but the gold, the cause of all this ruin.

Del Mar understood that as Europe had enslaved the world, gold had enslaved Europe. Why did mercantilism—that is, state-sponsored economics based on accumulating gold bullion—fall before the new faith in laissez-faire markets? Countless economists have pored over the equations of import, export, and employment, while ignoring the key syllogism: Since money is a story, it must act like one. And the motivations driving this story were clear: Mercantilism was a captivity narrative.

The desire for peripety — the desire to reverse the plot, to escape metallic servitude, and break the bonds of gold — was nowhere more evident than with those fanatics who purchased one-way tickets to the promised land. In 1874, Elias Derby, a descendant of one of the richest families in colonial America, came out with his *History of Paper Money*. The book noted the strange quality of early American transactions:

> The colonists of Massachusetts, when they sought an asylum on the rugged coast of New England, took with them a very small supply of gold and silver. A few years after they landed...the scarcity of money was so great that their land and cattle fell to one-fourth of their previous value. The colonists sent most of their masts, fur, and fish to England to purchase supplies of tools and clothing, or to Virginia for corn; and, as these proved insufficient, their coin followed. They were soon obliged to resort to wampum, the Indian currency, and to constitute their peas, barley, and corn legal tenders at specific rates; and although these were somewhat inconvenient for the ladies to use when they went a-shopping, they were easily divisible into small change.

The first thaler was made from the silver of Count Hieronymus von Schlick, but the first "buck" was a strip of deer hide recast as currency when there wasn't enough specie to go around. Of course, the dead skin of animals — like their bones and teeth — had long held a place of honor in the annals of money-as-ritual-sacrifice, money-as-relic, money-as-adornment, and money-as-mitigator of fear and risk. There was plenty of precedent for American deerskin money, as bearskins, goatskins, lambskins, ox hides, rabbit fur, otter fur, and mice fur can be found among medieval inventories, lists of commodities, brokerage fees, and wills. In sixteenth-century Russia, pelts of sable, marten, ermine, and fox — along with their snouts and ears — were exchanged alongside silver coins. In Mongolia, squirrel skin currency endured well into the twentieth century.

It may not strike us as strange that the settlers of New Netherland and New England made skins and fur legal tender, nor that enormous moose hides were more valuable than flimsy beaver. But an unprecedented abundance of pelts alongside a mountain of wampum wasn't enough to run the economy, even an economy as stunted and primitive as that of colonial America. As a result, just about anything in the new world became worth its weight: not only *reales*, *escudos*, francs, and pounds, but butter, oats, ginger, molasses, mahogany, rum from Barbados, and whiskey from Pennsylvania. In Virginia, salaries and taxes could be paid in currency backed by tobacco. In North Carolina, the underlying value was rice.

As this mishmash of commingled currencies permeated the colonies, Nicholas Barbon, one of London's premier real estate developers, wrote a "Discourse of Trade." Money, he observed in 1670, "is an imaginary value made by a law, for the convenience of exchange." It had become just as obvious to the seventeenth-century London land mogul as it was to the Congregationalists in Connecticut that money could be whatever the congregation deemed. The physical material did not matter. Thus the wampum, the whiskey, the deerskins, butter, peas, and rice propelled into legal tender by the desire to escape the shackles of the golden fleshpots of hell-bound Europe. To the quixotic American settler, steeped in dreams of utopia, personal perfectionism, and riches beyond wildest imagination, fiction didn't necessarily mean *not real*.

In 1686, the governors of the Province of Massachusetts Bay printed pieces of paper that announced they were worth something,

Three years after the Declaration of Independence, a sixty-dollar bill from South Carolina was worth ninety-seven pounds, ten shillings—that is, if you believe everything you read.

and subsequently declared that something to be "shillings." In 1733, Maryland's public land bank issued thirty thousand "pounds" of paper money intended to be given away, in equal shares, to each inhabitant of Maryland. Not to be outdone, South Carolina printed one million "dollars'" worth of sixty-dollar bills, although no one really knew what those sixty dollars alluded to, other than the phrase. The problems of foreign exchange that travelers encountered when they transported their fictions from one colony to another bordered on the absurd. But that didn't stop Connecticut, Rhode Island, Pennsylvania, and New Jersey from printing their own paper money, each in its own color, size, and denomination.

Meanwhile, a set of what must have been symbolically challenged British lawmakers were advancing what appears in retrospect to have been one of the more logical of mercantilist arguments: that the money of English colonies should have a modicum of connection to the money of the mother country. Therefore, went the political economic thinking, American currency should have an underlying value anchored in gold or silver — preferably in the same ratio as the British pound. This was immediately perceived to be an outrageous assault on American liberty.

England might have solved the problem by sending a few boatloads of precious metal across the Atlantic, but that would have violated the philosophy of bullionism: Once gold was got, it was to be kept — preferably in an underground vault. Instead, Parliament passed a series of Currency Acts aimed at constraining the creation of colonial paper money, money that escaped the clutches of gold. These laws, enacted in the decades prior to 1776, gave the rabble-rousers another reason to decry the tyrannical shackles of despotism. Their rhetoric proved so convincing that for many years after World War II, the most popular explanation for the American Revolution was economic.

Eventually, the historians got around to examining the net worth of the Founding Fathers and discovered that the patriots of Boston and the '76ers of Philadelphia hardly qualified as a phalanx of righteously indignant proletariat. Philip Livingston was typical of the fifty-six signers of the Declaration of Independence — a merchant specializing in sugar and slaves. Caesar Rodney's plantation in Delaware sold commodity wheat and barley to markets in Philadelphia and the West Indies. The great majority of Charles Carroll's wealth was invested in his ten-thousand-acre Maryland estate upon which toiled one thousand enslaved Africans. George Clymer of Pennsylvania, born an orphan, became the first president of the Philadelphia Bank. Carter Braxton of Virginia inherited great sums. Among the most famous of these founding fathers, Ben Franklin was a tech millionaire and John Hancock a shipping magnate. But the richest of them all was arguably George Washington, whose 52,000 acres of real-estate holdings stretched from Virginia north to New York, then east to the Ohio Valley. By some estimates, Washington's buying power, translated into today's dollars, would be in excess of $25 billion.

They were rich white men, slave owners, booze bankers, merchants of sugar and cotton. They already had more money than they needed. But if not gold, silver, sugar, rum, real estate, and slaves, what were they after? The answer was obvious. Like Henry Box Brown mailing himself north in a wooden coffin to be redeemed from slavery, they wanted to reverse the captivity narrative. They wanted that reversal so badly that the plot defined their economics, pushing them toward the unknown of a yet-undiscovered currency. They imagined an American dollar unfettered from the metallic monomania that had for so long locked money in the cursed cage of gold. Perhaps, in their more speculative moments, they imagined they were setting money free.

Soon they would produce their own sovereign currency, and the money they created would surpass their wildest dreams. The first American dollar of 1792 would eventually prove more powerful than the pound, the franc, the mark, the denarius, the shekel, and the snail shell. It would increase and multiply into trillions. Eventually, it would make gold its slave.

{7} THE BUCK
STARTS HERE

Wisdom consists not so much in knowing what to do in the ultimate as knowing what to do next.

— HERBERT HOOVER

MONEY OBEYS THE RULES OF MATH, but math does not rule money. When it comes to creating and sustaining faith in a currency, the principles of narrative reign supreme. Like great characters, great currencies develop. The dollar faltered for more than one hundred years after its founding. It teetered into the twentieth century, then much like an adolescent on the verge of adulthood, matured and regressed in equal measure until, by the middle of the same century, it was ready to rescue the franc, the lire, the mark, the pound, and the yen.

Heroes often discard logic and reason in favor of fury and passion; likewise, the impulses that motivated the greatest character ever invented. Molded from farmland, flesh, fish, forests, sugar, and slaves, the dollar was and always would be synonymous with the American spirit. It epitomized the vision of Alexander Hamilton, Andrew Jackson, Woodrow Wilson, Franklin Delano Roosevelt, Richard Nixon, and Ronald Reagan. Nothing would surpass it.

Gold tried to keep the dollar in check. And there would be those who would remain loyal to yellow metal, those who could not see that it, too, was just another myth. They would have understood why Emperor Tiberius had tossed Sextus Marius off the Tarpeian Rock, that it was all about the measurable weight of an element.

But by the latter half of the nineteenth century, the outlines of a more nuanced philosophy of money had begun to emerge in Europe, personified in the figure of the *haute financier*, from whose like would descend the modern derivatives trader, financial engineer, leveraged buyout artist, and hedge fund billionaire. The financier's assets were not hoarded in a hidden vault, nor locked in any single form. On the contrary, the financier's money was fluid. When Otto von Bismarck and Napoleon III disagreed about the fate of Austria, the *haute financiers* suggested they might handle the problem by brokering the sale of Luxembourg to France. Which is to say that for these men, money was not only credit and debt, but art and politics. They would have understood the modern neoliberal dollarization of the world, in which the all-pervasive spirit of money inhabits every blade of grass, every ounce of mineral, gallon of water, and patented strand of genetically modified DNA. For the financier, that old fatal choice — gold or not gold — was a primitive relic. Money was the opposite of *either/or*.

America was the first sovereign state to make the *haute financier*'s worldview official. When Woodrow Wilson signed the Federal Reserve Act on Christmas Eve, 1913, the dollar became a Federal Reserve *note* — neither paper nor gold, yet both. For a long time afterward it would be impossible to say with precision what the dollar was and what it was not. Instead of *either/or*, the dollar had become *both/and*.

The first law of logic is the identity principle, which states that everything must equal itself: A equals A, a rose is a rose is a rose.

From Aristotle to Zeno, philosophers had tested the limits of this proposition, all to no avail. Then came Woodrow Wilson and a Federal Reserve note that was and was not the same thing at the same time, a dollar with an identity that did not equal itself, a *literary* dollar, destined to become the most powerful thing on earth.

In rhetoric, the technical name for terminal doubt is *aporia*. This condition of undecidability, as impossible to parse as it may have been for philosophers, logicians, gold-loving conquistadors, and members of Congress, had been a long-standing cliché of literature. Some of the most renowned fictional figures present equivocal traits, for the simple reason that aporia gives characters depth and sophistication. That's why the history of fiction presents one conflicted protagonist after another, protagonists who conceal hypocrisy, hide secrets, and self-destruct. Think of Arthur Dimmesdale in *The Scarlet Letter*, Jay Gatsby in *The Great Gatsby*, Satan in *Paradise Lost*, Anna Karenina, or Emma Bovary. Iago could well have been speaking for Woodrow Wilson's Federal Reserve note when he said, "I am not what I am." Hamlet, most famously, could not decide. In fiction, ambiguity and paradox qualify as achievements. And now the same could be said for the fiction that is money.

Woodrow Wilson signed into law a gold-backed dollar that was not really backed by gold. The paradox went well with a Federal Reserve system constructed in such a way that the federal government would be both involved and not involved in the money supply. Only then could banks be both dependent on and independent of central banking policies. Of course, this raft of inconsistencies did not appear out of nowhere, fully formed. It had been the outcome of an epic struggle, centuries in the making.

The American dollar was the brainchild of Alexander Hamilton, who received his first lesson in the undecidability of money when he was eleven. One morning, the boy walked out the door of his Caribbean shack and instead of going to school headed to the docks. There he found bales of cotton, barrels of molasses, blocks of brown sugar, bolts of cloth, casks of rum, thousand-pound ropes of tobacco, precious metal coins of all shapes and sizes, enslaved black men and women yoked and harnessed, and business offices full of white men securitizing debt, signing letters of credit, crafting certificates of insurance, and drafting statements of limited liability.

As he stood on a wharf in the West Indies the boy could see all the plots and characters of money. He may not have known about kula magic, the metonymies of uncanny contagions, or the synecdochal leverage of medieval incorporations, but he could see versions of each as they shifted and reversed roles in an allegorical drama motivated by risk, fear, and ever-decaying time.

The boy understood that any of the commodities of trans-Atlantic trade could be substituted one for the other — or translated into Spanish *reales*, Portuguese escudos, Prussian thalers, English guineas, bills of exchange, deeds of maritime indemnification, or written promises to deliver or receive any or all of the above in whole or in part at a date, place, and time to be determined by endless other options and expirations. Each element of trade was materially different, and each was possessed by its own set of invisible *daimons*, which determined its price. And the boy saw that it was just this slipperiness of money that gave the small commercial port of Nevis its reach and strength.

What exactly was money? Alexander Hamilton saw that it was impossible to decide.

He talked his way into an apprenticeship as a clerk at the import-export firm of expatriate New York traders David Beekman and Nicholas Cruger. The mercantile house exchanged a wide variety of commodities, which gave Hamilton the opportunity to observe fluctuating markets in everything from timber to lard, iron, rope, cattle, and slaves. He soon proved himself an adept at the art of releasing metaphors from one restraint and enclosing them within another. That is, he showed a talent for making money, a gift too great to waste away in Nevis. When hurricanes devastated the islands six years later, a few of the Caribbean's richest merchants did the kid a favor and bought him a one-way ticket to the mainland. At seventeen, he landed in Boston, headed south, and not long thereafter found himself wandering through the port of New York.

Before he became the first secretary of the treasury and the new republic's greatest banker, Hamilton was a revolutionary, a composer of George Washington's correspondence, and one of the best lawyers in Manhattan. His hours-long streams of verbiage could hold a courtroom in thrall, and his feverish renditions convinced jury after jury. At the constitutional convention, William Pierce of Georgia compared the brilliance of his language to that of the great English novelist, Laurence Sterne.

Hamilton understood that American money would have to fit the stubborn inconsistencies of the American temperament, that American money would have to take into account the same sort of emotional stresses the sensational novels of his time were recounting in lurid detail. In a "Letter on Currency," Hamilton noted that people were "governed more by passion and prejudice" than by reason. In the sixth of *The Federalist Papers*, he noted the greatest threats to American independence: "rage, resentment, jealousy, avarice." It was a prescient observation. For the next two hundred years, these emotional antagonists would remain the dollar's enemies. And Hamilton understood that the best defense against such forces would be a set of equal and opposite energies. The word he used to describe such economic jujitsu was "sympathy."

In the winter of 1790, less than three years before the birth of his currency, Hamilton delivered his "Report on Public Credit," in which he declared that every credit should have "the nicest sympathy with every other part. Wound one limb and the whole tree shrinks and decays." To Robert Morris, America's wartime finance minister, he insisted that even the ultimate antagonist, debt, "if it is not too excessive, will be to us a national blessing. It will be powerful cement of our union."

The dollar Hamilton envisioned would be anchored in a matrix of opposed forces: foreign loans, domestic taxes, tariffs, post office revenues, and duties on coffee, tea, wine, and booze. Hamilton's amalgamation was so complicated that it was impossible for anyone to say what, in essence, a dollar was. And that was the point. The individual forces of the dollar's psychomachia could not be undone without unraveling the entire plot.

When Washington asked, "What is to be done with our terrible debt?" Hamilton had a quick and easy answer: "Bank on it as our only available capital." That was the terrifying beauty of aporia, and it has endured as a feature of American money ever since, incarnated in a national debt that presently exceeds $25 trillion — debt that other countries stand in line to purchase!

In 1792, Congress passed the first Coinage Act and established the United States Mint. As a matter of course, Hamilton had decided that the value of an ounce of gold would be worth twenty American dollars, an equivalence that would hold fast for almost 150 years. But Hamilton was far too clever to chain his dollar to gold and gold alone. From the outset, the dollar was not an *either/or* but a *both/and* arrangement, for the original American dollar was bimetallic: Its worth could be defined by either gold or silver. It was neither one nor the other, and there was no need to choose between the two.

Uncertainty about the world and fear of the future had goaded canoe traders to create magical tokens; it had encouraged chieftains to institute marriage ritual and enforce inheritance law; it had lurked behind the violence of domestication and motivated the legal armatures of mortgages and insurance. Uncertainty had made money *money*. And while Hamilton had exploited that uncertainty to create the fiction that would rule the world — that is, the almighty dollar — the currency's inherent instability would trigger a multitude of unforeseen consequences.

In the title of his 1815 book, the radical journalist William Cobbett defined what would be the great economic conflict of the nineteenth century: *Paper Against Gold*. The book's subtitle clarifies where Cobbett stood in regard to the conflict, as the title page promised to narrate "The history and mystery of the Bank of England, of the debt, of the stocks, of the sinking fund, and of all the other tricks and contrivances carried on by the means of paper money." Cobbett, who had initiated the work as a series of letters while in prison, began his diatribe in full-blown conspiracy mode:

> The time is now come, when every man...ought to make himself, if possible, well acquainted with all matters belonging to the Paper-Money System. It is that System, which has mainly contributed towards our present miseries; and indeed, without that System those miseries never could have existed in any thing approaching towards their present degree.

Within two years, the screed had sold hundreds of thousands of copies. Clearly, the charms of ambiguity inherent in a dollar based on wide-ranging sympathies with gold, silver, credit, debt, import duties, and taxes was not for everyone, and particularly not everyone in America, where a growing population of frontiersmen, boatmen, cattlemen, miners, and lumberjacks preferred less ambiguous ways of approaching the world.

"I cooks an eats my dead!" cried the otherwise unnoteworthy backwoodsman from Wolfville. John Wesley Harding "travelled with a gun in every hand," and committed his first murder when he was eleven. "My footsteps have often been marked with blood," declared Daniel Boone. If his musket wasn't handy, Davy Crockett strangled bears. The legendary American frontiersmen of the early nineteenth century did not see their new land as a delicate play of fine forces, each held in check by another. They wanted to kill, consume, and conquer, and to this end they plowed down forests, eviscerated mountains, drank rivers in a single gulp, and rained bullets on any indigenous people who dared stand in their way. It was just a matter of time before one of them would rise to the highest office in the land, and wage the first all-out attack on Hamilton's brilliant fiction.

Andrew Jackson was that man. He drank whiskey, loved to fight, loathed bourgeois culture, and felt quite comfortable massacring Creeks and Seminoles. He owned a thousand acres, enslaved hundreds, and kept thirty-seven sets of dueling pistols, more guns than any other president before or since. He believed in the merit and value of utterly demolishing his enemies, be they Native Americans in the godforsaken swamps of the Florida Panhandle, Whigs in Congress, bankers from Philadelphia, or any unfortunate who happened to insult him in print — and be summarily summoned to choose his weapons at dawn the next day. On his deathbed, when most mortals contemplate heaven, transcendence, and forgiveness, Jackson raged that his one regret in life was not having tried his vice president, John C. Calhoun, for treason, and seeing him hanged.

He was the richest president America had ever known and a famously ill-tempered son-of-a-bitch who exhibited a surprisingly unbiased and inclusive set of hatreds. A preliminary list would include aristocracy, lineage, pedigree, and protocol. He detested anyone or anything with more money, power, culture, or wealth than he, so naturally despised the East Coast banking elite, their ties to Old World nobility, and their elaborate private protocols for paying dividends, leveraging indemnities, and selling equity in their corporations.

At the time Jackson took office, Alexander Hamilton's national bank had reached a new incarnation. The so-called Second Bank of the United States helped regulate everybody's dollars, but shares in the bank's corporation were held by a closed circle of grandees, a clique of snobs who revered the customs and ceremonies of what Jackson contemptuously called "titles, gratuities, and exclusive privileges." To Jackson, the Second Bank of the United States was holding the American dollar captive in outdated and stultifying forms. He felt that this was "odious…most odious…more formidable and dangerous than the naval and military power of the enemy.…" And Jackson took it personally. "The bank is trying to kill me. But I will kill it."

Historians have traditionally described the ensuing "bank war" as a conflict of personalities — the brute politician versus the pedantic and pretentious bank president, Nicholas Biddle. And it is true that Biddle was the opposite of Jackson in every way. He graduated college at thirteen and two years later collected a second degree from Princeton, where in honor of his adoration of Latin rhetoric, he was nicknamed Grammaticus. After Princeton, the prodigy's well-to-do parents presented their teenage son with a custom-made, tailor-fitted, pseudo-military uniform with lots of shiny brass buttons. He dressed himself up and embarked upon a grand tour of Europe. Upon his return to Philadelphia, the future head of America's central bank decided, at long last, to which of the arts and sciences he would devote his brilliance. He would be a literary man.

Magazines such as *The Dial*, *The Atlantic*, and *The Knickerbocker* were still years away from their first issue, and only one person in America, Charles Brockden Brown, was making his living as a

GENERAL JACKSON SLAYING THE MANY HEADED MONSTER.

In this early nineteenth-century allegory of the bank war, Archangel Andrew Jackson slays the hydra-headed globalist dragon of Wall Street, Nicholas Biddle.

professional writer. Perhaps Biddle should have paid some attention to the content of Brown's fashionable fictions, which featured nothing akin to the high rhetorical modes of Gorgias and Pericles. Brown's tales of psychological horror presented madmen who murdered their own children, insomniac cowboys who drank panther blood, and most disconcerting of all, con men who printed and distributed counterfeit money.

Nicholas Biddle was a dandy in a barbaric land. He was a fop, an aristocrat, a conservative, a rich boy, and a prig who worshipped at the altar of classical art, drama, and philosophy. He readily assumed the most prestigious literary post in New York, the editorship of an urbane, upper crust, and sophisticated magazine called *The Portfolio*. His name would have been forgotten to all but the scholars if not for the fact that in the first decades of the nineteenth century, rhetorical knowledge and literary taste were considered essential qualities for public service, which included central banking. In fact, over the course of the magazine's twenty-five years of publication, *The Portfolio* published numerous merchants and politicians, including future president John Quincy Adams, who delivered two fables in verse — one about a fly, another about a dancing bear.

As a matter of course, Biddle the literary aesthete was elected to the Pennsylvania General Assembly, where in his first public address he praised the national bank. When the Bank of the United States was rechartered in 1816, President James Monroe appointed Biddle as a director. The following year, *The Portfolio* published a short story by James Hall, yet another writer-banker (the author of ten books, Hall also became the state treasurer of Illinois). The story was called "The Adventures of a One Dollar Note." "Be not surprised," the newly rechartered American dollar declares, "that in this age of wonders, you behold a bank note endowed with the powers of motion and speech."

Personification of money was nothing new, but Jacksonian America proved to be a dangerous time for currency that spoke like a gentleman. When the president of the Second Bank of the United States resigned in 1822, Nicholas Biddle became its president, and soon attracted the fury of a president.

It wasn't supposed to be that way. Mortal conflict was the last thing on Biddle's mind when he began to lay out plans to make the bank's headquarters in Philadelphia a replica of the Parthenon. That way, as he ruminated over the arcane structures Alexander Hamilton had come up with to collateralize debt, his thoughts might never stray too far from the achievement of his idols, those who held court in the agora, debating in high rhetorical style the nature of justice, truth, and beauty.

A great deal of study has been devoted to the plots and characters of the bank war. Some say that Jackson versus Biddle was a personification of South versus North, others that their antagonistic spirits embodied Main Street versus Wall Street, rural versus urban, populists versus coastal elites, or America First versus globalism. But in the end it wasn't much of a contest, as Jackson used his executive power to remove all federal deposits from the central bank, in one fell swoop eliminating one-fifth of the bank's capital. Then Jackson distributed the ten million federal dollars among his friends who owned their own banks.

Biddle retaliated by raising interest rates and calling in loans, trying to contract the economy, induce a recession, and blame it on the president. But the literary aesthete proved to be an inept politician. When American businessmen turned against him, Biddle withdrew from public life and spent the remainder of his career defending himself from million-dollar lawsuits and charges of criminal conspiracy. Meanwhile Jackson's thirty-two pet banks were leveraging their sudden windfall into $150 million in new loans.

Despite Jacksons attempts to banish the elite rhetoric of money and replace it with frontier fact, the true winner of the bank war was metaphor. Once the national bank had been obliterated and state banks took over, a liberalized set of rules and regulations allowed just about anyone to print notes on rectangular slips of paper, call them dollars, and loan them out so they could increase and multiply. (Even Andrew Jackson eventually expressed some regret regarding the "general evil influence" of such unbound financial excitements. Before he left office he declared that if anyone wanted to buy more than 320 acres of government land in the new territories, they would have to pay with gold or silver. As might have been expected, this reversal of paper back to metal threw into even greater disarray all the state-issued "money of account" Jackson's policies had previously inspired.)

The intensity and drama of the bank war underscored what objective observers had long perceived about American money: It was what Americans said it was. Incontrovertible evidence to this effect appeared the year after Jackson left office and the United States carved the twenty-sixth state of the union from the so-called Northwest Territory.

Michigan's first governor was Stevens Mason. Elected when he was all of twenty-three years old, he inherited a state roughly equal in size to the kingdom of the Visigoths when Alaric sacked Rome. Unlike the hinterlands of Austria, England, France, and Germany, Michigan was not inhabited by bloodthirsty barbarians, but by the Ojibwe people, who had settled where the fish were plenty and the wild rice grew. There is no count of how many natives were displaced by the influx of New Englanders, but it is clear that by 1840 just under a quarter of a million Americans had been seduced by the myth that among the ore, timber, and freshwater lakes larger than the Adriatic Sea, a new sort of money was breathing fresh air. After sixty thousand years of captivity to beads, shells, skulls, iron, copper, silver, and gold, this money would be free.

In emulation of their hero, Andrew Jackson, hundreds of frontier bankers armed themselves with corn whiskey and caplock revolving rifles designed by a twenty-two-year old American manufacturing genius named Samuel Colt. Then they headed into the wilderness. The state celebrated its first birthday with the establishment of forty new banks, one for every two thousand of its new citizens — the equivalent of twenty thousand new banks opening in California this year. The kicker was that each bank offered its own, independent dollar. In America, where self-reliance ruled as the ultimate virtue, everyone could have their own currency based on full faith and credit in themselves.

Such an egomaniacal money plot unleashed impudent and reckless breeds of land-boomers, speculators, and cowboy bankers, each of whom imbued money with his own particular character. No longer a concubine, no longer Juno Moneta, no longer "Lady Credit," frontier money was male money, and as such it prefigured the money of the corporate marauder, the Wall Street shark, the junk-bond king. Here were riches that could scarcely be differentiated from robbery, and the eventual results were memorialized in the trials and prison sentences doled out to 1980s plutocrats such as Charles Keating, Ivan Boesky, and Michael Milken, for whom making money and making a killing were synonymous terms.

The so-called wildcat bankers of the booming American Midwest were not timid men, but their one enduring fear was that a depositor might stumble upon William Cobbett's old tirade, *Paper Against Gold*, and demand that his banker transform promissory notes into metal that largely did not exist. The reserve capital of the Jackson County Bank, for instance, consisted of nothing more than a half-full drawer of lead, ten penny nails, and broken glass. The bankers reasoned that the harder to get to the bank, the more hidden the hoard, the more unlikely the prospect of redemption. So the pioneers made a point of setting up shop in the most inaccessible, impossible, and barren stretches of terrain, deep among the birch and maple, where the wildcats roamed.

By the middle of the nineteenth century, it had become clear to anyone paying attention that paper money was allegorical. These were the decades in which Laurence Oliphant's *The Autobiography of a Joint-Stock Company* appeared in print, and the phrase "fictitious capital" began to pop up with some regularity in the pages of *The Economist* and *The Morning Chronicle*. A "review" of a Bank of England note appeared in *Household Words,* a London magazine that often featured the work of Charles Dickens. Here, the banknote was treated not as a talking oddity as it had been in the days of Nicholas Biddle and *The Portfolio,* but as if it were a literary masterpiece: "There is a pithy terseness in the construction of the sentences; a downright, direct, straight-forward, coming to the point, which would be wisely imitated in much of the contemporaneous literature..."

The post-Jacksonian era of "free banking" began in 1837, and that year more than two hundred new banks were born in the United States, each issuing its own paper. That same year, twenty New York banks went bust, and all the notes and promises they had issued became worthless. From there, things went downhill. As Michigan banks went under, Stevens Mason, the young governor, fled to New York, leaving the state with two million dollars in bad debt. Fifty-five of Indiana's ninety-five banks collapsed. Half of Minnesota's "free banks" failed, along with eight out of ten in Illinois. The excitements of free money had devolved into an unending series of panics, depressions, and an unemployment rate that reached 25 percent. Not to mention eight thousand different kinds of dollars.

The "Texas redback" was perhaps the most ambitious and audacious failure of them all. It had been anchored in the poetic imagination of Mirabeau Buonaparte Lamar, whose otherwise obscure biography is worth summarizing if only for the insight it provides into the greatest metaphor he ever conceived. Born on a Georgia cotton plantation in 1798, Mirabeau and his older brother, Lucius Quintus Cincinnatus Lamar, spent long hours acquiring the gentlemanly skills of fencing and equestrianism. As the slaves sweated it out in the cotton fields the boys whiled away their afternoons in proper spats and dark cravats, immersing themselves in the arts of painting and dramatic recitation. Given such proclivities and upbringing, it was only natural that the brothers imagined themselves knights, crusaders, troubadours, and fairy-tale heroes. Mirabeau in particular became an incessant scribbler: A selection from the collected works:

> ... O radiant West!
> Thou seem'st, to Fancy's eye,
> A lovely land — a home of rest ...

There is no need to provide more of his dismal rhymes, which he most likely recited as he and brother Lucius strolled along the banks of the Oconee, dreaming of the philosopher's stone and the Holy Grail while keeping an eye out for stray Cherokee.

Unfortunately, Mirabeau never could figure out how to earn a living. He tried a general store and failed. He tried a newspaper and failed. When he was thirty-four his wife died of tuberculosis, and soon thereafter Lucius killed himself. At this point Mirabeau did like *el ingenioso hidalgo*, the medieval *peregrinatio*, and the kula traders of Melanesia. He got on his horse and followed the setting sun. Eight hundred miles later he came across an armed insurgency.

The conflict between those who lived in what is now called the state of Texas and the rulers of the Mexican Republic had been brewing for more than a decade before 1836, when the Republic of Texas declared its independence as a sovereign state. Mirabeau Lamar now stumbled upon a scene in which terrified caravans of refugees were fleeing their homes, their only hope of survival pinned upon a ragtag "Texian" army maneuvering to escape the troops of Antonio López de Santa Anna, Mexico's president and commander in chief, who had vowed to exact bloody revenge on the insolent upstarts who dared defy his authority. Any sane bystander would have fled the conflict zone. But Mirabeau Buonaparte Lamar had been named after a French emperor. He had trained since childhood to take his place at the round table. After a life of nothing much, he had at last found something.

Those who hold death in steely contempt make the best warriors, but a close second are the insane, those besotted with the romance of it all. Lamar possessed both traits. In the Battle of San Jacinto, the knight from Oconee unsheathed his saber, spurred his horse, and charged into a crowd of astonished enemy to rescue two captured Texian warriors. Here was idiocy worthy of Don Quixote charging the windmill, and the act shocked everyone on both sides of the battlefield, including the two captives, who realized, belatedly, that they had been redeemed. The act was so absurdly courageous that — Lone Star legend has it — the Mexican army, arrayed on the opposite field, stood to salute. The Battle of San Jacinto turned into the massacre of San Jacinto, a decisive victory of the Texas Revolution. General Santa Anna was captured, and Mirabeau Lamar's epic act entered the mythology.

The mad poet rose through the ranks to become secretary of war, and six months after San Jacinto, when a friend of Andrew Jackson's by the name of Sam Houston became the first president of the Republic of Texas, Mirabeau Lamar took the oath of office as the first vice president. In the next election he ran at the top of the ticket. It must have been a strange campaign, as before voting day one of his opponents committed suicide and the other drowned in Galveston Bay. Left with no one to run against, the daydreamer who couldn't manage a general store found himself chief executive officer of a republic larger than France.

Lamar's overwrought sensibilities began to wax. He envisioned Texas as a great nation, a realm stretching radiantly all the way from the Sabine River to the Pacific coast. There was only one thing he needed to sustain his holy crusade against the Mexicans, Cherokees, and Comanches who stood in his way, and that was money.

The first treasury secretary of the Republic of Texas had been a farmer named Henry Smith, who spent a great deal of his tenure begging President Sam Houston for permission to resign, as he was going broke. Henry Smith had tried and failed to raise revenue through real estate taxes just as Texas real estate went bust. He had tried to raise revenue through tariffs collected at the port of Galveston, but his efforts were met with widespread fraud. He eventually agreed to a system of promissory notes printed on one side with Texas stars and the other side left blank — a boon to counterfeiters of all stripes. The day President Mirabeau Lamar took the oath of office, Smith went back to his farm.

Lamar could not have cared less about real estate taxes and port tariffs, much less about bankruptcy, inflation, trade balances, and the fact that the Republic of Texas could not mint any coins because the Republic of Texas possessed no precious metal. Instead, Lamar embraced the paradox commonly known among ancient philosophers as *creatio ex nihilo* — that is, the divine power to create something out of nothing. He had discovered for himself an economic idea that would be articulated more than a century later by Luigi Einaudi, a scholar of early modern Europe, economist, and president of Italy, who would make the following historical observation:

> If one reads books on monetary subjects that were written in the period from the sixteenth to the eighteenth century, one frequently encounters the concept of "imaginary money." Other terms used are "ideal money," "political money," *moneta numeraria*, "money of account."

It is not inconceivable that at some point during those long afternoons overlooking the cotton fields, Mirabeau Lamar had read about Louis XIV and the non-existent money that built Versailles, or the Bank of England notes of 1691 that funded the war against

France — those three million pounds that have yet to be repaid. Perhaps he was familiar with Colonial financial history and knew of the 1686 paper emissions of Massachusetts, or had read Benjamin Franklin's autobiography, in which the future profile on the hundred-dollar bill recalled steering home a wheelbarrow of his own freshly printed Philadelphia cash. Perhaps Lamar had heard of the paper money of the Tang Dynasty, the parchment currency of Carthage, or the Swedish notes of 1661. He may have studied how the Alberti, the Abizzi, the Bardi, and lesser medieval banking houses of Florence, Milan, and Rome, had constructed financial empires upon mountains of debt. It is unlikely that news of the Yurok and their dentalia or Melanesian kula had spread to nineteenth-century Georgia, but it is possible he had read *The Travels of Marco Polo*, and knew that the great and murderous Khan had conjured tree bark into cash.

Lamar was a dreamer, a poet, and the president, so in January of 1839 he commanded the Texas Department of the Treasury in Austin to print 2.7 million Texas dollars.

The first Texas redback single featured a portrait of Daniel Boone carrying a rifle, dressed in buckskins, while a naked Native American woman paddled a birch bark canoe, looking back over her shoulder in fear. The two-dollar bill depicted a cowboy on a white horse, rounding up a longhorn, harnessing the uncouth forces of the west into commodity beef. The fifty boasted a portrait of the Father of the Republic, Stephen F. Austin, dressed in suit and tie alongside an adoring, naked woman. Blatant as the imagery might have been, it did not inspire faith. A mere decade after Lamar's *creatio ex nihilo* of money came a monstrous bankruptcy, as the Republic of Texas found itself in the hole for more than ten million of these redbacks, none of which had ever really existed in the first place.

Three years after Mirabeau Lamar left office, the eleventh President of the United States, James K. Polk of Tennessee, purchased the Republic of Texas for fifteen million United States dollars — the equivalent to about half a trillion today. In the end, Mirabeau's magic money had worked, as two years after that, *Banker's Magazine* became the first to print the phrase "the poetry of Banking." By then, Lamar had abandoned the muse of politics and the poetics of cash to devote himself to verses that had, in his own words, "dropped like wildflowers along the rugged path of public duty." His *Collected Works* appeared in 1857, to tepid reviews.

The decade preceding the American Civil War is generally considered the greatest era in the history of American literature. While imperial selfhood triumphed in Ralph Waldo Emerson, Henry David Thoreau, and Walt Whitman, undecidability and terminal doubt powered the works of Nathaniel Hawthorne and Herman Melville. The *A* of *The Scarlet Letter* proved to be as resistant to decoding as the white whale or the underlying value of a wildcat dollar. It is hard to overstate the volatility of the mid-nineteenth-century American mind as it fluctuated between the poles of spirituality and materialism. Spanning both sides of the split lay the half-material, half-fiction that was money. The North would need a lot of it to win the Civil War.

The number of dollars required was far beyond the horizon Hamilton envisioned when he first created the dollar, beyond what Jackson envisioned when he destroyed the central bank and left American money to the whims of his cronies, and far beyond the fantasies of Mirabeau Lamar. For Lincoln and his treasury secretary, Salmon P. Chase, were not considering 2.7 million redbacks, but a quarter of a billion *greenbacks*, so named because the reverse of each note was printed in green ink. And it was not only the outlandish volume of greenbacks that instilled shock and awe, but the existential origin of the currency, for the demands of war had brought the dollar's captivity narrative to its logical conclusion: a dollar defined by declaration. God's first words were *fiat lux*—let there be light. Now, Lincoln, Chase, and Congress had a new directive: Let there be money, fiat money.

The terror of what hundreds of millions of greenback dollars might unleash upon the world was the theme of an apocalyptic speech delivered in January of 1862, when the United States representative from Ohio, George Pendleton, took the floor and declared that if the members of Congress were to disengage money's material moorings in gold and silver, they would

> send these notes out into the world stamped with irredeemability. You put on them the mark of Cain, and, like Cain, they will go forth to be vagabonds and fugitives on the earth. What then will be the consequence? It requires no prophet to tell what will be their history. The currency will be expanded; prices will be inflated; fixed values will depreciate; incomes will be diminished; the savings of the poor will vanish; the hoardings of the widow will melt away; bonds, mortgages, and notes, everything of fixed value will lose their value; everything of changeable value will be appreciated; the necessaries of life will rise in value; the Government will pay twofold—certainly largely more than it ought—for everything that it goes into the market to buy; gold and silver will be driven out of the country. What then? The day of reckoning must come.

Once again, money was all mixed up with magic, spirits, doom, prophecy, redemption, and god. Pendleton's narrative through line started with Genesis and ended with Revelations, from Adam and Eve's firstborn to everyone's last day. When the next presidential elections came around in 1864, the Democratic National Convention nominated the great Union Major General George McClellan to run against Lincoln, and McClellan's running mate was none other than the antiwar Cassandra of the greenback apocalypse — that same representative from Ohio, George Pendleton.

Sixty-five thousand Union soldiers were killed in the long, bloody summer before that election. When Confederate forces under the command of Jubal Early advanced to within five miles of the White House, economic debate abruptly receded. Given the proximity of actual fire and brimstone, Americans decided they could survive without gold. Paper money would do just fine.

But the dollar's emancipation would not be smooth going, nor the ancient myth of gold so easily forgotten. What war could banish, war could resurrect. Five years after the Union's victory, soldiers from the French Empire and the German Confederation gathered on opposite sides of the Rhine. They fired lead bullets at each other, sprayed grapeshot from state-of-the-art breech-loading rifles, and inaugurated a new weapon of mass destruction, the 750-pound *Mitrailleuse*, precursor of the machine gun. The Franco-Prussian War left more than 900,000 casualties, and only ended when the German Confederation blockaded the road to Paris and all the dollars, francs, marks, pounds, silver, and gold in the world could not buy a baguette.

The French surrendered in the spring of 1871, and as summer rolled around the Germans wrote up a list of the outrages and crimes committed by their enemies and demanded five billion francs in reparations, a sum that would be worth around five-hundred billion dollars today. The victors gave their vanquished foes five years to pay up, but as it turned out, the French were hoarding more metal than anyone ever imagined. Much to Chancellor Otto von Bismarck's surprise, the French delivered the sum a year early, all of it in gold.

The melting and minting business returned in full force. The Germans fired up the cauldrons to just above one thousand degrees centigrade and tossed in the lot of their francs. They liquefied the image of Napoleon III and minted Heinrich XXII, Ludwig II, and Kaiser Wilhelm. And once the gold coins were ready, they pulled the plug on their silver mines, silver mints, and silver thalers and relegated silver to the realm of bracelets and earrings. Scandinavia, France, and Holland followed suit.

Gold had taken money captive once again.

The return of the gold standard struck the artists and writers who had been radicalized by the failed revolutions of mid-century Europe as tragically absurd. The German composer, Richard Wagner was typical of the type. So, while George Pendleton of Ohio had been terrified by the approaching apocalypse of greenbacks, Wagner began to work on a magnum opus that warned of the opposite: an apocalypse made of gold. His epic began and ended beneath the waters of the Rhine, which like the River Patoclus in which Midas had washed his cursed hands, flowed with gold. Here, Wagner imagined a vast hoard mined by the minions of Pluto, that long-forgotten race of gnomes known in German mythology as *nibelungs*.

The heroes and the villains of *Das Rheingold* ride horses with golden bridles, protect themselves with golden shields, drink wine from golden cups, and pray for treasure chests overflowing with red, silver, and yellow gold. They kill each other with golden weapons then lie for eternity in golden coffins. The maidens wear golden girdles and golden thongs, and say things like: "If thou lovest me, let me fill twenty travelling chests with gold…"

The story starts when Alberich, an evil *nibelung* dwarf, steals a sacred hoard of gold and concentrates its power in a ring. Wagner had mashed up nineteenth-century German nationalism, European Romanticism, the allure of primitive ring money, the age-old border dispute between France and Germany, and his own love-hate relationship with riches. No wonder the plot went right off the rails, proceeding to incest, suicide, castles in the sky, magic swords, giants, mermaids, dragons, and immortal furies known as Valkyries. But the metaphors incessantly return to gold, as much "as twelve huge wagons in four whole nights and days could carry from the mountain down to the salt sea bay; though to and fro each wagon thrice journeyed every day."

Adolf Hitler would read the character of Alberich as a veiled reference to Jewish bankers, but others saw it differently. George Bernard Shaw, a founder of the London School of Economics and a winner of the Nobel Prize for literature, devoted a book, *The Perfect Wagnerite*, to analyze what he called "the economic lines of the allegory." That is to say that by the beginning of the twentieth century, it was clear to fascist and socialist alike that money was an allegory, and that the central figure of money's final epic struggle would be gold.

George Bernard Shaw saw Alberich's underground realm of enslaved *nibelung* gold miners as a model of capitalist manufacture, that the scene

> ...need not be a mine: it might just as well be a match-factory, with yellow phosphorus...a large dividend, and plenty of clergymen shareholders. Or it might be a white lead factory, or a chemical works, or a pottery, or a railway shunting yard, or a tailoring shop, or a little gin-sodden laundry, or a bakehouse, or a big shop, or any other of the places where human life and welfare are daily sacrificed in order that some greedy foolish creature may be able to hymn exultantly to his Plutonic idol:

> *Thou mak'st me eat whilst others starve, And sing while others do lament: Such unto me Thy blessings are...*

On the coattails of Shaw's radical reading of the opera's allegorical money plot came the more sober musings of a German statistician named Georg Friedrich Knapp, whose book, *The State Theory of Money*, argued that the validity of a coin had little to do with its weight or the quality of its metal. Knapp had reached this conclusion during the 1870s, as alongside Wagner and Shaw he had witnessed the monetary outcomes of the Franco-Prussian War, when all previous state debts in silver were magically transformed into state debts in gold. When Germany changed the metal of the mark, it became clear to Knapp that the coins could just as easily have been stamped out of copper or nickel or tin. Money was a matter of law, and law was a matter of language.

For proof, Knapp needed look no farther than the fact that the 1905 silver thaler weighed less than the 1871 silver thaler, but they were both worth the same three marks. That was because a mark, like a Bitcoin and a dollar and any representation of property, is a name that doesn't necessarily have anything in common with the thing it names. Money was not gold or silver or grain or livestock or debt or credit or cash, but a yoke for any and all of them. We could choose whatever harness we wanted, but the most efficient and elastic yoke of all was language. That was why Georg Friedrich Knapp used a term he borrowed from the history of philosophy to describe the nature of money. Money, he said, was "nominal."

"If anyone says that my own aim has been to discover the soul of money," he wrote, "well, so be it."

On the one side, the spirit of names; on the other side, the spirit of gold. Never had the two fictions been so far apart. Never had money been so split. But the genius of Alexander Hamilton's original American dollar was that it had been engineered to embrace antagonisms. Conceived in aporia, the dollar's infancy was not only bimetallic, but equal parts credit and debt. This may explain the successful outcome of the dollar's long struggle, why after a century of strife the dollar would emerge as the most powerful currency ever, the world's reserve currency, the fiction everyone believes.

In 1872, President Ulysses S. Grant signed the General Mining Act, which ruled that prospectors could stake claims on public lands by piling up a few rocks or driving in a few stakes. They would then be free to dig in the dirt as much as they liked, and would own everything they found. Over the course of the next century, the American underground would yield more than $230 billion worth of metal, but hardly any of that copper, nickel, and silver would ever become money.

That was because the following year Grant signed the Coinage Act of 1873, which eliminated the silver dollar and directed the United States Treasury to stop accepting deposits in silver. The result was that even as industrialists and mining interests accumulated vast stores of non-gold metallic wealth, there would be no general increase in the money supply. Following Europe, the United States was back on the gold standard.

Grant had always teetered on the brink of personal bankruptcy. He was naive about finance. Perhaps that was the reason he decided money was gold. After all, no one genuinely wants money to be a white whale, its meaning impossible to decide. Considering how much time and energy we spend on it, everyone wants to believe money is real, not imaginary. It would be sad to see a Yurok at long last convinced that his cherished dentalia were nothing but clams.

But after rice money, whiskey money, and wampum, after wildcat ten-penny-nail money, after a federal buyout of Texas redbacks and a Civil War won on the strength of 450 million greenbacks, the United States dollar could not stand captivity in a golden cage. The Coinage Act of 1873 was followed by the Panic of 1873, which was in turn followed by the depressions of 1884 and 1890, followed by the Panic of 1893—when six hundred American banks failed, fifteen thousand companies went bankrupt, and for the second time in American history unemployment hit 25 percent.

To the rural Democrats who frequented the grain elevators and stockyards in the great markets of Chicago, money was a man standing up to his waist in blood, killing pigs. Money was wheat, corn, and hay. Money was bacon, ham, sausage, and steaks. And what was left over — the lard and the glue, the brushes, candles, and soap — that was money, too. So why, the farmers and ranchers asked, must the dollar be stuck in Plutonic captivity? Why must the dollar be gold and nothing but gold?

A political movement was born. For years, the Populists would rail against the ever-deflating price of their grain and beef. The fault, they argued, was American money. They wanted the government to make more of it. An increase in the money supply, reasoned the wheat growers, would inflate the price of wheat, and an inflated price of wheat would allow them to pay their debts to the banks with dollars worth less than the dollars originally borrowed. And the quickest, easiest, and most obvious way to increase the money supply was to make money silver again.

After thousands of years the Titans awoke. Once again, the metal gods went to war, and the demand to "Free Silver" became a rallying cry for Governor John Altgeld of Illinois, Representative Richard P. Bland of Missouri, and Governor Horace Boies of Iowa — all of whom called Grant's Coinage Act the "Crime of '73." The old story was new again, including The End. The Greek poet Hesiod had declared the apocalyptic results as far back as 800 BC: "evil war and terrible battle."

In 1896, the National Bank of Illinois collapsed, the largest bank to sicken and die up to that point in the history of the United States. If the financiers didn't make use of their Colt pistols, they drowned themselves in Lake Michigan. Waves of anti-Semitism erupted as the Populists blamed the Rothschilds of London for the international conspiracy of selling gold at exorbitant prices to the United States Treasury. The panic closed the Chicago Stock Exchange for three months. The dollar survived only after America's wealthiest banker, J. P. Morgan, injected 3.5 million ounces of his own gold into the US Treasury.

The Populists would have welcomed the chance to throw Morgan off the Tarpeian Rock, and submit Alfred de Rothschild to a dose of good old *sparagmos*. They were thirsting for a redeemer, and he came in the form of a thirty-six-year-old congressman from Nebraska scheduled to address the Democratic National Convention. On the third day — July 9, 1896 — he stood before the masses assembled in the Chicago Coliseum: "I come to speak to you in defense of a cause as holy as the cause of liberty..."

William Jennings Bryan's economic argument was so simple that it hardly qualified as economics, and for good reason. His dollar was founded on the plot, character, and metaphor that had mattered to him most since he had experienced a miraculous epiphany at a religious revival when he was fourteen. Like many a priest and poet, not to mention merchant kings like John D. Rockefeller and advertising executives like Bruce Barton, William Jennings Bryan had seen that the story of Jesus and the story of money were the same story. What made Bryan's version slightly different was that in his rendition, the archvillain of was gold. He stood on the podium in silence, his arms outstretched as though he were being crucified. Then he said, "You shall not press down upon the brow of labor this crown of thorns. You shall not crucify mankind upon a cross of gold."

A dramatic reenactment of Christ on the cross at the climax of an economic speech delivered at a political convention might strike some as strange. The crowd, as reported by the *Washington Post,* fell silent. Then, "bedlam broke loose, delirium reigned supreme." The masses lifted Bryan on their shoulders and carried him through the coliseum. Without a trace of irony, the *St. Louis Post-Dispatch* reported that the representative from Nebraska had immortalized himself.

It is hard to overstate the weirdness of the Cross of Gold speech going down in American history as perhaps the third most famous behind Martin Luther King's "I Have A Dream" and Lincoln's Gettysburg Address. But the Jesus-money moment landed Bryan the Democratic nomination and 46.7 percent of the popular vote. It wasn't enough to win, and he lost again in 1900 to William McKinley, who took office and signed the Gold Standard Act with a golden pen. Eighteen months later, McKinley was assassinated and the New York Stock Exchange bottomed out at 53. The Trust Company of America failed, alongside Lincoln Trust, Knickerbocker Trust, and International Trust. The Bank of New York also failed. Its constitution had been written by Alexander Hamilton.

Worse was to come. Over the course of three terrifying weeks in October of 1907, the New York Stock Exchange lost half its value, and this time Morgan and the plutocrats had to pony up more dozens of millions of dollars, and even Congress had to admit that the gold story no longer made much sense. The result was the creation of the third central bank in American history, known as the Federal Reserve.

A reserve is that portion of land held back for posterity, that portion of the military held back for full-scale attack, the grain set aside in case of famine, the cash a bank keeps to remain solvent. It's something you don't see, but trust is there. It's the money you don't use, without which money couldn't be used. A reserve is always two things at the same time, something both present and absent. As Georg Friedrich Knapp noted: "Gold reserves . . . must, of course, be inviolable, i.e., they must not be used in any form of State expenditure but such as involves conversion."

What he meant was that the gold held in the reserves of a country's sovereign bank could only be used as money in deals with other sovereign banks of other nations. The international interchangeability of gold would eventually power the final reversal of the dollar's captivity narrative, but in 1913, the idea of releasing United States sovereign gold to other sovereign banks was theoretical.

In 1913, the gold bullion held by the Federal Reserve was worth its weight because of the emotional response it elicited. Knapp provided a rationale as to why this would be so. "The natural man's *feelings* are autometallistic," he wrote. Whatever the reason, the autometallistic feeling that emanated from the Federal Reserve brought immense relief.

Confidence that the United States government kept a hoard of gold locked up somewhere no one could reach provided widespread assurance, the *feeling* that dollars that might not reside anywhere in particular—or even exist—could always somehow be made to materialize. As a result, America became the land of credit-based acquisition. Here, washing machines, refrigerators, and vacuum cleaners could be purchased by all. Twenty-six million cars were manufactured and sold during the 1920s. The Dow increased and multiplied sixfold. At the Republican National Convention of 1928, Treasury Secretary Andrew Mellon (worth about $300 million at the time) threw his support behind a mining magnate named Herbert Hoover (worth about $100 million), who became president in a landslide and promised a final triumph over poverty. "Anyone not only can be rich," he proclaimed in his inaugural address, "but ought to be rich."

Economists and historians debate the causes of what happened next. Buying stock with borrowed money was obvious trouble, along with bank deposits lacking insurance. The list of other culprits includes stagnant wages, higher tariffs, Midwest drought, international debt structure, and growing income inequality. But such economic phenomena are not uncommon. Perhaps that autometallistic feeling just wasn't enough to carry the economy. Whatever the cause, within a year of Hoover's election he would be presiding over a 600 percent jump in United States unemployment. That, at a time when eight out of ten Americans had no savings whatsoever.

Some say the president was unlucky. After all, he had been an orphan, and spent his childhood shuttling across the country from one relative to the next, looking for something solid and stable to latch onto. Perhaps that was why he fixated on rocks, which tended to stay in one place. He failed his entrance exams for college, all except for math, but that was good enough to gain admission to a school in Northern California that had just opened for business and was willing to accept just about anyone. It was called Stanford.

He graduated with a degree in geology but couldn't find a job, so the future president entered the workforce at a Northern California mine, pushing an ore cart for seventy hours a week. Friends in San Francisco eventually told him about an opening for someone willing to survey geological sites in the deserts of Australia and Asia, someone who would trek into wastelands without food or water in order to tell others where to dig and drill and blast the planet open to extract its treasures.

After a few years overseas Hoover was fluent in Mandarin, had opened his own consulting business, and taken stakes in silver and lead mines. But it was Burmese zinc that made his fortune. Zinc lends itself to commercial applications: batteries, deodorants, dandruff shampoos, paint, toothpaste, galvanized nails, and throat lozenges. Before his fortieth birthday, the poor boy was rich as Croesus.

Hoover believed that a dollar was no more nor less than its weight in gold, and that weight was 23.22 grains. He believed that the dollar linked all the world's currencies in ratios, $4.86 for each pound sterling, and so on down the line of marks and francs and rubles in a great chain of being, fifty-nine countries on earth bound together in metal, which was itself bound by the laws of mechanics, which were in turn bound by the laws of reason. Hoover had the best intentions to combat the Great Depression with every ounce of scientific, technological, engineering, and mathematical know-how and can-do. He summoned captains of industry to the White House, he insisted that business owners maintain wages, he increased lending to banks, farmers, and construction companies. He raised taxes.

None of it worked. Between 1929 and 1933, five thousand American banks collapsed, and it looked to many as though Karl Marx had been right after all, that gold was a fetish as worthy of full faith and credit as a snail shell. The End was at hand. In desperation, the Federal Reserve recalled $300 million in bullion from across the Atlantic to be socked away in its underground vaults, as though a return of Montezuma's treasures might reverse the plot.

The British economist John Maynard Keynes ridiculed the tactic as a holdover from the days of primitive money. Money was not bullion to be unloaded, packed up, and shipped from one place to another, like white and red shell armbands. The Federal Reserve's recall of metal was like the recalling of "little household gods," he wrote, to be swallowed by the "single golden image" which "lives underground and is not seen."

Hoover may have possessed more money than even he could count, but it never occurred to him he didn't know what it was. The soul of money wasn't metal, and it wasn't math. That was what Franklin Delano Roosevelt understood. On his first day in office he closed every bank in the United States. Then he decided that gold would no longer be street legal, and ordered that all gold coins be turned in to the central banking system to be melted down into bullion, cooled into ingots, and locked in cages in the subbasements of the Federal Reserve. As per the Gold Reserve Act of January 30, 1934: "No gold coin shall thereafter be coined, no gold coins shall hereafter be paid out or delivered by the United States..."

Eleven years later, FDR died in office. Five months after that, as radioactive clouds hovered over the ruins of Hiroshima and Nagasaki, the economic dust of the American money plot had settled into irony: A dollar that could not be made of gold had endowed its sovereign state with more gold than any other country in the history of the world. The hoard amounted to more than five hundred million physical ounces unambiguously corralled within the underground caverns of the Federal Reserve.

Gold had been exiled to the land of the *nibelungs*. Considering the damage done, it was poetic justice.

{8} THE FLOAT

... any attempt at understanding the complex and basically alien phenomena in an archaic civilization must be oriented along the lines in which this civilization itself conceived of them. In dealing with a literate civilization, the most efficient means of reaching this understanding is to study the semantics of selected key terms...

— A. LEO OPPENHEIM

All technology has the property of the Midas touch.

— MARSHALL MCLUHAN

IN THE THIRTEENTH CHAPTER of *The Poetics*, Aristotle noted that the tragic hero must have two characteristics. The first was "great reputation and prosperity." The second was a fatal flaw. That defect, according to Aristotle, could not be "vice and depravity, but ... some error of judgment"—as basic and simple as numbers not adding up to the correct sum.

The story of the dollar's greatest crisis began like a lot of other stories: with a hero up a tree and a villain throwing rocks. Such a beginning may suggest the reassuring probability that the crisis would play out like other crises, that the plot would match other plots, that the hero would avoid the rocks, climb down from the tree, vanquish the villain, and live to fight another day. But at the time, no one was reassured. At the time, it looked like tragedy.

Throughout the 1960s, the story of the dollar had left bankers, economists, and financiers increasingly muddled and perplexed. Their bewilderment had been based upon increased volatility in foreign exchange rates, balances of international payments that didn't quite balance, and the still-debated mystery of the Great Stagflation, that blend of increasing prices and unemployment in the midst of decreasing economic activity.

Richard Nixon knew the dollar was suspect when he took office in 1968. That was one reason why he appointed his own chairman of the Federal Reserve, the business cycle expert Arthur Burns. The previous chairman, William McChesney Martin, Jr., had served five presidents over a nineteen-year span, and his retirement dinner was a black-tie affair for one hundred and ten.

"I wish I could turn the bank over to Arthur Burns as I would have liked," said Martin. "But we are in very deep trouble."

A brewing energy crisis exacerbated the dollar's troubles. After United States spare crude oil capacity was exhausted in the first quarter of 1971, the Organization of Petroleum Exporting Countries (OPEC) made it clear that henceforth, they would take charge of the supply chain. OPEC consisted of Iran, Iraq, Kuwait, Saudi Arabia, and Venezuela — countries not generally recognized for their love of America. Savants in the Nixon administration knew then that the price of gasoline would skyrocket, bringing everything along with it. Most politically damning would be the rise in unemployment.

So on Friday the 13th of August, 1971, Richard Nixon retreated to Camp David with a group of fifteen bankers, economists, politicians, and speechwriters. Many traveled by secret routes. Most did not know why they had been summoned until they were herded into in the Aspen Room and informed of their mission by Nixon's secretary of the treasury, a Texas lawyer named John B. Connally. They were there to float the dollar.

The captain of this effort, Connally told them, would be John Connally. He was tall and handsome, a natural leading man who on more than one occasion had appeared on the cover of *Time* magazine in his cowboy hat, oil wells spouting petrodollars in the background, steely eyes set with the look of a man who relished risks, stared down fear, and lived the life of capitalist dreams. John Connally knew that Nixon was counting on him to save the dollar, direct the next act, and write the denouement. But while Connally knew something about oil, he knew virtually nothing about foreign exchange rates, balances of international payments that didn't quite balance, and stagflation.

Another potential problem was that not everyone in the Aspen Room understood what was meant by a floating dollar — although the metaphor of money as water was as old as money itself. Personified figures of rivers such as the Meander, the Istros, the Anthios, the Hypios, and the Samos had all appeared on coins of the Roman Empire. Some of the waters personified were handsome and clean-shaven, others old and bearded; some reclined, some embraced horns of plenty. One Roman coin depicted the Tiber and the Nile holding hands. One portrayed the Danube grasping another river by the neck.

The power to float over bodies of water had long been associated with the power of money. But the float Connally proposed that Friday afternoon at Camp David was a bit different than money floating across the Atlantic, up and down the Mississippi or the Erie Canal, or back and forth among the islands of Melanesia. The 1971 dollar would float on words.

Perhaps it was not coincidental that once again, money and language had reached the same conclusion at the same time. Only two decades before that secret summer meeting at Camp David, the anthropologist and ethnologist Claude Lévi-Strauss had published a book devoted to the theories of magic, sacrifice, and gift exchange developed by a French sociologist named Marcel Mauss. Here, Lévi-Strauss introduced what would become a famous phrase throughout departments of anthropology, sociology, and English. The term was *floating signifier*, by which Lévi-Strauss meant that not only could a word's meaning shift, but that words themselves were relentlessly shifty.

Richard Nixon was not an expert in cowries, kula, the coinage of classical Greece and Rome, or the *rogadias*, *ricorsas*, and *societas* of medieval merchants. But he had studied history in college, so was most likely familiar with the biographies of Alexander Hamilton, Andrew Jackson, and Nicholas Biddle, if not Mirabeau Buonaparte Lamar. No doubt he could recite the details of the currency debates that underlay Federalism, Jacksonianism, the Civil War, the Gilded Age, and the founding of the Federal Reserve. And even if he had never heard of Claude Lévi-Strauss, Nixon was an expert when it came to shifting words.

His first fiction-writing lesson came in the winter of 1960, when John F. Kennedy invited his erstwhile adversary to the Oval Office for a conciliatory meeting in which the newly elected president suggested that his defeated opponent take some time off to write a book. *Profiles in Courage* had boosted Kennedy, so why not Nixon? It was good advice, and the brooding, infuriated, and resentful former vice president set out to accomplish the task with the help of a ghostwriter provided by Simon and Schuster.

Nixon had never written a book before, but soon discovered that the best way to generate a narrative was to anchor a story in a series of episodes in which the protagonist demonstrates his expertise at managing risk and fear under severe constraints of time, combating one reversal after the next to emerge victorious. (That is, the money plot.) One of the episodes Nixon evoked to illustrate his strength of character in a time of crisis centered around an accusation that he had put together a political slush fund. The scandal that ensued had threatened his standing as Dwight Eisenhower's running mate in 1952. As Nixon's political career hung in the balance, he decided to go on air to deliver his infamous Checkers speech, in which he compared his fund of campaign contributions to the gift of a "little cocker spaniel dog," which his six-year-old daughter had named Checkers. The speech drew sixty million viewers, the largest television audience recorded up to that time.

While the Nixon family did indeed possess a cocker spaniel named Checkers, no one had ever believed that the dog had anything whatsoever to do with the collection and expenditure of illegal campaign funds. Yet Nixon's rhetorical reconstruction of himself in front of millions of viewers turned the political crisis into political gain, and the success of the Checkers speech in 1952 as recounted by Nixon in his memoir of 1962 helped put him on the path to political victory in 1968.

Six Crises consisted of Nixonian captivity narratives in which the hero always managed to escape. And it would redound to Nixon's credit that he would eventually apply all he had learned about plot, character, and metaphor to money, for money was not in Nixon's blood. Like Alexander Hamilton, Herbert Hoover, and Abraham Lincoln, Nixon came from a family with none of it.

He was born in 1913, the same year as the Federal Reserve, and grew up surrounded by citrus groves and fields of commodity alfalfa and beans. His father, Francis, had built their mail-order house between the San Bernardino mountains and the Pacific Ocean. But Yorba Linda, California, population 300, was not quite Mirabeau Lamar's radiant west. It was economically depressed, and when the Nixon family farm failed, Francis moved to Whittier and took out a $5,000 loan for a spot of land right off the road to La Habra. Here, he built a gas station. Then he built The Nixon Market, site of the future president's first job.

> Each morning I got up at four in order to be at the Seventh Street market in Los Angeles by five o'clock, I chose the best fruits and vegetables, bargained with the farmers and wholesalers for a good price, and then drove back to East Whittier to wash, sort, and arrange the produce in the store and be off to school by eight.

Money, Nixon learned, was anchored in necessities — agriculture and gasoline. There was no sign of gold anywhere on the road from Seventh Street to Whittier.

The family was poor, but Dick was brilliant. Harvard accepted him on a full scholarship but he could not go because his family could not pay for his travel to and from the East Coast. Instead, he attended Whittier College, where the student athletes were known as the Poets. Here, he read the works of Shakespeare and starred in college drama. His interest in dictation, speech, and words bordered on the compulsive.

Over the three year span in which he served as vice president under Eisenhower, Nixon delivered five million words to his Edison Voicewriter Dictaphone, and kept the platters on which they were recorded for posterity. "I cannot remember why I started or why I stopped making them," he would later write. "They cover such a wide variety of subjects and personalities that there does not seem to have been any single purpose behind them."

By the time of the 1971 dollar crisis, Nixon had served in the military, served as a senator and vice president, and was in the third year of his first term as president. He had delivered innumerable speeches and become a master of American political rhetoric. Writing Six Crises had taught him a great deal that would come in handy with the dollar, but he could not have created the most extraordinary fiction of the twentieth century without the help of his secretary of the treasury, John Connally.

Like Nixon's father, Connally's father had tried his hand at farming. Like Nixon's family, Connally's family was poor. The house was in Floresville, a dusty western town outside San Antonio, Texas, just a few miles down the road from the hallowed ground of the Alamo. The geography influenced the boy's taste in literature, as his favorite poem while growing up was the tragic-heroic ballad, "The Siege of the Alamo," which he memorized and declaimed to the cows and pigs. Like his fellow Texan, Mirabeau Lamar, hero of the battle of San Jacinto, Connally was drawn in equal measure to poetry and dreams of apocalyptic war. He graduated from "The Siege of the Alamo" to dramatic recitations of Patrick Henry's portentous address to the Virginia House of Delegates: "Gentlemen may cry, Peace! But there is no peace. The war is actually begun! The next gale that sweeps from the north will bring to our ears the clash of resounding arms!"

As the Depression deepened, Connally pledged that he would master the art of rhetoric. He made his way to San Antonio, found a public speaking coach, and began to enter forensics tournaments. While nine thousand banks were going under and $140 billion was withering away, Connally was memorizing the locutions of the Federalists in one dazzling speech after the next.

At the University of Texas at Austin he became president of the drama club, but his acting career did not advance past the starring role of Peanut King at the Floresville peanut festival. At twenty, he committed his intellectual, rhetorical, and theatrical gifts to yet another professor of public speaking, a twenty-nine-year-old Democrat named Lyndon B. Johnson who was running for his first term in the United States House of Representatives.

LBJ won, and Connally joined the Navy, left the Navy, went to law school, left law school, went to work for Fort Worth's oil magnate, the "Bachelor Billionaire" Sid Richardson, left the job, and returned to the side of Lyndon Johnson to help with the future President's senate campaign. Connally's responsibilities had now grown. His job was to gather and distribute the money.

Connally looked nothing like a bagman so was perfect for the job, and soon began to log long hours on private planes, picking up bundles of cash from landing strips on secluded islands in the Gulf of Mexico and delivering them to wherever in Texas the boss decided to land the helicopter. On one such evening, Connally picked up a brown bag in Houston. In the bag were five hundred one-hundred-dollar bills. He carried the $50,000 with him onto a plane to Austin, and after the flight decided to grab a bite. Unfortunately, he left his carry-on at the local diner. Connally eventually got the money back, but that didn't make him any more careful in the future, as he subsequently lost track of $40,000 left in the pockets of a suit he mistakenly sent to the cleaners. Such was the apprenticeship of the future secretary of the treasury.

A dozen years after he won that first Texas senate campaign by eighty-seven still-disputed votes, "Landslide Lyndon" had become vice president Johnson, and he suggested to President Kennedy that his bagman oversee the expenditure of more than eleven billion dollars as United States secretary of the Navy, which was then the nation's largest consumer of oil. Coincidentally, Connally's home state was the nation's largest *producer* of oil.

In the early 1960s, West Texas Intermediate, the grade of crude oil used as a benchmark in oil pricing, was selling for just under three dollars a barrel. By buying all the Navy's oil with none of his own money from oilmen who would eventually contribute to his political campaigns, the secretary of the Navy learned a lesson about floating signifiers: that politics could turn jet fuel into petrodollars, then back into politics.

It is hard to overstate Connally's role in creating a dollar freed from the confines of gold, silver, shell, gong, or bead, a dollar that would rule the world by means of attributes more commonly associated with plots, characters, and metaphors, a dollar that would share the aporia of language. The only traditional element of the money plot missing from Connally's politics was anagogy. But apocalypse was about to overtake Connally—to be followed by an epic reversal.

During John Connally's eleven-month tenure as secretary of the Navy, he supervised more than one million employees, oversaw a budget of billions of dollars, and kept close watch over the Navy's newest darlings, more than six hundred 35,000-pound submarine-launched two-stage solid-fueled Polaris ballistic missiles, made by the Lockheed Corporation, each armed with a nuclear warhead. President Kennedy had promised to exceed President Eisenhower's military budget, and to this end was considering the construction of six more Polaris-launching submarines, at a cost beyond most people's imagination.

Secretary of the Navy was a big job, so perhaps Connally could be forgiven for overlooking some of the details. For instance, at one point during his tenure, Connally received a letter from a former marine, humbly requesting that the secretary ameliorate his hardship discharge. In classic bureaucrat-from-Washington style, Connally's office sent the supplicant a boilerplate denial, the envelope adorned with a smiley face and a sticker printed with a succinct message: "John Connally for Governor." The name of that ex-marine who had unsuccessfully appealed for an honorable discharge was Lee Harvey Oswald.

Two years after John Connally left his post in Washington he was elected Governor of Texas, and soon after that President Kennedy and Vice President Lyndon Johnson flew in. JFK planned to visit old friends, attend events and fundraisers, and deliver a speech about the federal deficit at the Dallas Merchandise Mart. In order to give the president maximum political exposure, the Secret Service mapped out a ten-mile route for a motorcade from suburban to downtown Dallas. John Connally and his wife, Nellie, sat in the jump seat of a black stretch Lincoln convertible as the president waved from the back seat next to his wife, Jackie, who had dressed in pink. It was a little after noon on November 22 when the motorcade passed the Texas Schoolbook Depository.

Connally's bloodstained, white Arrow shirt remains on display in the Texas state archives. But from the moment Oswald pulled the trigger, Connally's story shifts and swerves. The declaimer of apocalyptic poetry, the high school debater, college actor, peanut king, lawyer, bagman, military bureaucrat, yes-man to Lyndon Johnson, and Democratic governor of Texas — that man was over.

As Connally recovered from his bullet wounds the national news media descended on Parkland Memorial Hospital in Dallas to interview him. He lay beneath a white sheet, Nellie sitting by his side, and rambled on and on into the cameras and microphones. "There have been many thoughts on many subjects," he told Martin Agronsky, from NBC News. "You wonder all sorts of things."

As the sedatives waned and his national prominence waxed, Connally expatiated on live television about the Kennedy assassination. Within his mind, a unique scenario had begun to take shape, for he recalled the letter Lee Harvey Oswald had sent him in 1960, and was now convinced that Oswald remembered that letter, too. As he had veered from conscious to comatose, Connally reached the conclusion that he had been Oswald's target, not John Kennedy.

The governor of Texas thought the Kennedy assassination was all about him, that he was the protagonist, and it did not matter to Connally that virtually no one else would ever believe the story. According to John Connally, the central character of the central assassination of the twentieth century was John Connally. "I personally felt that I had been killed, too," he told Martin Agronsky. "It makes you reflect, ponder, wonder..." Perhaps most perplexing of all was the fact that Connally awoke from anesthesia to find himself a Republican.

"God often gives us an inner conviction or prompting to confirm which way He wants us to go. This prompting comes from the Holy Spirit." The quote is from neither Connally nor Nixon, but from a man who knew them both well, and who defined for twentieth-century America the evangelical spirit that can be summed up in two words: *born again*. For it wasn't personal ambition and political expediency alone that brought Nixon and Connally together. It never would have happened without the help of a preacher convinced of the urgent need for repentance, salvation, and repeat visits to the West Wing.

The End of Days had appeared imminent in medieval Europe, riddled as it was with crusades, famine, plague, serfdom, and menacing infidels. But that was nothing compared to the forebodings that rippled through popular culture after the bombs dropped on Hiroshima and Nagasaki. So it was par for the course when an obscure, thirty-year-old president of Northwestern Bible College in Minneapolis had a vision that shook him with such force he had to commit it to paper: "We are on the brink of a world catastrophe and impending judgement."

Within three years, the president of that Bible college resigned to become a full-time revivalist, and founded a group he called the "Youth for Christ" religious campaign. Billy Graham was on his way to becoming America's most famous religious figure, and pastor to Presidents from Truman to Obama. But of all the men Graham knew who occupied the Oval Office, he was closest to Richard Nixon, who attended Graham's services and hosted him on Air Force One. The two spent long hours in conversation and prayer.

Over the course of a lifetime preaching the gospel while eating steak and eggs at national prayer breakfasts with despots, kings, and country music stars, Graham conducted more than forty crusades in 185 countries and preached to more people in person than any other individual in history, including Jesus Christ. "Crusades" was Graham's word, implying that his Southern Baptist–style tent shows, camp meetings, and sold-out arenas of revelation and rapture had something in common with Sir Bors, Sir Percival, and Sir Galahad murdering Muslim apostates in order to recover the Holy Grail from Jerusalem, and establish a Christian state replete with gold and silver coins graced with the face of Jesus on the heads side, the holy cross on which he died on the tails.

The late 1960s and early 1970s were awash in visions of doomsday. At the movies, there was *Dr. Strangelove*, *Fail Safe*, *This Is Not a Test*, and *Soylent Green*, a postapocalyptic tale of euthanasia and cannibalism. *Planet of the Apes* took place in the year 3978, when the human race has destroyed itself and the Statue of Liberty drifted out to sea. Talking monkeys made for an unlikely hit, but such was the curiosity about post-human life that the original was followed in quick succession by a slew of sequels.

In publishing, a book prophesying impending global starvation, *The Population Bomb*, was such a hit that its author, Paul R. Ehrlich, landed an interview with Johnny Carson on *The Tonight Show*. Another best seller, *The Late, Great Planet Earth*, was a countdown to the rapture, and its author, Hal Lindsey, a self-proclaimed "Christian Zionist," followed up with sequels such as *There's a New World*

Coming, The Terminal Generation, Satan Is Alive and Well on Planet Earth, and eleven others. In 1971, the then governor of California Ronald Reagan noted: "For the first time ever, everything is in place for the battle of Armageddon and the second coming of Christ." The feeling was pervasive: a born-again youth movement of self-identifying "Jesus freaks" sprang up across the country in waves of Christian counterculture. Their motto: "Jesus Is God's Atom Bomb."

Three weeks before Nixon and Connally convened at Camp David to float the dollar, "The Jesus Revolution" graced the cover of *Time* magazine. "The movement," editorialized Richard Ostling, *Time*'s senior religious correspondent, "is amorphous, evasive, going on everywhere and nowhere."

But of all the preachers, writers, directors, politicians, freaks, and televangelists, Billy Graham was the most powerful, prestigious, and political. "There are two great forces," he told Larry King in an interview on CNN. "God's force of good and the devil's force of evil, and I believe Satan is alive and he is working, and he is working harder than ever." Graham's critics admonished him for advertising religion like toothpaste, but he embraced the criticism. "I am selling the greatest product in the world," he said.

Sermons that transferred so effectively into belief and fundraising fascinated Richard Nixon, and he instructed his press office to tune in. "You can see the effectiveness of the parable technique," he told his chief speechwriter, William Safire.

Nixon's need to plot his way out of political predicaments had led to a long-standing interest in resurrection and redemption. *Six Crises* not only narrated the story of the Checkers speech, but the ominous threat posed by the dapper communist Alger Hiss; and then there was the time Nixon had faced down death in a riot in Caracas. Above all, there was the soul-crushing defeat in the presidential election of 1960. After each crisis, Nixon had risen from the dead. Perhaps it was in this regard that the death of John Connally the Democrat and his resurrection as a Republican entered the conversation with Billy Graham. Here was a plot reversal that dovetailed with Nixon's need for a new base of political contributors in Texas, a state he had lost in 1968. It was at the president's behest that Billy Graham called Connally in 1968 and asked him to join the cabinet as secretary of the treasury.

Connally politely declined. Two years later, after the failure and resignation of Nixon's first treasury secretary, David Kennedy, Graham called again. Jesus, the country's leading revivalist preacher likely explained, had not only been a businessman but a politician. His gospel was prosperity. He was the man nobody knew.

When news of the appointment hit, Governor Francis Sargent of Massachusetts had only one question: "Can John add?"

Connally was now fifty-four, eight years into his post-JFK-assassination life, and his first task at Treasury was to bring a corporate body back from the dead; specifically, to acquire $250 million funding from Congress for a company that had gone bankrupt — not once, but three times. The Lockheed Corporation employed 72,000 people in Southern California. They sold U-2 spy planes to the CIA, Poseidon missiles to the Navy, and Cheyenne helicopters to the Army. They filled the night sky over Hanoi with SR-71 Blackbirds, MC-130 Combat Talons, and AC-130H Spectres. Lockheed's F-104 Starfighter had been the first fighter jet to fly at twice the speed of sound. But most magnificent of all was the submarine-launched Trident intercontinental ballistic missile system, armed with nuclear warheads.

The company's founding brothers, Allan and Malcolm, had at one point planned to make their fortune prospecting for gold in the rivers of Northern California, but had gone bankrupt there, too. By 1971 the brothers were no longer in charge of Lockheed, but the nation's largest defense contractor was, once again, teetering into insolvency. It was the L-1011 that was doing them in this time, a wide-body civilian aircraft with Rolls Royce engines ordered just as Rolls Royce went belly up. Before England could nationalize their storied company, one of Lockheed's prototype helicopters that had overrun its research and development budget by 233 percent crashed into flames during a Nevada test flight. The Army dropped the order, resulting in a loss of $125 million for Lockheed, who were, according to *The Congressional Record*, "stunned by the cancellation."

Flat out of cash, Lockheed executives sent a letter to the Department of Defense, who forwarded it to the commander in chief, who brought it to the attention of Congress, who sent it to the Senate Banking and Currency Committee. The company was asking for a federal bailout. When Lockheed hearings began in the summer of 1971, Nixon sent John Connally as his star witness. The secretary of the treasury knew that Lockheed was the president's favorite arms dealer. So the Peanut King, who had moved from Texas to Washington with a collection of string ties and monogrammed cowboy boots, ambled over to Capitol Hill, intent on deploying the rhetorical skills he had honed in San Antonio.

The committee called the secretary as their first witness, and Connally may have been surprised to discover that after his request for a couple of hundred million, instead of filling his azure and delphinium two-toned suit with hundred dollar bills, the senators asked him to stick around for a few follow-up questions. The most memorable was put to him by William Proxmire of Wisconsin, the senator who had spent his life refusing campaign contributions, clamoring for finance reform, and doing sit-ups and push-ups on the floor of his Senate office, as gym membership would have been an extravagance.

"It is the beginning of a welfare program for large corporations," Proxmire said. "In this case the government gives the guarantee and there is no requirement on the part of Lockheed to perform."

Connally's response to William Proxmire indicated he would be different from all previous secretaries of the treasury, but just the right secretary of the treasury to solve the dollar's problems. Instead of answering the senator's question, Connally asked one of his own: "What do we care whether they perform?"

Lockheed got the $250 million.

The following Thursday, the crisis began. The British ambassador to the United States appeared at the Treasury Department in Washington, D.C., and gave John Connally a heads up that his government was about to ask that the Federal Reserve transform three billion paper dollars held by England's central bank into more than five million pounds of gold. This was not a typical request, but it was more or less predictable, as the dollar of 1971 was not the dollar that had led global currencies out from the ruins of World War II. The pound, the franc, the yen, and the mark were pushing American money out of its safe space, making it reveal, once and for all, to what extent it was the slavish captive of precious metal kept in Uncle Sam's basement.

The British could make such a demand because unlike dollars held in the bank accounts and wallets of individuals, United States dollars held by the central banks of foreign governments could still be exchanged for United States gold. The technical term was that pending foreign demand, the dollar would be "convertible." The only problem was that five million pounds of gold amounted to roughly one-third of the total gold reserves held at that time by the United States. And rumors had it that a French demand would be next.

One day before Nixon and his men went to Camp David, that is, on the evening of Thursday, August 12, 1971, John Connally and George Shultz — the man who would succeed Connally as secretary of the treasury—walked into the Oval Office and sat down across the desk from the president. The men in the room already knew that gold and the dollar were over, so Connally got right to the point. "So we can't pay it," he said. "I don't know that it's that big of a deal."

"What's unanimous," said Nixon, perhaps recalling the title of his best-selling book, *"is we're in a crisis."*

On the White House tapes there is a long silence, eventually broken by Connally.

"It has to come," he said. "There's not a question of whether, it's a question of when."

Another long silence.

"We owe thirty billion," Connally said. "So what?"

More silence.

"Why," Connally continued, "do we have to be reasonable?"

The tapes reveal that all that previous week Nixon had been considering the historical case of William Jennings Bryan. The president respected the power of speeches at political conventions. He revered the power of speeches delivered on national television. But he also knew that Bryan had lost twice.

"What I was thinking we would do," Nixon said to Shultz and Connally, "is call the whole working group together, and we could whip up to Camp David tomorrow, and spend Friday, Saturday, and Sunday, and then on Monday, we announce the whole program."

The next day, Richard Nixon and his men escaped to Camp David. The topic of conversation that Friday evening was gold, but not the type that came in eighteen-karat trinkets. Nor did they concern themselves with kings Croesus, Casper, Midas, Montezuma, or Tut. The only story about gold that meant anything to the men at Camp David had begun twenty-five years before. As the war had come to an end in the summer of 1944, 730 delegates from forty-four countries showed up for two weeks of drinking, espionage, and economic negotiations at a United Nations conference held at the Mount Washington Hotel in Bretton Woods, New Hampshire. It was here that the dollar was anointed king of the world's currencies.

In the aftermath of Bretton Woods, while the economies of Europe struggled to reclaim the magic of plenty, the United States possessed more gold than Atahualpa of the Incas, Alberich of *Das Rheingold*, Louis XIV, Herod, Hitler, and Jack's Golden Goose combined. For the next quarter century no one dared question the power or the glory of the paper dollar, every one of which was assured a slice of America's stupefyingly immense hoard, each piece of paper guaranteed to be worth one thirty-fifth of an ounce of the metal — even if the metal were locked deep within the underground vaults of the Federal Reserve. No one ever asked to see it.

"Gold reserves," to repeat the prophetic wisdom of the nineteenth-century German Chartalist, Georg Friedrich Knapp, "must not be used in any form of state expenditure *but such as involves conversion*." The core element of the Federal Reserve's policy of conversion was known as the gold window. That was why, since Bretton Woods, the central banks of France, England, Germany, Japan, Italy, Switzerland, and all the great realms and domains on the planet had been buying and holding dollars.

The gold window possessed the power of conversion, transfer, trope, and metaphor; because a dollar that could be converted into gold by means of a magic window was a better insurance policy for monetary meltdown than a lire, a peso, a franc, a mark or any of the other currencies that littered the economic landscapes of the postwar world, currencies that could only be converted into other marks, francs, pesos, or lire. As a result of the magic gold window and the confidence of foreign central bankers, the United States dollar became the world's reserve currency, the general equivalent of all money everywhere. The story would have continued to work indefinitely—as long as no one insisted on converting their ever-increasing supply of paper dollars. The story stopped on Thursday, August 12, 1971, when the British asked to transform the material of a story into material reality.

The president and his secretary of the treasury may not have understood the parallels between central banking and Plutonic myth, nor the semiotic parallels of linguistic exchange and foreign exchange, nor the details of how silver thalers bowed to gold marks in the wake of the Franco-Prussian War, but they could tell the difference between gold bricks stacked in the cages of the Federal Reserve and paper notes piled in the back of the United States Bureau of Engraving and Printing. Connally and Nixon understood that countries that did not use the paper dollar as their currency were hoarding more than $80 billion worth of those paper dollars in the vaults of their central banks, while the United States held less than $10 billion worth of gold bullion in the vaults of its central bank. They understood that eighty was more than ten.

They understood that if the Swiss and the Canadians and the Mexicans were to follow England and demand that their bundle of metaphors be spun into gold, then all the precious metal of the richest country on earth would not be able to make up the sum. That would be the day the United States said goodbye to the last ounce of gold in its treasure chests. And when there was nothing left and still, foreign countries called for more, the dollar would share the fate of the aureus, the *dudu*, the kroon, the hecte, the solidus, the yang, and the *zuz*. It would share the fate of the coconut currency of Nicobar, the cranberry currency of Turkmenistan, skull money, feather money, the cowrie, and the ostrich egg bead.

How could such a thing have happened? How could there be more dollars than gold when each American dollar came with the promise that a magic window could turn it into gold at the rate of

$35 per ounce? Those who generally respect arithmetic could only see contradiction, defect, and impossibility, for math could not elucidate the paradox that lay at the bottom of the dollar's character: that it had to be gold yet could not be gold. The dollar's aporia, its undecidability as to what it really was, could no longer be locked up and concealed within the vault, and leveraged into ever-larger sums. The dollar's tragic flaw had been revealed.

One solution was to close borders and shut down all foreign exchange. The other solution was a return to money's liquid history, and to let the dollar float. A floating dollar would mean that a dollar would no longer be anchored to any underlying value. A floating dollar would mean that the Federal Reserve notes of the most powerful country on earth would establish their worth only as compared to all the other promises written on other paper banknotes issued by the treasuries of all the other, less powerful countries on earth. The dollar would be a floating signifier, equal in status to a word.

There was opposition within the Aspen Room that evening, most vehemently expressed by the Ukrainian-born, virulently anti-communist Columbia University professor of economics, Arthur Burns, chairman of the Federal Reserve. If dollars could no longer transform into gold, if dollars were just another metaphor, if the dollar was *nothing but a story*, Burns was convinced that Canada, England, France, Japan, Switzerland, and all the other countries that held dollars in the vaults of their central banks would sell all they had. The price would plummet, and the only solution would be to print more. After which would come a tumult of anarchy, disaster, and revolution. The world had not witnessed such a scenario since 1923, when more than a thousand German printing presses were churning out so much paper money the paper mills could hardly keep up, and a loaf of bread cost 28 billion marks.

To Arthur Burns, a floating dollar meant hippies and Jesus freaks running riot on the south lawn of the White House. A floating dollar meant the fall of Saigon, and Russia advancing west across Europe and north from Cuba to Key West. The stock market would collapse, the rest of the world would pounce. Burns was convinced the news would blast its way to the front page of *Pravda*. It would spell the fall of capitalism. It was, said Burns, "a tragedy for mankind."

But the president did not ask his men to provide political, social, historical, or literary analysis. He did not ask for numbers, statistics, regressions, or math of any sort to back up his decision. Nixon simply said, "Get me language on that." It had been decided. From the beginning, money had been a fiction. At long last, the world's reserve currency would have to act like one. Either that, or die.

At dinner that Friday evening the future head of the Federal Reserve, Paul Volcker, sat next to William Safire, Nixon's chief speechwriter, who still did not grasp the extent to which the two thousand words he was about to write would reverberate across the global economy. Volcker tried to explain. "Give me a billion dollars and a free hand on Monday," he said. With that, he joked that with a few strategic bets, he could make up the entire federal budget deficit, which in the summer of 1971 amounted to $23 billion. Safire had no idea what Volcker talking about. The speechwriter had begun his career in public relations, where his clients had included an ice cream manufacturer and a laxative maker. The first he had heard of "the gold window" was on the helicopter ride from Washington to Camp David. After dinner he began to write The Challenge of Peace.

The next day the president settled into a chair next to Camp David's swimming pool and rewrote what Safire had drafted. That night, Nixon got up at three in the morning and kept writing. At four-thirty in the morning he woke his chief of staff, H. R. "Bob" Haldeman.

Haldeman had been the head of J. Walter Thompson, the agency in charge of advertisements for Shake-a-Puddin', NBC, and Walt Disney. He had no qualms about words being money and money being words. He was a writer, too, and had a habit of writing every day. The number of words in his diary of the Nixon years comes in at just under 750,000, which is the rough equivalent of ten books in four years.

In addition to being chief of staff, Haldeman was Nixon's S.O.B. and Iron Chancellor, and he ended up in prison for his role in Watergate. But his diaries exhibited a gift for scene setting. Late that Saturday night, he recounted, "We walked in and the living room was empty, the President was down in his study with the lights off and the fire going in the fireplace, even though it was a hot night out. He was in one of his sort of mystic moods..."

The fire in the middle of summer, the ambience of deep-think with a dash of end-of-history. How romantic and literary the new dollar would be! Nixon the mystic looked up at Haldeman and ordered him to make sure Safire reported for duty first thing that morning.

After the president's men posed for the commemorative photograph on Sunday afternoon, August 15, phone calls went out to hold the front pages of Monday's national newspapers. Soon thereafter Marine One touched down on the south lawn of the White House and Nixon returned to the chair behind his desk in the Oval Office. He flipped through the pages Safire had written and rewritten over the long weekend.

He called the attorney general to make sure what he was about to do wasn't illegal. He called his daughter, Julie. He called Bob Haldeman. He called Safire. He spent a few minutes with his makeup consultant, Ray Voege, whom the administration had on loan from *The Tonight Show*.

A royal blue curtain had been draped in front of the windows facing the south lawn. That would be the backdrop. In the foreground, the mahogany Wilson Desk — the one with five secret microphones installed — was flanked by the stars and stripes and the flag of the President of the United States. Nixon wore a suit to match the curtains, a white shirt, cuff links, and patterned tie. As the sun set a small crew entered and began setting up the lights and video monitors.

During the 1950s, as Nixon was learning firsthand the power and scope of words broadcast on television — that they could mesmerize sixty million viewers, that they could elicit outpourings of emotional support, that they could destroy or redeem political careers — a Catholic mystic had also begun to study television and teach an unprecedented series of courses at the University of Toronto. He had been writing books and essays about something he called "communication theory," for it was in the technologies of communication that Marshall McLuhan had seen the future of money. As an engineering student fascinated by the humanities, it was only natural that McLuhan became interested in the structure of stories, which had inevitably led him back to myth. "The classic curse of Midas," he wrote,

> his power of translating all he touched into gold, is in some degree the character of any medium, including language. This myth draws attention to a magic aspect of all extensions of human sense and body; that is, to all technology whatever. All technology has the Midas touch.

Like John Maynard Keynes and Georg Friedrich Knapp, Marshall McLuhan had seen that the technologies that enabled globalization, market liberalization, and commercial culture had no particular requirement for gold or coinage of any specific sort. Anything that could be annexed by greed, fear, security, or the endless volatilities of desire could be money. The store of value, media of exchange, and unit of account could just as easily be a television address as anything else. Money was representation, and television just happened to be the best "extension of human sense and body" yet invented. Just as Midas had dispersed his gold curse in the river, Nixon would dissolve the gold dollar in an electronic stream. For it would be by telling that story, simply by saying the words, that Nixon would float the dollar. Nothing more would be required. No legislation, no law, no change to the United States Treasury or the Mint. One set of floating signifiers would anoint another.

In this regard, the idea of evaluating money not by assaying its underlying value but by counting its face value goes by an interesting name. It's called valuation by "tale." Which appeared to indicate that the float would come down to a simple question: How well could Nixon tell the tale?

At 9:00 p.m. Eastern Standard Time, the president began. He reminded his audience that he had spoken to them before about "the problems of ending a war." This rhetorical strategy—starting by citing conflict in order to prepare the way for apparently unrelated resolutions—was as old as Thucydides, who reported that Pericles, Archidamus, and Hermocrates had each in turn asserted in their orations to Athenians, Spartans, and Syracusans that when it came to waging war, the most important factor was neither troops nor weapons, but money.

Commander-in-chief Nixon did not mention the price tag of half a million troops in Cambodia, Vietnam, and Laos, nor their associated glide bombs, cluster bombs, daisy cutters, Smith & Wessons, Carbines, Sten guns, fighter-bombers, Chinook helicopters,

9:00 p.m., EST, Sunday, August 15, 1971. Nixon turns money into words.

and Sidewinder missiles — all of which had to be paid for in United States dollars. Nor did he mention the fact that The Great Society required monthly unemployment checks for hosts of shell-shocked veterans. Nor a word about Lockheed's free $250 million. Instead, he said, "The time has come for a new economic policy for the United States. This not only requires bold leadership ready to take bold action — it calls forth the greatness in a great people."

Perhaps it was the density of Safire's language — the doubled use of bold and bold, greatness and great — that was making the president stutter and sweat. "Every action I have taken tonight is designed to nurture and stimulate that competitive spirit..." Haldeman had watched Nixon by the fireplace in the middle of the night at Camp David, and observed his "sort of mystic mood." Now, Nixon was saying that the dollar would be possessed by a competitive spirit, and only through the force of that spirit could the dollar's bold boldness and great greatness emerge to fight any other currencies that dared question its authority.

"We must protect the dollar from the attacks of international money speculators." Thus did he gird and arm the dollar for war against the National Bank of England, the Banque de France, Swiss gnomes, Plutonic speculators, Mephistopheles, and the Communists.

"In recent weeks, the speculators have been waging an all-out war on the American dollar..." As had enraged Andrew Jackson a century and a half before, the innocent character Nixon described was a victim of a global conspiracy. "We must protect the position of the American dollar as a pillar of monetary stability around the world...We must protect the dollar from the attacks of international money speculators..." The maiden in distress was being threatened by a tribe of savage Pequots, and so the dollar took its place in a long line of American captivity narratives: "I am determined that the American dollar must never again be a hostage in the hands of international speculators."

Then: "I have directed Secretary Connally to suspend temporarily the convertibility of the dollar into gold..." "Suspend temporarily" had been Connally's idea. What it meant was the opposite: Going forward, the dollar would never again be anything other than a story.

"Let us raise our spirits," Nixon concluded, invoking 65,000 years of shell and metal possessed by ghosts. "Let us raise our sights...Let us invest in our nation's future. And let us revitalize that faith in ourselves that built a great nation in the past, and that will shape the world of the future. Thank you, and good evening."

The end of one epoch and the beginning of another had happened mid-sentence—and no one had noticed. Going forward, the dollar was just a word—and there was no uproar from the central bankers, no vote in Congress, no murmurs from Wall Street.

Everything stayed the same. The float hadn't mattered a bit, because money had always been a fiction.

As John Connally had predicted, abolishing gold was as easy as raising a few hundred million for Lockheed or running back to the diner to get that grocery bag of bills someone had left behind. It was almost as if everyone had been waiting for it. Instead of panic, there was a primitive yet pervasive premonition that vast sums of money were about to be made.

Nixon, Connally, Safire, Shultz, and Volcker had delivered a parable worthy of Billy Graham. The ancient silver thaler had been seized by the rapture. It had become an airy nothing, and Nixon a greater poet than Shakespeare. For what fiction would ever transcend the floating dollar? What plot would be more widely accepted, loved, and envied? What poem more revered, reviled, and recited? What redemption more sought? The Koran, the Torah, the Gospels, the Upanishads, the Tao-Te-Ching, the *Mahabarata* — all pale beside the dollar.

Arthur Burns woke up that Monday morning and went to his office at the Federal Reserve. He read the news reports, and there were no hippies rioting on the south lawn, no *Pravda* headlines. It was not The End.

Later that morning, a triumphant John Connally fielded questions in the first televised press conference ever broadcast from the Treasury building on Pennsylvania Avenue. The Dow Jones Industrial Average had just surged thirty-three points, the greatest daily percentage gain in its history.

Three months later, Connally arrived in Germany to address the "Group of Ten." It was one thing for Nixon to suspend the convertibility of the dollar on national television, another for his secretary of the treasury to explain the decision in front of the representatives of the world's greatest economic powers. The dollar might float as much at it liked at home, but, as Burns had warned, the decision to close the gold window and allow the dollar to float against other international currencies was a bit more ambitious. The greatest theorist of state-chartered money, Georg Friedrich Knapp, had drawn the line half a century earlier: "The Chartal form can never be effective internationally." So it came as something of a surprise when Connally explained himself in the following manner: The dollar was "our currency," he told the gathering of finance ministers—"*but your problem.*" One month after that, in December of 1971, the member countries of the G-10 did exactly what Nixon and Connally had predicted, and signed the Smithsonian Agreement, a document that replaced the world's fixed exchange rate with a floating exchange rate.

Which is, in many ways, the end of the story. We are no longer shocked to learn that the US dollar is made of words, particularly not the men and women of Wall Street, who for a half century and counting have abandoned the idea that money need be physical, bounded, constrained, or defined by anything other than someone's ability to tell a story about it. By the end of the twentieth century these men and women would be aiming the full force of their creativity, intellect, and analytical power at the problem of transforming ethereal concepts like risk, fear, and time into plot, character, and metaphor for the sake of their single, abiding goal. The bankers had come to understand that whatever they could imagine, they could plot, whatever they could plot they could monetize, and whatever they could monetize they could bank.

Lifestyles of the Rich and Famous, Dallas, and *Fantasy Island* were the hit TV shows of the following decade—a time of junk bonds, bull markets, leveraged buyouts, hostile takeovers, white knights, poison pills, and derivatives swaps. Anxiety-ridden voices shrieked that soon, everything on earth would be branded and patented, that the dollar would be the last metaphor standing. For some, the prospect was enticing. Wall Street prepared to place the infinite bet.

This chapter might end here, too, with the dollar unbound, spreading its wings and soaring to the four corners of the earth. But the matter was not entirely settled. Less well known than Nixon's political disgrace is the fate of John Connally, who soon after the float resigned as treasury secretary and began to think long-term about his own political future. He was a Democrat turned Republican who had come back from the dead, turned the Navy into a political money machine, made cash from congressional testimony, and vanquished the ancient prison house of gold. On the strength of this résumé, he conjured a $12 million war chest, spent all of it on his 1980 campaign for president, paraded into the Republican National Convention in Detroit, and came away with a single delegate. Other peoples' money gone, Connally congratulated Ronald Reagan on the nomination, returned to his home state, and retired from politics.

He had been secretary of the Navy, secretary of the treasury, and governor of Texas. He had survived an assassination attempt, floated the dollar, and run for president. Now Connally wanted to be a tycoon in the epic Texas mold, a Plutonomist like the oil baron Perry Bass, rancher Sid Richardson, metal maven Nelson Hunt, buyout artist T. Boone Pickens, and Dallas Cowboys founder Clint Murchison, Jr. And Connally's capitalist second act began auspiciously, as described in a puff piece that ran in *Texas Monthly*:

> Connally's Sandhill and Picosa acreage are justifiably the most breathtaking spreads in the area. Sandhill covers 2400 acres; Picosa, the site of Connally's ranch house, more than seven-thousand acres.

Another ranch, the Four C, belonging to Connally's children and named for them, encompasses another 1200 acres, and Connally owns another 500 acres nearby. In addition, Connally bought 250 acres of his family's original homestead, with his brother Merrill purchasing the remainder. In 1965 Connally bought the Tortuga Ranch in Zavala and Dimmitt Counties: 14,270 acres purchased from Delhi Properties for about $300,000...

He secured loans from dozens of banks and began to build malls and office buildings, bridges, country clubs, conference centers, a housing subdivision near a racetrack, and beachfront condos in Padre Island, Mexico. He bought a barbecue restaurant in Austin, a 909-mile gas pipeline in Kansas, an insurance company, and an airline hangar.

Then, in September of 1986, *The New York Times* published a surprising report. "The former Secretary of the Treasury...finds himself being sued by the tiny Texana National Bank of Belton because he does not have enough cash flow to meet a $3,237 monthly lease payment for furniture at the Padre Island condominiums." The story behind the story was that John Connally had notched up more than $90 million in personal debt, including the $9,600 he owed the local pizza delivery joint.

As if the sonorous money gongs of Burma had gone silent and the jar money of Indonesia had stopped dancing, John Connally had run out of stories. His voice could no longer propitiate the spirits, much less Texana National Bank, Western Savings of Dallas, and Bell Savings and Loan of San Mateo (the last being Connally's largest single source of credit, due $11 million). In Connnally's infamous, arrogant words to his foreign counterparts, the dollar was "our currency, *but your problem.*" And so it became his. The dollar—*his dollar*—had betrayed him.

Even bankrupt, John B. Connally believed that money was a matter of names—specifically, his own. At Hart Galleries, "the Southwest's premier antique auction house," he transformed a paltry $3,000 into $60,000 by selling signed $1 bills for $20.

Connally was not alone. In 1982, Ronald Reagan signed the Garn–St. Germain Depository Institutions Act, removing interest-rate caps at savings banks, allowing money to increase and multiply at the banker's command. Reagan called the law "the emancipation proclamation of America's savings institutions." The result: From 1983 to 1992 more than 1,500 savings and loan institutions would go belly up, $150 billion vanishing alongside.

In dire circumstances, Connally did what he could. He sold his ranches. He sold his prized cattle. He sold his stable of more than ten dozen horses. He sold six trailer trucks' worth of miscellaneous knickknacks. A sea of secondhand gubernatorial gewgaws eventually stretched across the showroom floor of the Hart Galleries, "the Southwest's premier antique auction house."

The auctioneers priced his collection of Winchester rifles, his Tanzanian elephant tusks, his two hundred oil paintings, his collection of Chippendale and Louis XIV furniture, and his ceremonial horse saddles with the initials, JC, inlaid in gold. When he and his wife Nellie showed up at the auction house, two thousand bidders greeted them with applause, as though the greatness of his bankruptcy indicated the greatness of the man who had made the dollar into a story so powerful, independent, and free that it could elude the grasp of its author.

As a final recourse, Connally was reduced to selling money itself: three thousand one-dollar bills printed with his signature from his days as secretary of the treasury. Autographed by John Connally, the singles went for twenty bucks apiece, which raised an extra $60,000. But it was nowhere near enough. After the last Persian rug, porcelain vase, and Rolex hit the block, all that was left was the Connally family ranch on fifteen lonely acres in Floresville, and creditors had to accept ten cents on the dollar.

John Connally died five years after that in 1993, and was buried with no coin in his mouth, no token to pay his way downriver, and nothing of value but those fragments from Lee Harvey Oswald's bullets lodged in his thigh. The FBI inquired if they might extract the metal splinters for ballistic testing. The family said no.

{9} HOW TO MAKE MONEY

...the daemonic world is one where supernatural energies and consuming appetites are the sole means to existence.

— ANGUS FLETCHER

EVENTUALLY, every story that could be told had been told. At least that was the perception throughout the late 1970s and '80s, a literary era marked by a proliferation of postmodern narratives that were purposefully emptied of long-established elements — stories that could be read out of order, stories that had no order, stories peopled by absurdist characters in search of authors, stories that rejected the idea of an author.

The belief that narrative was a formula that could be deconstructed and reconstructed at will, that an author was simply taking dictation from a series of cultural clichés about character and plot, and that the analysis of a story was far more profound than the story itself — all these phenomena paralleled the development of a formulaic approach to finance. The rise of the computer as a tool of analysis quickened the dream that money could be distilled into elementary particles, and supported the long-standing ambition that one might rearrange the story of buying and selling in such a way as to never again have to face the terrifying consequences of a gamble gone wrong. Here was the hope of the hedge fund: No matter the direction *Regina Pecunia*'s chariot took, the one who knew the formula might already be there at the end, waiting.

The bedrock of this new approach to money was calculus, invented in the seventeenth century by Gottfried Wilhelm Leibniz and Sir Isaac Newton. No set of techniques would have as deep and lasting an effect on modern science, engineering, and economics. The discovery of mathematical derivatives introduced a method to measure infinitesimal elements as they shifted speed and direction through increasingly small increments of time. Before calculus, uncertainty had undergone its most rigorous and sustained analysis in the realms of literature, philosophy, poetry, and religion. After calculus, uncertainty changed.

No one was more enmeshed within the ambiguities of money than the great physicist himself. Sir Isaac spent the last three decades of his life working in the Tower of London as Master of the British Mint, where he coddled and cared for all manner of coinage, overseeing the reminting and modernization of English currency, some of which dated back more than two-hundred years. Even in 1700, the globalization of banking and currency demanded intense technical prowess, as every country from Portugal to Japan maintained their own practices and policies regarding how to assay and value their gold and silver coinage — not to mention small change stamped from brass, copper, lead, pewter, and tin. So it was perhaps inevitable that the greatest king in the world would ask the greatest mathematician in the world to ensure the security of the greatest money in the world, so that no one would cheat the British Empire out of its hard-earned cash.

If Newton had never been given charge of the mint it is possible he might have advanced to Einsteinian insights, if not beyond. We shall never know, as he had to spend long hours in the Tower, perusing coins and dealing with the particularly complex problem of computing how much of one currency amounted to how much of another, as the master explained in endless streams of professional reports.

> ...a Doppio Moeda of Portugal was coined for ten Crusados of Silver...In France a pound weight of fine gold is re-coined worth fifteen pounds weight of fine silver...The Ducats of Holland and Hungary and the Empire were lately current...at five Guilders in specie, and five styvers...

Newton divided ducats and guilders and crusados and *styvers* just as he had dissected time and space, and ended up with a unified field theory—otherwise known as foreign exchange rates. He understood the equations required to balance and settle the most complex transactions, but what lay behind the relative excitements and torpors of different currencies—the reason why one money became more desired and another less so, why one was hoarded and another dispersed, why one nation's economy strengthened while another weakened—that logic eluded him. To unlock such secrets, a new generation of mathematical techniques would be required. Money, physics, and calculus would have to wait another four centuries before their long-anticipated embrace.

Moreover, while Newton's math satisfied the requirements of the mint, it ignored the needs of an economic sector arguably even more important in the history of finance, the casino. Twenty-seven years after Newton died, the infamous scam artist, diarist, and womanizer Giacomo Girolamo Casanova reported that a certain type of high-stakes game had come into vogue at the world's first government-approved gambling establishment, the Ridotto Casino in Venice. The bet was called a martingale, and it referred to a wager made in a most exacting, immediate, and dramatic form. The martingale was a coin toss, the betting options limited to heads or tails. There was no middle ground. In a matter of seconds, the martingale could deliver dizzying jackpots or equally as often, ruination. That was the thrill of it.

The most intoxicating part of betting on martingales was the fact that everybody knew there was an infallible strategy for winning: If a player were to put money on the same outcome every time, again and again ad infinitum, the laws of probability dictated that not only would he win back all he may have previously lost, he would double his money. The only catch was that he would have to double down each time, a strategy that could be sustained only as long as the gambler remained solvent. Casanova reported that on numerous occasions, martingales left him bankrupt.

Of course, games of chance predate both Casanova and coinage. Ever since humans began using tools, that is, about three million years ago, they have been deploying sticks, stones, and primitive dice to divine the will of the gods. As soon as there were coins, people began to toss them. The Romans — who often stamped images of rowing galleys on the obverse of their heavy brass denarii and sestertii — had a name for this betting game: *navia aut caput*, ship or head?

In modern finance, the coin toss has come to represent a great deal more than heads or tails. The concept of the martingale is a bulwark of what economists call the efficient market hypothesis, the meaning of which can be grasped by a simple binary: For every person who believes a stock will rise — the buyer — there will be some other equal and opposite person who believes the stock will fall — the seller. Even as markets go haywire, brokers and traders repeat the mantra: For every buyer there is a seller. Heads or tails.

Martingale can also mean a bridle, perhaps because the either/or of heads/tails and buy/sell is as confining as the yoke that restricts a domesticated animal to the uncompromising back-and-forth demanded by the plow. No doubt, the martingale ensures that the racehorse stay on the path toward what appears to be the goal. But what if the bridle, instead of locking everything and everyone in its thrall, could itself be brought under control? Imagine the prize money at the end of that finish line.

To restate the problem as a matter of a coin toss: Was there a way out of the prison house of either/or other than doubling your money or going bankrupt? Was there a way around the binary oppositions of buy or sell, heads or tails, and the market's inexorable rise or fall? Or was the zero-sum game an inescapable characteristic of all money?

Writers and poets had mastered their art of aporia. They had learned to utilize ambiguity, equivocation, and undecidability to create depths of meaning. But the possibility that one might discover a rigorous *mathematical* formula to circumvent — or at the very least, neutralize — the binaries of a martingale universe first began to tantalize mathematicians in 1827, when a Scottish botanist named Robert Brown peered through his microscope at a pollen particle floating across the surface of a drop of water. The pollen was on a path from some point A to another point B, but Brown noted that the trajectory was neither a straight line nor a curve, but an apparently random zigzag, as though at each point along the journey the speck of dust might have had to make a choice: up or down, left or right, slow or fast, backward or forward. The seemingly patternless plot of this jittery journey came to be known as "Brownian Motion."

Once discovered, Brownian Motion turned up everywhere. In chemistry, the process took the name diffusion, and could be used to explain everything from how incense permeated a room to how a bottle of soda, left open, would go flat; in biology, Brownian Motion described the way oxygen moved through cell membranes, thus elucidating the way we breathe; in physics, the motion not only described the movement of colors in stained glass, but of atoms and molecules; in geography, the zigzag was suddenly apparent in maps of jagged coastline; in biostatistics, the model clarified everything from the spread of infectious disease to the dynamics of a mosquito infestation Karl Pearson had famously dubbed "the problem of the random walk." In finance, Brownian Motion appeared as the peaks and valleys of an asset price, or the ragged spikes and dips of a day in the life of the Dow Jones Industrial Average. The similarities among divergent fields are not coincidental. In each instance, the phenomenon had emerged as the outcome of either/or events, some found in nature, some replicated in models of nature — such as the allegory of money.

Rahul Bhattacharya's *Book of Greeks* is a typical example of a twenty-first century financial engineering textbook for those who look forward to careers as derivatives traders and hedge fund managers. It begins with the declaration that prices follow "a geometric Brownian motion." This erratic up and down, explains Bhattacharya, conforms to natural processes governed by the "coefficient of diffusion." Furthermore, "asset price is like the molecule following a random walk suspended in a medium, where the 'molecule' was the stock (asset) and the 'medium' was the volatility."

The sentence combines physics, math, finance, and narrative, and defines the way a modern banker envisions the world: Nature, knowledge, history, and drama had prepared the way for the single most important epic of them all — buying and selling.

Think of Robert Brown's microscopic particle — that is, the "price" — traveling from A to B as a miniscule canoe floating on a journey through a vast sea — that is, a drop of water. As the microscopic boat floats along, the intensity of the elements that deflect the trajectory one way or the other — that is, the "volatility" — are the storms, the monsters, the enchantresses, the witches, and the enemies that the hero must outwit in order to continue his erratic and wayward path to Ithaca. That is the so-called random walk of the asset price. Thus, the title of Burton Malkiel's 1973 best seller, *A Random Walk Down Wall Street*. "There's a tremendous battle going on," Malkiel had observed about the market. "It has all the ingredients of high drama."

The plot is familiar to the point of cliché. It's the picaresque tale, the romance of the crusader, the adventures of Huck Finn, Tom Jones, and the Boyowas who braved the elements in order to exchange white shell armbands for red shell necklaces. It was the travels of Marco Polo and the wanderings of the intrepid medieval merchant. It is the psychomachia of every allegorical pilgrim as he or she progresses toward redemption.

Traditionally, poets and writers have found the choices that accompany such journeys not only dramatic, but philosophically profound. Just as a coin toss presents the opportunity for either fortune or bankruptcy, so do writers delight in describing characters who reach a crossroads and find themselves confronted by two options. From the cliché of the lady or the tiger to *Antigone* to *Sophie's Choice*, the fatal choice is a constant.

> *Two roads diverged in a wood, and I —*
> *I took the one less traveled by,*
> *And that has made all the difference.*

Robert Frost's "The Road Not Taken" is not generally considered a poem about Wall Street. But as any investor knows, the path of finance presents endless bifurcations, each of which can be summed up by a stark choice: buy or sell. There is no in between. Yet the dream of the financier had always been to take both paths at the same time in order to know which would be most profitable. The dream was to transcend either/or, to possess another option, to solve in a single equation the seeming unpredictability of Brownian Motion, and thereby remove the random from the walk.

A premonition as to how such a feat might be accomplished appeared one year after the Ridotto Casino closed, when an obscure eighteenth-century financial writer named Nicolas Magens published his *Essay on Insurances*. It is in this essay that the word "option" first appears as a technical term of finance. "The Sum given is called Premium, and the Liberty that the Giver of the Premium has to have the Contract fulfilled or not, is called Option..."

From 1775 on, the word "option" would have a financial definition: the possibility of escaping the captivity of either/or for the liberty of buying and selling the same thing at the same time. Ever so slightly, the fatality of choice could be suspended. It would have saved Giacomo Casanova a lot of money.

Within one hundred years, the option would come to rule the central chamber of the Paris Bourse. Here, among Corinthian columns carved to evoke the riches of a Roman temple, nineteenth-century French financiers bought and sold assets known as *rentes*.

These rentes were state-sponsored bonds. They guaranteed a 3 percent return in annual interest, and their underlying value was secured by the income generated by France's tax on wine, which is to say they were secure. As the expiration dates of these bonds came and went, their prices fluctuated in relationship to one another. Thus did traders on the Bourse buy and sell.

Among these traders was a young man named Louis Bachelier. He had wanted to attend college, but unfortunately his parents had died while he was a teenager. Before he could consider higher education, Bachelier had to multiply what remained of his family's money. His maternal grandfather had been a banker, so he got the kid a job on the Bourse.

Here, Bachelier became an expert in rentes. He made enough money that by the age of twenty-three he was able to achieve his dreams and enroll in the Sorbonne, where he immediately excelled. But Bachelier did not forget what got him there. In 1900, he submitted as his doctoral dissertation to the faculty at the University of Paris a mathematical analysis of option trading on rentes.

Bachelier's dissertation, "The Theory of Speculation," was the first to use calculus to analyze trading on the floor of an exchange. His committee, supervised by the renowned mathematician and theoretical physicist Henri Poincaré was confounded. "The subject chosen by M. Bachelier is rather far away from those usually treated by our candidates," noted the report. For work that would forever transform finance and generate untold billions for derivatives traders and hedge fund managers, Bachelier received a grade of *honorable* instead of *très honorable*. Essentially, he got a B. No teaching position was forthcoming.

Bachelier had scrutinized the practices of the finest traders of rentes, and noted their propensity to take an extraordinary array of diverse and contradictory positions on the exchange, each coming due at a variety of expiration dates. By doing so, they could eliminate the risk of betting either one way or the other — and the risk of losing money on the ever-fluctuating value of rentes. Bachelier became convinced that there was a mathematical way to express their actions, to describe within a single equation two seemingly incommensurable decisions: buy or sell.

His dissertation began with a startling claim: "I have in fact known for several years that it would be possible…to imagine transactions where one of the parties makes a profit at all prices." Here was an idea that contravened either/or, buy/sell, and the supposed invisibility of the hand that guided price. Here was an idea that abolished the uncertainty of the random walk. It was also an idea that destroyed the money plot.

Faced with the enormous complexities of a market of more than 100 billion francs that could change volume, speed, and direction in a thousand different ways at a moment's notice — an exchange in which buyers became sellers, sellers buyers, and many both at the same time — Bachelier's dissertation applied a concept in calculus called the partial derivative. Since the market in rentes was an example of what mathematicians call a multivariable world, Bachelier's first step was to isolate each of the variables that determined change in price. And since the Bourse was in a constant state of flux, in order to define the behavior of a single variable, Bachelier had to pretend that he could freeze all the others. Holding everything in place in order to define the path of a single character simplified the problem, but only told a fraction of the story. Thus the term, *partial* derivative.

Of course, Bachelier's goal was not a partial explanation of the Bourse's daily movement, but to express the entire drama. In order to articulate the story of all prices at all times, the partials would have to interact, and that was where Bachelier showed his genius. He figured out a way to sum and tally all of his equations, to fit them together in such a way that each individual character — no matter how big or small the role, no matter how strong or weak the impulse, no matter his or her motivation — combined into a single and seamless if extraordinarily complicated formula that would deliver the true price of any rente at any given time, and thus provide the key to profit at all prices.

From the canoe trade of the South Pacific to Roman slave galleys to oil tankers that cross the Persian Gulf, boats ballasted with commodities left the dock to float into uncertainty. Before calculus, the direction, speed, and capacity of these ships were the partial derivatives. Along with these factors came measures of time, such as the duration of the journey and the season of the year. Added to these considerations were estimates of risk: the danger of the route, the experience of the captain and crew, and innumerable other factors such as the odds of shipwreck, the threat of piracy, and shifting weather. Each of these variables — capacity, catastrophe, directionality, fear, daring, speed, time, uncertainty, risk, and volatility — was just as important for the journey of an asset price on a stock exchange as a journey on a merchant ship, and Bachelier transformed each element into a mathematical expression that could not only be isolated, but interact with all the others.

He then selected a cast of characters from the Greek alphabet, although the dramatis personae had nothing in particular to do with anything Greek. Risk and volatility he called vega. Fear he named gamma. Time and interest were theta and rho. These Greek letters, alongside ersatz nomenclatures like vanna, vomma, veta, and vera, endure as characters in the field of financial engineering. Some people know the meaning of these letters — that they are the ghosts in the machine, the motivations that make money money. But most people don't. Some people can break the code. Most people can't.

Bachelier's drama of the rentes, represented by a battle of partial derivatives, had suggested one of the oldest of all literary forms. It was as if the symbolic forces had come straight out of the late Middle Ages, when poetic allegories illuminated psychological struggles in which discipline fought desire, cowardice fought bravery, virtue fought vice, and confidence fought fear. The outcome of these allegorical encounters decided the salvation or damnation of the soul. Here was the same psychomachia on the Paris Bourse — enacted by gamma, theta, rho, and vega — except that the conflict and redemption revolved around money.

l'origine et qui présente deux points d'inflexion pour

$$x = \pm \frac{1}{p_0\sqrt{2\pi}} = \pm \sqrt{2\pi}\,k\sqrt{t}.$$

Ces mêmes valeurs de x sont aussi les abscisses des maxima et minima des courbes d'espérance mathématique, dont l'équation est

$$y = \pm px.$$

La probabilité du cours x est une fonction de t; elle croît jusqu'à une certaine époque et décroît ensuite. La dérivée $\frac{dp}{dt} = 0$ lorsque $t = \frac{x^2}{2\pi k^2}$. La probabilité du cours x est donc maxima quand ce cours correspond au point d'inflexion de la courbe des probabilités.

Probabilité dans un intervalle donné. — L'intégrale

$$\frac{1}{2\pi k\sqrt{t}}\int_0^x e^{-\frac{x^2}{4\pi k^2 t}}\,dx = \frac{c}{\sqrt{\pi}}\int_0^x e^{-c^2 x^2}\,dx$$

n'est pas exprimable en termes finis, mais on peut donner son développement en série.

$$\frac{1}{\sqrt{\pi}}\left[cx - \frac{1}{3}\frac{(cx)^3}{1} + \frac{1}{5}\frac{(cx)^5}{1.2} - \frac{1}{7}\frac{(cx)^7}{1.2.3} + \dots\right].$$

Cette série converge assez lentement pour les valeurs très fortes de cx. Laplace a donné ce cas l'intégrale définie sous la forme d'une fraction continue fort aisée à calculer

$$\frac{1}{2} - \frac{e^{-c^2 x^2}}{2cx\sqrt{\pi}}\cfrac{1}{1 + \cfrac{\alpha}{1 + \cfrac{2\alpha}{1 + \cfrac{3\alpha}{1 + \dots}}}}$$

dans laquelle $\alpha = \frac{1}{2c^2 x^2}$.

Les réduites successives sont

$$\frac{1}{1+\alpha'},\quad \frac{1+2\alpha}{1+3\alpha'},\quad \frac{1+5\alpha}{1+6\alpha+3\alpha^2},\quad \frac{1+9\alpha+8\alpha^2}{1+10\alpha+15\alpha^2},$$

Il existe un autre procédé permettant de calculer l'intégrale ci-dessus quand x est un grand nombre.

On a

$$\int_x^\infty e^{-x^2}dx = \int_x^\infty \frac{1}{2x}e^{-x^2}\,2x\,dx;$$

en intégrant par parties, on obtient alors

$$\int_x^\infty e^{-x^2}dx = \frac{e^{-x^2}}{2x} - \int_x^\infty e^{-x^2}\frac{dx}{2x^2}$$
$$= \frac{e^{-x^2}}{2x} - \frac{e^{-x^2}}{4x^3} + \int_x^\infty e^{-x^2}\frac{1.3}{4x^4}\,dx$$
$$= \frac{e^{-x^2}}{2x} - \frac{e^{-x^2}}{4x^3} + \frac{e^{-x^2}1.3}{8x^5} - \int_x^\infty e^{-x^2}\frac{1.3.5}{8x^6}\,dx.$$

Le terme général de la série a pour expression

$$\frac{1.3.5\dots(2n-1)}{2^{2n-1}x^{2n-1}}e^{-x^2}.$$

Le rapport d'un terme au précédent dépasse l'unité lorsque $2n+1 > 4x^2$. La série diverge donc à partir d'un certain terme. On peut obtenir une limite supérieure de l'intégrale qui sert de reste.

On a, en effet,

$$\frac{1.3.5\dots(2n+1)}{2^{2n-1}}\int_x^\infty \frac{e^{-x^2}}{x^{2n+2}}dx < \frac{1.3.5\dots(2n+1)}{2^{2n-1}}e^{-x^2}\int_x^\infty \frac{dx}{x^{2n+2}}$$
$$= \frac{1.3.5\dots(2n-1)}{2^{2n-1}x^{2n+1}}e^{-x^2}.$$

Or cette dernière quantité est le terme qui précédait l'intégrale. Le terme complémentaire est donc toujours plus petit que celui qui le précède.

On a édité des tables donnant les valeurs de l'intégrale

$$\Theta(y) = \frac{2}{\sqrt{\pi}}\int_0^y e^{-y^2}\,dy.$$

Some of the calculations Louis Bachelier presented in his dissertation, "The Theory of Speculation." The late-medieval allegorical court of Regina Pecunia *— notably, the figures of Fear and Greed — at long last translated into partial derivatives, would create the modern soothsayer known as the "financial quant."*

Bachelier had mathematized the plot of asset price. By defining and redefining each force as one or the other gained or lost strength as time lengthened or decayed, and by bringing them all together and pitting them all against each other in the same arena, Bachelier was able to formalize the calculation of what the best traders of rentes had known in their guts. He could predict the end of the story before it ended, which meant he could profit no matter which way the market moved. Without the literary legerdemain of metonymy, synecdoche, catachresis, or the printing press, Bachelier had discovered how to make money. Science had caught up to stories.

Yet his achievement contravened Rule #1 of fiction: Never reveal the ending in advance. A reader who knows the end before the end is the reader who stops reading. The rule parallels Rule #1 of properly functioning free markets: no trusts, monopolies, and cornering the market. They fix the ending before the end, and thereby ruin the story that is money.

While Bachelier was writing his dissertation at the beginning of the twentieth century, the analysis of plot, character, and metaphor had caught the attention of a new subset of literary critics. Instead of collecting bones, seeds, shells, and teeth like the anthropologists and ethnologists who had devoted themselves to the study of primitive money, these scholars collected folktales, myths, and reports of magic ritual. They were not interested in primitive economics, ethics, or religion. They were not even particularly interested in the meaning of the stories they collected. They did not consider their work a contribution to the field of humanities so much as a contribution to the sciences. Their goal was to develop a rigorous, systematic, and technical account of plot, character, and metaphor to see if, given the beginning of a story, they could predict how it would end.

The Russian Structuralists were not invested in names, places, or any of the specifics that fill myths, legends, folktales, epics, and lyric poetry with detail, emotion, and color. To them, plot and character were interchangeable from one narrative to the next, a set of variables to be thrown into an equation. They tabulated realizations, reversals, risks, fears, doubts, choices, and all the other constituents of narrative as though they were axioms of geometry, elements in the periodic table, or numbers on a spreadsheet. Like Louis Bachelier, who had channeled the seeming randomness of Brownian Motion into a single law, the Russian Structuralists sought to reduce all story to a single plot.

Viktor Shklovsky argued that plots were mechanisms, and that an astute reader could uncover the hydraulics. Yury Tynyanov suggested that plot was an engine controlled by a system of regulators, belts, and gears. Andrey Markov applied statistical theory to the great romantic Russian poem "Eugene Onegin" thereby transforming its ardent iambic tetrameters into a lifeless set of graphemes.

Boris Tomashevsky was an engineer and a statistician who began to study Russian folktales on the assumption that every element of every story ever told—from the most ancient myth to the most sophisticated comedy of manners—could be approached with the same tedious and repetitive methodology as a structural engineer might approach the torques and stresses of a bridge. When he was thirty-eight, Tomashevsky published *The Writer and the Book: An Outline of Textology*, which sucked the music out of verse, quashed the spirit of prose, and converted storytelling into predigested bits and pieces.

These men promoted the notion that behind every surprise of every story lay mandatory prescriptions and inviolable principles that had little to do with creativity and absolutely nothing to do with originality. The details of character, coincidence, and dilemma were superfluous. Romeo and Juliet were the same as Samson and Delilah were the same as boy meets girl, tragedy.

And that wasn't all. The Structuralists stripped stories of all their cultural, ethical, and philosophical relevance, too. The sins of villains and the sublime self-sacrifice of heroes became nothing more than encrypted functions that certain characters, given specific trajectories, had to enact at predetermined intersections. Neither love nor hate were judged tragic, justified, scandalous, redemptive, or even historically relevant. They were numerical requirements, as essential as passing 3 in order to get from 2 to 4. Marriage was a cliché, murder was a cliché, hidden treasure was a cliché. When viewed through the lens of textology, comedy and tragedy were no more than different slopes on the same coordinate system.

One particularly enduring rendition of structural analysis descended from the research of a high school teacher named Vladimir Propp, who took the study to a length that bordered on absurdity. He saw his life's work as the tabulation of plots, and to this end he tracked down one hundred Russian folktales and cataloged every reason a protagonist might find himself up a tree, every kind of projectile that might be hurled at his head, and every friend or enemy he or she might acquire or eliminate along the path back to safety. Like Tomashevsky, Propp outlined beginnings, middles, and ends as sets of impersonal "functions." Propp enumerated thirty-one of these, which he arranged in sequence along a narrative number line. Not every function had to appear in every story, nor did every story have to begin at the first function. A plot could just as easily get going at number 16 as at 26; but once the story did begin, it had to proceed in order. Like yoked oxen, all stories must follow the path.

Viewed in its entirety, the course tended toward redemption, as function 1 suggested that someone, somewhere, would have to be rescued. Function 6 described ransom, 8 articulated abduction, 10, 13, and 19 various extrications, liberations, and recoveries. If the story ever made it to plot point 21, there would be yet another capture. The final function brought the narrative back to the beginning, as point 31 was a wedding. Propp did not mention the procession, the vows, the ring, or the harnessed bride. Still, Propp's structure mirrored the captivity narrative.

If there was only one plot, it looked like the money plot.

Propp's conclusions were not received with widespread joy, nor acclaim, nor even a great deal of respect among the elites of literary analysis. Much like Louis Bachelier's dissertation, Propp's *Morphology of the Folktale* went virtually unnoticed for decades after it was published. Then, in 1958 came the English translation, and a new generation of linguists, historians, sociologists, anthropologists, psychoanalysts, and other professors of the humanities and social sciences — with the exception of the economists — came to the conclusion that Russian Structuralism could illuminate not only the inner workings of the *Iliad*, the *Odyssey*, and the *Mahabarata*, but also the complete works of Shakespeare, Tolstoy, Proust, the Brothers Grimm, and Mother Goose.

The postulations of a half dozen literary quants in the 1910s found their intellectual moment in the 1960s and blossomed into numerous theories of plot and the plot's set of *actants* — the name the Lithuanian literary theorist A. J. Greimas came up with in 1966 to describe archetypal characters. That same year the French philosopher Roland Barthes published an essay called "An Introduction to the Structural Analysis of Narrative," in which he spoke of stories using technical terms such as "catalyses" and "nuclei." In 1969, the Bulgarian-French philosopher Tzvetan Todorov published his own "Structural Analysis of Narrative," suggesting "a future science of literature." Todorov refined and reduced Propp's theory, arguing that all narratives progress through five stages, not thirty-one. Todorov then illustrated his theory by means of schematic notation, and developed the argument that plot shifted from one "equilibrium" to the next, much like the movement of oxygen molecules in a chamber of increasing or decreasing pressure. The underlying value of narrative was tending toward a programmed series of functions and numbers, so perhaps it was not entirely coincidental that Propp's morphology of story and Bachelier's morphology of finance united in the summer of 1971, when dollars became words.

Alongside Bhattacharya's *Book of Greeks* is the inarguably less literary *Option Volatility and Pricing: Advanced Trading Strategies and Techniques*, a legendary best seller originally published in 1988, written by a bespectacled and professorial options trader named

Sheldon Natenberg. From its first page, the book immerses its readers in a new universe. Money lives among self-referential signs and symbols, and travels along arcane geographies that lead to its demise or triumph. Here's an excerpt:

> If a call can be purchased (sold) for less (more) than its theoretical value, it will, in the long run, be more profitable to take a long (short) market position by purchasing (selling) calls than by purchasing (selling) the underlying contract. In the same way, if a put can be purchased (sold) for less (more) than its theoretical value, it will, in the long run, be more profitable to take a short (long) market position by purchasing (selling) puts than by selling (buying) the underlying contract.

On first read, this makes no sense. But the literary key emerges from the verbs. Note how they are doubled, that purchasing a "call" is equivalent to selling a "put" and purchasing a "put" is equivalent to selling a "call," so that buying and selling effectively become the same thing. This was precisely the observation that perplexed Bronisław Malinowski one hundred years ago, as he observed the circular trade of cowrie shells. Consider the verbs as you might the rhymes of the witches in the opening scene of *Macbeth*: "the foul that is fair," "the fair that is foul." Macbeth was confused when the witches predicted he would be king when the battle's "lost and won."

If the ancient Greek philosophers had read Sheldon Natenberg, they would have recognized such doubleness as further proof of their hypothesis that the universe consisted of a single substance, that a mysterious and transcendental force united all that appeared antagonistic — including such seemingly opposed and opposite activities as buying and selling. It is no coincidence that the first person to propose that oppositions were illusions, that the universe was a gigantic unity, that to buy was to sell and to go long was to go short was the first option trader. His name was Thales of Miletus, and he lived during the time precious metal coinage first became popular, around 600 BC. Like neoliberal theorists who see money in everything, everywhere, all the time, Thales believed the single substance of the universe was liquidity. But unlike the merchants, capitalists, canoe traders, conquistadors, and all other floaters of credit and debt, Thales of Miletus did not identify liquidity with assets and cash, but with something much more basic. He believed the single substance of the universe was water. As a result of the liquid universe, any movement in one part of the pool would create movement in every other part.

Mere mortals were consigned to be confused by onslaughts of unrelated epiphenomena, but Thales proposed a theory of the everything. He saw relationships no one else could see, which proved invaluable for his reputation. First, he pulled off the feat of correctly predicting the solar eclipse of 585 BC. Amid the stunned silence and amazement that followed, it is rumored that a voice rose from the crowd, asking the great philosopher a question that has echoed through the ages: "If you're so smart, why aren't you rich?"

At this point the question for Thales became: How could he direct the ripples of the universe to wash the world's coins into his pocket? The ancient answer was the same as the modern answer. It was the way to make money, heads or tails. It was the language of having it all, the language of both/and. Which is Wall Street's favorite language.

That year, Thales foresaw a particularly abundant olive harvest. Anticipating the relationships that would ensue when a sudden glut of perishable fruit met the urgent need to be transformed into non-perishable olive oil, the philosopher began to make the rounds of Greek olive presses. The owners of these machines were accustomed to renting their works out during harvest season, thereby relieving themselves of the stresses of procuring fresh olives at a wholesaler's discount, pressing them into oil, discarding the pits and skins, bottling the commodity, and distributing the finished product. To reiterate: The owners of the presses were neither the growers of the olives nor the marketers of the oil. Their job was the transition of one commodity to the other. Thales understood that in order to make the money spirit flow his way, he would need to dig into the core of *tropos*. Only in transition would the moneyness of money reveal itself.

As he made his rounds of olive presses, Thales asked each owner if, instead of a normal rental agreement for their manufacturing works, he might give them a smaller payment in advance to secure the right — *but not the obligation* — to rent their presses when harvest time came. If at some point before the harvest season he exercised his option to rent, he would pay whatever they asked, stipulated in advance. If not, they could keep his money, and rent their presses to someone else.

The owners proved amenable to such a deal. After all, if the nutty professor who had never engaged in commerce — much less sold a pint of olive oil — eventually decided to rent for their preset asking price, they would make money. If he decided not to exercise his option, they would get to keep what he had already given them and not have to give him anything in return. They ran no risk, so they signed.

If they had cared to consider the old man's motivations, the press owners may have figured that he wanted to get in on the lucrative oil business. But nothing could have been farther from the truth. Thales had no interest in agrinions, amfissas, and kalamatas. His interest was getting rich. So he didn't haggle when the owners of the presses named their rental price. He didn't care about the number. He planned to be out of the deal long before the crush.

Thales wandered up and down the Peloponesse, negotiating with every olive oil manufacturing conglomerate he could find, in each case purchasing the right but not the obligation to rent within a time period defined by the execution and expiration of the contract. In the language of Sheldon Natenberg's *Option Volatility and Pricing: Advanced Trading Strategies and Techniques*, Thales was going "long on a call" — that is, he was betting on the possibility that within a certain period of time the price of what he had the right but not the obligation to purchase would go up.

What the owners of the olive presses did not understand was that by pawning off their risk to Thales, they had given away their most valuable asset — namely, the allegorical force that one day in the distant future would be known among quantitative finance wonks as vega. It was true that no matter what happened, the olive press owners would make money, either through the rent of their machines or through keeping their premium and renting to someone else. But their agreement with Thales had preset and bounded their profits. At the same time, Thales had managed to secure a position for himself wherein his potential loss was bounded, but his potential for profit unlimited. Recall Nicolas Magens: "The Sum given is called Premium, and the Liberty that the Giver of the Premium has to have the Contract fulfilled or not, is called Option..."

As it turned out, the olive harvest was tremendous, and Thales exercised his option to rent the presses for the duration. In a matter of weeks, the roads of Greece were jammed with wagons overflowing with fresh berries, a harvest such as no one had ever before seen the likes. And the old man, who had no interest in manufacturing amphoras of extra virgin, did nothing. Like Aristotle, Vladimir Propp, and the medieval Scholastics counting down to Armageddon, Thales understood that once the story had begun a certain way, it could only end a certain way. So he waited for the plot to unfold as it must.

Thales knew there would be a lot of people out there wanting to rent olive presses as soon as possible, and that they would eventually discover that someone other than the olive press owners possessed the rights. He observed the growing frenzy among growers whose fruits were about to rot, and the growing fury of olive oil manufacturers who realized they were being denied the chance at the biggest payday ever. As time (eventually to be known as theta) dwindled down to nothing, fear and frenzy (eventually to be known as gamma) went through the roof, Thales sat back and watched. Meanwhile, the owners of the olive presses, those who should have been at the center of the action, had been effectively removed from the picture. They had already sold the option to use their presses to the grizzled and bearded old man. Imagine the owners' dismay and wonder as they belatedly realized that risk was more valuable than olives.

Eventually, Thales offered the leases he had acquired to the highest bidder. To give a sense of how much money he might have made, Greece produced 300 million tons of olive oil last year. If Thales had subleased his rights to the olive presses for only ten shekels per ton above what he had paid for them, he would have become a shekel billionaire three times over.

To be sure, the plot Thales had divined was complicated, featuring more than a few reversals. The man who had seen everything as a single thing had considered the soil, the sun, the rain, the buyers, the sellers, the execution and expiration dates, the olives, the olive oil, and the various pricing agreements as if all were elements of a single story, the ending of which only he knew in advance. The philosopher had understood that the battle of contrary forces which most had perceived to be olive tree versus weather, or man versus nature, or buyer versus seller, was actually occurring on a level one step removed in the metaverse of money, where the jeopardy of the drama translated into profits. He had not cornered a market in olive presses so much as he had mastered the forces of an allegory in which gamma, theta, and vega were the central players.

Thales of Miletus did not have to touch an olive to get rich, but he had to visit a lot of olive presses. He had to go out and negotiate each agreement separately, and if he had been wrong about the volume of that olive harvest 2,600 years ago, he would have had to take a loss. What he lacked was a centralized platform for buying and selling his olive harvest options. It wasn't until August of 1999 that the Chicago Mercantile Exchange received approval from the United States Commodity Futures Trading Commission to list an exchange-traded product called Heating and Cooling Degree Day futures. In short, bets on the weather.

Banks like Barclays, Citi, Deutsche, Merrill Lynch, JPMorgan Chase, State Street, UBS, and Bankers Trust continue in the tradition of Thales, even if olive oil has been displaced by palm oil and petroleum and other commodities—most notably money itself. Every hour of the day from New York to London to Tokyo to Sydney they stake bets on the future of money—paying special attention to the character Louis Bachelier called rho, the price of money's accrual, otherwise known as the interest rate. The great banks buy, sell, option, and swap between $4 and $5 trillion worth of these bets every day and conduct their business on central trading platforms like the Boston Options Exchange (BOX), the CME, the Eurex Exchange, the Moscow Exchange, New York's NASDAQ, the Shanghai Futures Exchange, the National Stock Exchange of India, and Euronext Paris, descendant of the Bourse.

The greatest piles of money the world has ever seen are now being presided over by the largest banks and exchanges the world has ever seen. And when a bank has a trillion or so under management, it may not be easy to find a safe spot to hoard it. You can't put it in a safe, because it's not material. You can't put it in the bank, because you *are* the bank. And that's where the universe of financial swaps and options comes in. On an electronic derivatives exchange managed by a third party like the CME Globex, bankers can execute trades of every size, shape, and combination in order to mitigate every possible fear or risk, and anticipate the end of every story before it ends. On such exchanges, buying and selling the same thing at the same time happens all the time.

Here, then, is a short primer on how to make money: Let's say you are considering the idea of throwing a backyard barbecue in two weeks, but are concerned you might have to cancel at the last minute because of rain. Unlike Thales, who was entirely convinced that the upcoming olive harvest would be huge, you honestly do not know if your barbecue will be rained out or not. What you do know is that if you go ahead with your plans you will need to purchase two hundred hamburger patties, three hundred hot dogs, one hundred steaks, and forty chicken breasts. (It's a big party.) You also know that unless you order in advance, your local butcher will likely not have enough burgers and dogs in stock when you need them. You are reluctant to shell out payment for everything so far in the future because the weather may turn, and you do not want to get stuck with a ton of food you don't need. By the same token, the butcher is happy to place your order as long as he has some assurance that he won't get stuck with all of the inventory in the event that you cancel at the last minute. Amid all these uncertainties, this complicated array of time, change, desire, and anxiety — what would be the best course of action?

The first step is to analyze the options inherent within the plot. Only after conceptualizing all possible forks in the road of the narrative will you be in a position to increase the odds of getting what you want no matter what happens, and in Louis Bachelier's immortal words, "profit at all prices."

After assessing the situation, an options trader might suggest that you agree to give the butcher a nonrefundable payment of one hundred dollars to order the meat and hold it in his freezer, as long as the butcher, in turn, promises to sell the meat to you at a preset price—one thousand dollars, say—on the day before the party. In addition, you promise that by noon on the day before the party you will have made up your mind about the event, at which point you will either exercise your option to purchase the burgers at the set price for the set delivery date (minus the hundred-dollar prepayment), or let the option expire without purchasing anything, in which case the butcher would get to keep the meat, resell it if he likes, and keep your hundred bucks for good measure. In the parlance of the option trader, by holding the right but not the obligation to buy you have gone "long" on hot dogs and hamburgers (what Sheldon Natenberg calls a "call"), while the butcher, by putting himself in a position wherein he may be required to sell, has gone "short" (a so-called put).

As in the case of the ancient olive oil, the option mitigates the economic risk of both buyer and seller by generating a narrative with a predetermined set of endings. The option provides you with the security of knowing that if you do indeed decide to go forward with your barbecue you will be able to feed your guests, and you are willing to pay one hundred dollars for the privilege. The butcher, in turn, has been provided a measure of protection for his purchase of hot dogs, hamburgers, steaks, and chicken breasts by the hundred dollars he gets to keep no matter what, plus the fact that if you decide not to exercise your option to buy, he will be at liberty to sell the meat and poultry as he pleases at whatever price he pleases, to whomever he pleases, whenever he pleases. In the language of option trading, that hundred bucks is the option's premium and the end of the two-week period is known as the option's expiration. Both buyer and seller have embraced all the possibilities of the future barbecue, mitigated risk, and defined the end of the story from the start, so that in the great narrative tradition of anagogy, time is no longer measured from the beginning to some obscure future, but counts down from a predetermined moment known in the world of storytelling as The End.

After a day or two you may decide that you don't care so much about hosting your own barbecue, particularly since you have learned that your next door neighbor is considering hosting one of his own at the same time. As the expiration date of your option approaches, you may even consider selling your neighbor your right-without-obligation to purchase all those burgers, dogs, chicken breasts, and marinated strip steaks. And if the butcher's freezer is full, the sun is shining brightly and the weather report is propitious, your neighbor may decide he wants to have his own barbecue so badly he may be willing to purchase your option for more than you paid for it, say for $125.

At that point, if you decide to sell, you will have made a profit of twenty-five dollars without buying, selling, or flipping a single burger. And if you had not taken an option with one butcher for one barbecue for $100, but with one thousand butchers for one thousand barbecues from Maine to Long Island for a total premium of $100,000, then sold each one twenty-four hours before expiration for $125, you would have made $25,000. Of course, if the forecast were rain and nothing but rain, your options would become virtually worthless to you and to everyone else and you would be, as option traders say, "out of the money."

So far, the story has not progressed beyond the classical money plot, the conflict of forces Thales of Miletus had mastered to release the spirit of money inherent within olive oil into his own pocket. But as we have seen in previous chapters, the technology of money and the technology of narrative have progressed together. When Pope Innocent IV declared the corporation a *persona ficta*, so did money enter a new phase, more confident than ever of its independent character. Modern fiction began when Don Quixote realized he was a character in a best-selling book called *Don Quixote*, and ever since characters have been able to break loose from their captivity, and address their own imaginary existence. This is precisely what happens on commodity markets, where futures and options can be bought and sold as independent beings, with virtually no relationship to their underlying value, whether hot dog, hamburger, West Texas Intermediate, or gold. Derivatives possess a life of their own in which the binary rules of buying and selling — the limitations of either/or — may no longer apply.

Now imagine that those barbecue options were not a matter of a personal agreement between you and the butcher, but were selling on a centralized trading platform of buyers and sellers, not the BOX, the CME, or the NASDAQ, but the Barbecue Option Exchange, the BOE. (Just to be clear, such a thing does not exist.) And let's say you never really cared one way or the other about having a barbecue in your backyard; that like Thales of Miletus, you only cared about making money. Which is to say, your scenarios about buying and selling hot dogs and steaks were not only stories you made up, but stories about another story.

On the BOE, you would have the opportunity to purchase what financiers call a replication (and what English professors call an allegory) of the barbecuer's position, the position of the right but not the obligation to buy the meat, also known as the "long" position, or the "call." At the same time, you could purchase a replication or allegory of the butcher's position, the position of the possible requirement of selling the meat at a preset price, or of keeping the premium. You would then possess a replication of both sides of the deal, the buyer's and the seller's. On our imaginary central barbecue trading exchange, even more choices would be available. You could buy the option to buy, buy the option to sell, sell the option to buy, or sell the option to sell. None of which has anything to do with whether or not you own a hot dog or have any intention of eating one.

At the same time as you are placing bets within the BOE's metaverse of money, you could be buying equity shares in an actual hot dog and hamburger producer like Hormel or Tyson Foods, while also establishing long and short positions in livestock futures on commodities exchanges — all to further mitigate risk, and further complicate the story. Which brings us back to the question that plagued the mind of medieval monks: What happens when time's up?

If clouds gather and it becomes obvious to you that thunderstorms are fast approaching, you might sell as many of your "long" options as soon as possible (before they lose all value) and buy as many equal and opposite "short" options as possible (as they increase in value), essentially transferring your replicated position closer to the economic situation of the butcher. If you are able to execute the change in your position before too much time ran out, you would successfully mitigate your risk by offsetting your losses with equal and opposite gains. Of course, the longer you wait and the more everyone hears the weatherman forecasting rain, the "buy" options you have purchased will become increasingly harder to sell (and thus cheaper) while the butcher's "sell" options would become increasingly harder to buy (and thus more expensive).

One final scenario: Imagine it's two days before all the options expire, that it's cloudy and raining, but you are feeling lucky.

Something tells you the sun is going to shine, so following your hunch you buy one thousand of those "buy" options no one wants on the cheap — say for a deeply discounted $25 per option. Things are looking dim, but the next day your dream comes true. The weather clears up, and there is a sudden demand for the options you hold for tens of thousands of hamburgers, hot dogs, and steaks, without which no one can have a picnic. You sell your barbecue rights for $200 apiece, everyone on the eastern seaboard gets a hot dog, and you take home $175,000. On the allegorical level, the waxing power of vega (volatility) amid the waning tenure of theta (time) had torqued the suspense of the money plot and led to the ascendance of that high-strung maniac, the alternately anxious and greedy gamma (fear). It is increased gamma that can make the actions of buying or selling more profitable (or more devastating) in a situation of accelerated action and suspense. As a screenwriter might put it, a scene of a fistfight in a schoolyard during recess is one thing; that same fistfight between a hijacker and the pilot of a packed Boeing 737 as the plane plummets toward earth is quite another.

In today's landscape of high-frequency trading, the moment that differentiates profit from loss can be measured in fractions of a second. As infinitesimal time decays, some traders gain, others lose. These are the traders harnessed by the either/or of the martingale. But there is another group of traders on the floor of the options exchange, those who by means of mathematical formulae have programmed so-called "multi-asset risk parities" that will stabilize their story no matter which way the market turns. They are the ones who emerge unscathed when the battle's "lost and won."

Finding the path to "profit at all prices" may have driven Bachelier's dissertation, but at the heart of the problem lay another question: What would be the correct price of *any* option at *any* particular point in time? Was one hundred dollars the right price for the hypothetical butcher-barbecue option previously considered? Two days before the option expired, when the skies were gray, was $25 correct? Or should it have been $2.50? Twenty-four hours before expiration, when the sun was bright in the sky, was $200 the right price? Or should it have been $400? Or, perhaps, $401.87? Was there a way to calculate the right price? If such a thing were possible, then a central options exchange like the (imaginary) BOE might be able to set that price, and act as a clearinghouse for large-scale barbecue betting.

During the 1960s, as gold-backed currency teetered to the end of its reign and the floating dollar loomed just beyond the horizon, Louis Bachelier's dissertation of 1900 was rediscovered by Nobel Prize winner Paul Samuelson, author of the best-selling economics textbook of all time. Samuelson began to circulate "A Theory of Speculation," and among the recipients were two of his fellow MIT Professors, Fischer Black and Myron Scholes, who read the dissertation and, in a 1973 issue of the *Journal of Political Economy,* published what would come to be known as the Black-Scholes model of option pricing. "Profit at all prices" had joined the mainstream of economic thought.

The Black-Scholes world is entirely allegorical. To review the characters: Vega, or volatility, is commonly defined as the historical excitement of the stock, the bond, the interest rate, the currency, or any other underlying value. Vega measures the ups and downs or amplitude of price over a period of time. For example, the price of grains and oilseeds shows increased vega during June, July, and August, when the risk of drought is highest in the Midwest, and the price is most vulnerable to boom and bust. Thus had the ancient weather gods finally succumbed to calculus, their names, propitiations, and worship subsumed by vega.

Gamma measures the speed of vega and is particularly sympathetic. When vega gets into a mood, gamma accelerates. Louis

Bachelier called that fear the "coefficient of instability," which in turn measured the "the excitability of the security," and the more excited the security, the more "anxiety"; by contrast, a security's "calm state" would be an indicator of low gamma.

Delta measures the relative strength or weakness of the relationship between the price of the option and the price of whatever it may represent. One way financiers deploy delta is by generating what is commonly referred to as the "delta hedge." By buying or selling whatever may be the underlying value of an option while selling or buying an equal and opposite relationship to that underlying value — i.e., the delta — a trader can generate money by mitigating risk in every direction at the same time, as if the kula trader set off in a virtual ocean with one thousand different canoes, but only had to be on board the one that returned with the most white shell armbands. Bankers say that delta corresponds to the "moneyness" of the option, implying that they no longer think of money as dollars, euros, or yen; that money is no longer gold, grain, or oil; that money is not even risk, fear, or time, but a relationship among characters. Money is the money plot.

Two years after Nixon made dollars into words, the Chicago Board Options Exchange opened, and floating money found a welcoming home. Eleven years after that, MIT Professor Myron Scholes joined the board of directors of the Greenwich, Connecticut–based hedge fund Long-Term Capital Management, which in the first three years of its life brought in returns of 21, 43, and 41 percent, respectively. Unfortunately, the theorem was not foolproof. There were plot twists Black-Scholes had not anticipated.

In 1998, financial collapses in Asia and Russia caught Long-Term Capital Management by surprise, and in four months the fund lost more than $4 billion. But that did not stop Myron Scholes from winning the Nobel Prize in economics later that year. Nor did the failure of the Black-Scholes algorithms and metrics dissuade future hordes of quants from seeking better paths through the stochastic forest. And so the search for that elusive integration or leverage or game theory or behavior modification continues to haunt the quantamental world.

Perhaps that missing x was a nuance of time itself, known as theta. For Bachelier's allegory of finance had opened the door to a new kind of time. His equations introduced "the infinitesimal future," "optional time," "the square root of time," and "decomposed time." If these concepts stretched human understanding, perhaps it was because the characters in the story had not been made to serve our hearts and minds in quite the same way as the old allegories had engaged with common human themes.

The Greek letters portrayed the journey of money through a sea of volatility as a war for domination, a battle among risk, fear, and expiration date. The conflict may have had its roots in religion, poetry, and literature. But the new plot had come under the sway of protocols best suited for machines. This has occasionally been perceived to be a problem, as in the aftermath of the flash crash of 2010, which began at 2:45 p.m. Eastern Standard Time on May 6 and ended thirty-six minutes later. In just over two thousand seconds the Dow Jones, S&P 500, and NASDAQ lost $1 trillion — then gained it all back. The humans thought it was doomsday, and realized belatedly that machines would be just fine with a continual state of apocalypse.

This brings us to the present state of affairs, when a mini "flash crash" in some exchange-traded equity happens every day, and no one at *The Wall Street Journal* or Bloomberg News bothers too much about it. Today, the money engineers spend their days and weeks monitoring how efficiently their machines are offsetting long delta against short delta, long vega against short vega, long gamma against short gamma. The acolytes of Bachelier, Bhattacharya, Black, Scholes, and Natenberg live in a world only they can perceive; a world where the delta hedge is simply one of a multitude of back spreads, front spreads, diagonals, Christmas trees, butterflies, condors, strangles, and other baroque trading strategies.

"A synthetic position acts very much like its real equivalent," Natenberg reassured those who might have been unnerved by the delusion of it all, unmoored by the allegorical alternate reality. Later in *Option Volatility and Pricing* he would wax more confident, until he finally said it plainly: "There is no difference between the synthetic and its real equivalent."

Black-Scholes touched primitive emotions and revived the ancient genies long dormant in the shamans' shells, oxen, and beads. The grammar and rhetoric of delta, gamma, theta, and vega had been founded upon thousands of years of plots, characters, and metaphors, and the men who created the formulae were the first to admit its basis. "In options and warrants," Fischer Black would write, "people see the beauty."

At long last, the bankers had outdone the poets.

{10} THE END OF MONEY

There are means of payment which are not yet money; then those which are money; later still those which have ceased to be money.

— GEORG FRIEDRICH KNAPP, 1905

THE FIRST STORIES ever told have been lost, but the relics that come down to us suggest that they addressed the hopes, fears, and confusions of our ancestors in the face of an indifferent universe. Those long-lost plots, characters, and metaphors helped people come to terms with the volatility, unpredictability, and deadly hazards of their time on earth, and manage the terror of what might come after.

Then something happened to those stories, something that changed everything. Someone realized that fictions could do more than assuage anxieties, that stories could do more than unfold the unknowable and explain the inexplicable. Someone realized that stories could be used to achieve their purposes on earth, that fiction could make things real. That was the most powerful idea ever, and it came to rule the world. That idea was money, and it has been with us since the first ostrich eggshell beads of neolithic Kenya.

Today, stories are everywhere and nowhere, flickering fragments binged upon or broken into a barrage of memes, TikToks, and posts befitting attention spans gutted by flurries of meaningless multitasking. There is no coherent beginning or end to the stream of snippets, seductions, likes, and hates. It doesn't take much acuity to observe that the customary structures that have governed stories for millennia have collapsed into a feed.

That same fate awaits the money plot.

The first signs that the plot had peaked appeared in 1971, when Nixon and Connally made it clear that the world's most powerful money was the world's most powerful story. The myth that had taken more than sixty thousand years to compose could not get any more epic than that, and three thousand miles west of the Oval Office, the eleventh largest bank in the United States had already begun to strategize next steps.

It happened in the heart of what would within a quarter century come to be known as Silicon Valley. The bank was Wells Fargo, and five years before Nixon floated the dollar, the CEO, Ransom Cook, was coming to the end of a long career, and noticing something new. He had become convinced that computer algorithms could do more for banks than belch out data so that the printers of the day could spew out account balances at six hundred lines per minute. The dot matrix printers then in use sprayed ink bidirectionally across the margins of a page, and had thus reintroduced computer companies like Digital Equipment Corporation, Hewlett-Packard, and OKI Data to the ancient term boustrophedon — the back-and-forth movement of reading, writing, and domesticated livestock that had all appeared together at the same revolutionary moment.

Ransom Cook perceived that harnessing computers to money would be as extraordinary an innovation as harnessing an animal with a yoke, thus turning cattle into capital. The problem was, Cook didn't know how such a thing could be done. So in the great tradition of bankers, he threw money at the problem. In 1964 Cook created an entity called the "Investment Decision Making" group, a think tank led by a mechanical engineer and self-proclaimed data hog named

John "Mac" McQuown — the man who would earn the distinction of being finance's first bona fide computer geek.

Like earlier analysts of narrative engineering — notably, the Russian Structuralists, led by Tomashevsky, Tynyanov, and Propp — Mac McQuown's group could not have cared less about individual characters, plots, or metaphors. In the world of investing, that meant they were not concerned about the performance of Polaroid, Teledyne, Texas Instruments, or any of the other surging stocks of the 1960s. Their investment strategy had nothing to do with whether or not the sales of a company had increased or decreased, if the company were vulnerable to a leveraged buyout, or looking to swallow the competition. They did not care about price-to-earnings ratios or debt levels or the background and character of CEOs.

The investment vehicle McQuown's group envisioned would be a new kind of ostrich egg, a strictly mathematical aggregation defined by the behavior not of individual corporations but of the market as a whole. And in order to balance, manage, and weigh the massive onslaught of fluctuating numbers the market in its entirety presented, they needed power far beyond the capacity of the human brain. Their approach demanded that they back their way into a story that already existed. Instead of working to transform, anticipate, or analyze the plot, they labored to create an index.

The linguistic study of indices is known as *deictics*, and one of the basic tenets of the field is that the elements of an index make no sense without an understanding of the underlying material — that is, the text to which the index refers. An index cannot help to explain the meaning of a metaphor or the significance of a character. Decisive moments in a plot do not exist, for the index sucks time and place out of a story. Nor does an index stimulate an emotional response. No one has ever cried for joy or started with fear while reading an index. For an index is not a narrative. It is a story that has been dispersed and reassembled into an entirely different form, a story once removed.

Of course, McQuown and his data hogs were not concerned with the fine distinctions of deictics. Their job was to utilize the processing speed and storage capacity of computers to generate a constantly fluctuating database that did not replicate a single transaction or a group of transactions, but a sum of all the transactions at the same time. McQuown was not concerned that within his data machine, none of the usual differentiations of asset allocation counted. He understood that his product might utterly ignore distinctions made between financial, health-care, industrial, or manufacturing sectors of the stock exchange. Instead, the Investment Decision Making group aimed to capture the exchange as if all its disparate elements comprised the metabolism of a single, enormous beast. Their goal was to harness that beast, enclose it within the confines of a computer—then let others invest in its behavior.

In 1971, McQuown finally figured it out, and Wells Fargo immediately deployed the new technology as the vehicle for the $6 million pension fund of a company that had been founded in 1910 by a Denver-based luggage salesman who had named his business after the Bible's strongest man. The product Wells Fargo sold to Samsonite required no industry analysts, no stock pickers, and no portfolio managers. It was the earliest ancestor of the so-called *index fund*, an invention, McQuown would later observe, that "launched me into an entirely new life."

McQuown was Wall Street's first certifiable quant, and he continued his run of banking success. In 1972 he cofounded Wells Fargo Investment Advisors, a unit that was eventually sold to BlackRock, the world's largest asset manager, with more than $7 trillion under management—more than four trillion of which reside in index funds. These days, McQuown lives in Sonoma County, where his indexical approach to money allows him to invest in 30,000 stocks, all at the same time. His sizable fortune safely diversified, Mac McQuown has returned to the simple life, raising heirloom vegetables, pressing olive oil, and making a highly-rated Cabernet Sauvignon at his Stone Edge Farm Estate Vineyard and Winery.

Five years after Wells Fargo introduced the Samsonite index fund, a Princeton graduate named John C. Bogle came up with a similar, if much more ambitious notion: He would create an investment trust based on an index of the entire S&P 500 — that is, an index of an index — and sell it retail. Anyone who wanted could purchase a share. Nobel Prize winner Paul Samuelson called Bogle's product as great an invention as "the wheel, the alphabet, Gutenberg printer."

The company Bogle founded is still around today. It is The Vanguard Group, with more than $5 trillion under management. Needless to say, Bogle became a very rich man, and the indexical approach to money was widely imitated. By 2012, the number of index funds had mushroomed to one thousand. Within half a decade after that, Dow Jones would be offering more than 130,000 of them, and the global total would explode to more than three million, including funds that index double-short and double-long Euros, leveraged and inversed commodities, and endless aggregates of equities indexed to real estate, trade tensions, social media, environmental sustainability, ethical virtue, and the threat of epidemic disease, not to mention a new universe of so-called multi-strategy products, and countless funds of funds. According to the World Bank, there are fewer than 50,000 public companies, which means that indices now outweigh the stories they index by a ratio of sixty to one. Which is to say, the story is over.

The index most closely resembles the sleight of hand of magicians and charlatans, in that its purpose is to direct attention to something other than itself, as in itself it is nothing. For the value of an index resides nowhere within the index. The value of the index lies with those who do the indexing—and the beauty of the whole thing is that no one ever sees the indexers of an index, the gatekeepers who exact a toll but run no risk. They are like the guardians of the market of Ouidah, a West African kingdom that controlled the eighteenth-century slave trade. Its ten miles of coastline in present-day Benin were governed by a distinct set of port authorities whose power went unquestioned, as most of them were spirits of the dead.

Think of an index like that old slave trading post, a bounded space governed by characters beyond reach: ghosts, gods, and immortals. Think of an index as a world within which the old metaphors, characters, and plots no longer matter, a precinct with an entirely new set of manners and customs, a universe behind a firewall. Think of an index every time you enter the borders of Amazon, Facebook, or Google, themselves governed by a trove of invisible guardian spirits, where the cadence of your clicks, the rhythm of your attention span, and the pattern of your retinal blood vessels are duly noted and stored. These companies, which have a combined capitalization of well over $2 trillion dollars, generate hundreds of billions in revenue by selling indices so vast they can only be organized by other indices.

Think of an index when you visit a casino, and watch your money transform into multicolored plastic chips. If you are lucky enough to own one, the index is the place where you can write the rules of the game, then invite everyone to play. This is why the indexers of Wall Street inhabit the safest of safe spaces, owed a debt from all, responsible to none.

A little more than two decades after the appearance of the first index funds, the product took the next step toward financial domination. In 1993, the year John Connally died, the American Stock

Exchange offered its first "Exchange-Traded Fund," commonly known as an ETF, which would become the model of the modern, multitrillion dollar business in exchange-traded indices that generates $3 billion of profit every day. Bogle's index had been a standalone product, but the ETF was an element that could be bought and sold within the same product it indexed. In other words, *the index of the exchange could now be traded on the exchange.* It was as if money had swallowed itself.

The Securities and Exchange Commission, the federal agency in charge of protecting investors and ensuring the fair and orderly functioning of securities markets, didn't know what to make of such a thing. Yes, the index was a container — but all that it contained were other containers. It was neither metal nor oil nor oxen nor grain, though there would soon be indices of each — weighted, balanced, blended, commingled, and reduced from a complicated collection of real things into a mathematical formula that could be expressed as a single manifestation. Nor was the index a piece of paper telling a story — like a promissory note or a bill — although an index of all those pieces of paper from every corner of the earth would soon be available, and in every conceivable combination.

One might purchase a share of the index, but the whole was not a single corporate body but the widest dispersion of such bodies, thus turning synecdoche on its head. Nor was the exchange-traded index fund in the tradition of the *campagnia* or *societas,* where everyone was "in the same boat," or "eating the same bread," as those who ran the index were not in the index. Nor was the ETF a kula ring. It was more akin to the ocean itself, an ocean wherein everyone had to pay a fee to float. The ETF didn't fit any previous definition of money, so the SEC simply granted it an exemption.

ETFs were followed by an even more elusive contrivance, the ETP, or Exchange-Traded Product. The first of these, StreetTRACKS

Gold Trust, debuted on the New York Stock Exchange in 2004. StreetTRACKS turned gold into a price equation based on the input of guardian spirits: the Bank of China, Goldman Sachs, Morgan Stanley, the commodities giant Koch, and the hedge fund Jane Street Global Trading. Over the course of ten millennia, gold nuggets had transformed from ornament into coin, bullion, a gift for baby Jesus, a harness for a trophy wife, the cross that crucified William Jennings Bryan, the ring of Alberich, the gold-backed paper money of the Federal Reserve, and an option priced by the Black-Scholes theorem and traded on the Chicago Mercantile Exchange. What had once been the sovereign of all value had at long last dissolved into crypto-cosmic muck.

In 1993, the Chicago Board Options Exchange initiated trading on yet another new product, a volatility index called the VIX, commonly known as the Fear Index. The VIX was comprised of neither snail shells nor dollars nor stocks nor bonds nor gamma nor vega nor the expectation of vega but the square root of an index of theoretical expectations of volatility based on all the options taken on the S&P 500. In other words, the true nature of the VIX remains a mystery to all but the most ardent acolytes of quantitative finance. Yet it is the VIX that has become one of the market's most important bellwethers.

The term bellwether is itself instructive. The word goes back to the Middle English, when the word *wether* referred to a castrated ram. The bell around that ram's neck — the *bellwether* — would lead the flock of sheep. For most of the twentieth century, the financial bellwether — that is, the leading indicator of money's mood — was a stock. JPMorgan Chase, for instance, has at one time or another been perceived to be a barometer of the market as a whole, as Tata is for tech stocks in India. Today, the bell that leads the sheep is an electronically traded index with an underlying value that does not exist. The VIX is a story about nothing — because it isn't a story.

Which is not to say that fear and panic hadn't struck the financial hearts of bankers as far back as ancient Rome, medieval Florence, and nineteenth-century Chicago. In 1866, when London's so-called banker's bank, Overend, Gurney, and Company, collapsed, the trust was carrying debt equivalent to more than $1000 million of today's dollars. In the aftermath of the disaster, the editor of *The Economist*, Walter Bagehot, sought to calm the markets. "Panic," he dismissed as simply a "technical" term, and noted that there were credit panics, capital panics, and bullion panics. "The stock market literally lives, in a great measure, upon this kind of excitement," the English financial journalist David Morier Evans concurred.

No doubt, panic was an old-fashioned financial motivation — the traditional product of bad harvests, overextended credit, gruesome quarterly reports, and depleted gold reserves. But the VIX added an ominous twist. During the pandemic panic of 2020, with the global death spiral still in its incipient phase, amid skyrocketing unemployment, crashing global markets, and political chaos, the VIX boomed. The index could thrive on the worst possible scenarios because the VIX divorced panic from its context, thereby creating a well-documented formation of language narratologists call *deixis* — a pointer without a point, a boundless space with no there there. The VIX was a bellwether in reverse, breathtaking in its detachment.

Since 2006, the Chicago Board Options Exchange has not only offered trading on the VIX, but trading in *options* on the VIX. That is, an option to buy or sell the square root of all options on an index. Recently, VelocityShares debuted a daily double VIX and an inverse VIX, the definitions of which are beyond dizzying.

The new financial world rests upon such foundations. It is unlikely that anyone believes that a share of a Credit Suisse index that replicates the inverse volatility of the twenty-five most highly capitalized technology stocks on the NASDAQ is anything real. The share, the index, the volatility, the inverse, and the basket of equities are each many steps removed from olive oil or a barbecue on a lazy summer afternoon. What you own is a metaphor of a metaphor of a metaphor.

By describing the illusion of money in the light of primitive belief, classical mythology, Christian ethos, and political propaganda, my hope is that going forward we might no longer be locked into believing the cant of financiers, the deceit of free and competitive markets as the essence of economic life. Instead, we might begin to understand that those who control money are less scientist than shaman, seer, storyteller, and soothsayer — those who spun ancient tales about sticks and stones, convincing others of their fiction.

In a financial world increasingly defined by indices, it is unlikely that money will ever make its way back to its origins — the empty shell, the hollow bead, the silver coin. Nor might such a homecoming bring happiness and prosperity to all. They say disruption is the key to progress. But there are hazards, and the stakes are high. If we cannot decrypt how the 1 percent are controlling and containing the fiction within new boundaries they are increasingly setting for themselves, we run the risk of being pawns and shells ourselves. We will become other people's money.

acknowledgments

THE ORIGINS OF THIS BOOK date back to a stifling September afternoon in 2013. I was pitching projects to a literary agent and getting nowhere.

"Don't you have any ideas people can relate to?" she asked.

It was getting late in the day. I gathered the cash from my pocket and let the bills scatter across the floor.

"How about that?"

"Money's good," she said. "What's the chapter outline?"

Which is my way — seven years later — of expressing gratitude for Elyse Cheney.

That said, there would be no *Money Plot* without the insistence on perfection and ever-abiding intensity of Judith Gurewich, to whom I am deeply grateful. Many additional thanks to Adam Eaglin, for unfailingly excellent counsel. I would also like to express appreciation for the enthusiasm and support of Janice Goldklang, Yvonne Cárdenas, and to the rest of the staff at Other Press.

Professor Anne Humpherys of the Graduate Center of the City University of New York first introduced me to the world of narrative theory. Others from the College of Staten Island and the Craig Newmark Graduate School of Journalism who have supported this project include Sarah Bartlett, Ashley Dawson, Lee Papa, Andrew Mendelson, and Judith Watson.

Kevin Conley first connected money and narrative in my mind when many years ago he asked for a "biography of gold" — even if the article that eventually appeared in *Town and Country* was about a golden pocketbook. A few years later I began producing articles for *Harper's Magazine* under the expert tutelage of Luke Mitchell, who not only insisted I learn everything there was to know about commodity futures, but taught me that the story is always about the story.

I am indebted to those who helped explain technical aspects of index funds, futures and option trading, swaps, and derivatives, most notably Eunice Bet-Mansour, Steve Kessler, and Steven Williams; and to Kevin Carde, for helping to clarify what were to me obscure mathematical formulae.

Special thanks to Paul Freedman for opening doors to the Middle Ages, and to Rachel Barkay, for sharing her research in numismatics.

General and pervasive gratitude for Elizabeth Beier, Jonathan Bulkeley, John Bunzel, Craig Chesley, Robin Doupe, Göette Lyffe, Rebecca Mead, Elke Phelan, Bob Potter, George Prochnik, Greg Stern, Linwood Warren, and David Yaffe. Damon Brandt brought me through many a perilous writerly moment. This book could not have been written without the wisdom of Jimmy Burgio and Anne Kahn; nor without the camaraderie of Lori Barnhill and John Gainor.

Isla, Griffin, Audrey, and Liam — thank you for accommodating the strange customs and habits of an itinerant scribbler. Phoebe and Julian — no amount of currency, real or imaginary, can match your kula. Lorraine Kaufman's insights and worldview are present on every page of this book; pages that were, in turn, haunted by Millard Kaufman's *Plots and Characters*.

The most credit and greatest debt is due Patty Laxton, to whom my bond is no fiction.

timeline

65,000 BC – Ostrich eggshell money; the first allegorical materializations of fear and security; before markets, money appears as metonomies and personifications.

10,000 BC – Plant and animal domestication begin.

7,000 BC – The first written language is developed in ancient Sumer to write a royal accountant's list of the emperor's properties.

1,600 BC – Landlocked Hittite empire uses money based on domesticated grains and livestock.

1,500 BC – Early kula trade: money as circulation and insurance.

1,000 BC – Dharmashastras define the laws of marriage rituals, trophy wives, and prenuptial contracts.

700 BC – Hesiod's *Works and Days*, allegory of the metals.

600 BC – Aesop's fables are written, and allegory emerges as a full-fledged literary form.

500 BC – The first precious metal coins, made of a silver-gold mixture known as electrum, are minted. Greek tragedy is born.

427 BC – Gorgias preaches the art of sophistry in the Agora.

405 BC – Euripedes' *The Bacchae* premieres in Athens. The play ends with the protagonist, King Pentheus, ripped to pieces in a ritual act of violence known as *sparagmos*.

325 BC – Aristotle's *Rhetoric* and *Poetics* define terms of drama, including "plot" and "reversal."

100 BC – Tryphon of Alexandria publishes his book on rhetoric, providing written definitions of metonymy, synecdoche, catachresis, and other tropes.

32 AD – Christ upsets the tables of the moneychangers; shareholders in his corporate body conform to a synecdochal model.

95 – Marcus Fabius Quintilian publishes his *Institutio Oratoria*, a twelve-volume textbook on the theory and practice of rhetoric.

400 – John Cassian publishes his *Institutes*, in which he defines four ways of reading; introduces anagogical reading.

480 – Battle of Tolbiac; Christians of Europe begin their long wait for the Second Coming.

500 – Prudentius publishes the *Psychomachia*.

725 – The word *wife* enters the English language, originally meaning a woman engaged in trade.

1086 – William the Conqueror's *Domesday Book* appears.

1250 – Pope Innocent IV institutes the idea of the corporate *persona ficta*.

1100–1500 – Series of Lateran Council rulings about the price of redemption; commercial culture expands; highly rendered medieval allegories include *The Romance of the Rose*, *The Divine Comedy*, *Everyman*, *Piers Plowman*, *The Pearl*.

1425 – *Monte delle Doti* commoditizes marriage as an interest-bearing account.

1518 – Silver thaler born in Germany.

1519 – Cortés asks Montezuma, "Where's the gold?"

1554 – *Lazarillo de Tormes* appears, birth of the novel.

1615 – Cervantes publishes the second part of *Don Quixote*, in which the hero claims to have read about himself in the first part of the book; birth of metafiction.

1659 – First personal check written.

1666 – The word *plutocracy* enters the English language.

1670 – Nicholas Barbon publishes "Discourse of Trade," in which he observes that money is "an imaginary value."

1682 – Mary Rowlandson publishes *A Narrative of the Captivity*, inaugurating the genre of the "captivity narrative," which would eventually include the nineteenth-century slave narratives of Henry Box Brown, Olaudah Equiano, Frederick Douglass, Harriet Jacobs, etc.

1690 – Massachusetts issues paper money, predating the paper notes of the Bank of England by four years.

1694 – The Bank of England Act enables the issue of Bank of England banknotes, as opposed to pounds sterling.

1696 – Sir Isaac Newton becomes "Warden of the Royal Mint."

1776 – Adam Smith publishes *The Wealth of Nations*, in which he suggests his own currency creation myth, that money began with barter, and introduces the personified "invisible hand."

1789 – United States dollar invented.

1798–1819 – The Bank of England floats the pound.

1816–1836 – The twenty-year lifespan of The Second Bank of the United States.

1839 – Texas redback dollar born.

1850 – Texas redback dollar dies.

1861–1865 – Unbacked Union greenback dollars issued.

1869 – Wagner's *Das Rheingold* premieres at the Munich National Theater.

1871 – France pays Germany five billion francs in reparations for Franco-Prussian War, all of it in gold.

1873 – Germany moves to the gold standard; the rest of Europe follows.

1889 – Andrew Carnegie publishes *The Gospel of Wealth*.

1896 – The Populist Silverite William Jennings Bryan delivers the Cross of Gold speech and wins the nomination at the Democratic National Convention. He loses the national election that year and again in 1900.

1900 – Louis Bachelier defends a dissertation that uses partial derivatives to calculate the "true" price of rentes, marking the birth of mathematical finance.

1913 – Woodrow Wilson signs into law the United States Federal Reserve.

1922 – Bronisław Malinowski publishes *Argonauts of the Western Pacific*, in which he recounts his travels to Melanesia and the mysterious kula ring.

1923 – Georg Friedrich Knapp's *The State Theory of Money* first appears in English translation.

1925 – Alfred Kroeber publishes *Handbook of the Indians of California*, in which he notes that the more a Yurok Indian thinks about acquiring dentalia, their shellfish currency, the more he acquires.

1932 – Berle and Gardiner publish *The Modern Corporation and Private Property*, and note the latent fictionality of shareholding.

1958 – Vladimir Propp's *Morpology of the Folktale* appears in English translation.

1970 – Angus Fletcher publishes *Allegory: Theory of a Symbolic Mode*, in which he demonstrates the relationship between modern thought and medieval allegorical thought.

1971 – Richard Nixon floats the dollar. That same year, Wells Fargo introduces the first index fund as a vehicle for the Samsonite Corporation's $6 million pension fund.

1973 – Inspired by Louis Bachelier, MIT Professors Fischer Black and Myron Scholes publish the most famous paper in all of quantitative finance, on option pricing. The Chicago Board Options Exchange opens for business, and Texas Instruments introduces a calculator with a built-in Black-Scholes formula, which traders immediately begin using on exchange floors. Burton Malkiel's *A Random Walk Down Wall Street* becomes a best seller.

1987 – Volatility is theorized as an underlying asset; earliest ancestor of the VIX.

1989 – The phrase "trophy wife" first appears in print in an article by Julie Connelly published by *Fortune* magazine.

1993 – The first index fund offered by the American Stock Exchange, the S&P 500 Trust.

2007 – Warren Buffet loses $900 million in the debt hole created by the leveraged buyout of Energy Future Holdings.

2008 – The first global financial meltdown of the twenty-first century occurs.

2009 – The "Genesis Block" of fifty Bitcoin released, followed by digital currencies Ethereum, CannabisCoin, Dentacoin, Whoppercoin, and hundreds of others.

2018 – On February 5, the VIX doubles in value (up 103.99 percent from previous close).

2020 – Covid-19 pandemic sends global markets into turmoil. VIX and gamma skyrocket. In order to avoid a credit meltdown, the United States establishes the Secondary Market Corporate Credit Facility, through which the Federal Reserve Bank purchases bond ETFs.

glossary: selected terms

ALLEGORY – A form of literary expression in which every character and metaphor stands in a strict one-to-once correspondence with that which it represents.

ANAGOGY – A form of reading in which the end of the story defines every moment of the plot.

APORIA – A literary term that indicates undecidability and instability of meaning. Ambiguity, equivocation, oxymoron, and paradox are all varieties of aporia.

BOUSTROPHEDON – A form of reading and writing that "follows the oxen" back and forth from right to left, then left to right; may also refer to the bidirectional mode of dot matrix printers.

BROWNIAN MOTION – The apparently random movement, originally observed in a speck of dust as it progressed through a drop of water; visually and mathematically similar to the movement of markets. In 1905 the English biostatistician Karl Pearson defined the motion as a "random walk."

CAMBIUM ET RECAMBIUM – Medieval foreign exchange contract the church sanctioned in order to normalize interest bearing instruments.

CAMPAGNIA – Medieval contract that limited liability of shareholders in a commercial venture; from the Latin *cumpanis* — one eating the same bread.

CAPTIVITY NARRATIVE – A term of literary analysis to describe a form of narrative that became popular in seventeenth-century America, first typified by stories in which indigenous populations took white Europeans hostages; later applied to a wide variety of stories.

CATACHRESIS – "Violent naming" or yoking of a word to a thing.

CHARTALISM – Georg Friedrich Knapp's nineteenth-century monetary theory, which defined money as a legal construct, an idea not necessarily connected to any material, such as gold or silver.

COMMENDA – Medieval contract, "all in the same boat."

CYPRAEA MONETA – Snailshell money, also known as the cowrie, the most pervasive form of primitive money. Used in trade, as gambling chips, and to forecast the future.

DAIMON – A term of analysis for allegory; the demon or spirit that inhabits each object and character, providing energy and motivation.

DEIXIS – A word or phrase that needs other words or phrases in order to become comprehensible. Examples include "here," "there," "me," or "you," none of which can be precisely defined without further contextualization.

DENOUEMENT – Settlement of the plot.

DENTALIA – A form of mollusk shell money popular among the Yurok indigenous group of the American Northwest.

DELTA – A mathematical construct used by derivatives traders to indicate the level of sympathy between an asset and its underlying value.

ETF, ETN, ETP – Exchange-Traded Fund; Exchange-Traded Note; Exchange-Traded Product.

GAMMA – A mathematical construct used by derivatives traders to indicate levels of fear and panic.

HOMO ECONOMICUS – Personification of a theory asserting that people are strictly economic beings, and markets perfectly efficient.

IRONY – Literary term used to describe those instances when the implied meaning of a word or phrase is the opposite of the literal meaning.

JUNO MONETA – Ancient Roman goddess, personifying both money and "warning."

KOSMOI – Term of analysis for allegory; the character or object that is inhabited by a ghost or *daimon*.

KULA – A form of circular Melanesian bead and trinket exchange that dumbfounded the anthropologist Bronisław Malinowski.

MARTINGALE – A popular wager: heads or tails; also, the bridle of a horse; also, a model for efficient markets in which every participant faces a set of binary options, buy or sell.

METAFICTION – Recognition within a fiction that the fiction is a fiction.

METAPHOR – Something that represents something else, often abstract; from the Greek *metaphorá*, meaning "to transfer." Metaphors can turn or *trope* one thing into another.

METONYMY – Metaphor of contiguity and magical sympathy; such as using the word "crown" to stand for the king.

NIBELUNG – Mythical character from ancient German mythology who lives underground, mining gold and precious metals.

OPTION – A financial strategy that seeks to evade the binary of either/or choices.

PAROUSIA – Greek term for epiphany; also a term for classical coinage.

PEREGRINATIO – The epic journey of a crusading knight.

PACTUM – First medieval transnational credit agreement.

PARADOX – A literary term for the logical impossibility of something being both "A" and "not-A" at the same time.

PERMUTATIO – A church-sanctioned system of interest-bearing foreign exchange.

PERIPETEIA, OR PERIPETY – Originated by Aristotle, a term that refers to the moment of plot reversal.

PERSONA FICTA – Medieval version of corporate personhood, instituted by Pope Innocent IV, c. 1250.

PERSONIFICATION – Metaphor in which human attributes are given to nonhuman objects; e.g., "rosy-fingered dawn."

PICARESQUE – The "horse-drawn" tale; form of the first novel, popularized during the Spanish Golden Age of literature.

PLOT POINT – Based on the theory of the Russian Structuralist, Vladimir Propp; the idea that there is only one plot, but that it can begin or end at various "points" along a single line.

PLUTO, MAMMON, MEPHISTOPHELES, OGUN, SATAN – Sad and violent gods of underworld riches.

PLUTONOMY – the rulership of the planet by those with a minimum net worth of $100 million.

PSYCHOMACHIA – Term of analysis for the plot of allegory, in which a number of contrary forces such as fear, bravery, greed, and charity vie for the soul of a protagonist.

QUIXOTIC – Pertaining to the character of Don Quixote, eponymous hero of what is often considered the first modern novel. The term may imply metafictionality, as the book refers to itself as a book. This idea of fiction's awareness of itself as a fiction was a key step forward in the history of imaginary money, or "money of account."

RESERVE CURRENCY – The money central banks of sovereign states hold in order to help stabilize their own currency.

RHO – Modern "Greek" term of mathematical finance used to indicate the interest rate.

ROGADIA – Medieval commercial contract meaning "partner in prayer."

SEMIOTICS – The scientific study of signs; rooted in the ancient Greek word *seme*, which can mean either "word" or "coin."

SOCIETAS – A medieval contractual formula by means of which ever-larger groups of people could join in commercial ventures while limiting their liability.

SPARAGMOS – Greek term for the tearing apart and violent dismemberment of a protagonist.

SYNECDOCHE – Metaphor of "part for whole," or that which makes the "invisible visible." One of the concepts behind both coinage and leveraged debt.

TELOS – Greek work that can mean either goal or payment.

THETA – Modern "Greek" term of mathematical finance that indicates the passage or decay of time.

TROPE – Greek word for "turn," a figure of speech used to indicate all sorts of metaphoric transfer mechanisms; related to words such as trophy and apotropaic.

UNDERLYING VALUE – The idea that a metaphor, such as money, stands for something other than itself, commonly conceived to be precious metal; historically, either gold or silver.

VEGA – A mathematical construct used by derivatives traders to indicate the level of sympathy between an asset and the excitement or "volatility" of its underlying value.

VIX – Introduced in exchange-traded form in 1993, an index of the volatility of stocks; the "fear index"; money's new bellwether.

WAMPUM – Indigenous American shell money immediately utilized by European colonists, who soon after landing in the New World ran out of the precious metal coinage they had brought with them from the Old World; also a form of recounting history and treaties; that is, a form of writing.

WILDCAT DOLLAR – Following Andrew Jackson's destruction of the Second Bank of the United States, bank-chartered money of nineteenth-century America that led to numerous booms, busts, panics, and depressions.

bibliography

Aeschylus. *The Oresteia: Agamemnon; The Libation Bearers; The Eumenides.* New York: Penguin Classics, 1984.

Aesop. *The Complete Fables.* Translated by Robert and Olivia Temple. New York: Penguin Classics, 1998.

Agricola, Georgius. *De Re Metallica.* Translated by Herbert Hoover and Lou Hoover. Mansfield, CT: Martino Publishing, 2014.

Ahamed, Liaquat. *Lords of Finance: The Bankers Who Broke the World.* New York: Penguin Books, 2009.

Ancell, Kate. "The Generation of the First Index Fund." In *Chicago Booth Magazine.* Chicago: Alumni Magazine for the University of Chicago Booth School of Business, 2012.

Andrews, Robert. "Equilibrium in Biblical Exegesis: Why Evangelicals Need the Catholic Church." (2015). *Dissertations.* Paper 1628. http://ecommons.luc.edu/luc_diss/1628

Anonymous. *The Adventures of a Bank-Note, In Two Volumes.* London: T. Davies, 1772.

Anonymous. *Chrysal; or The Adventures of a Guinea.* London: Hector M'Lean, 1821.

Anonymous. *Everyman and Other Miracle and Morality Plays.* New York: Dover Publications, 1995.

Anonymous. *The Life of Lazarillo de Tormes.* Translated by W. S. Merwin. New York: NYRB Classics, 2004.

Anonymous. *The Tain: Translated from the Irish Epic Tain Bo Cuailnge.*
Translated by Thomas Kinsella. Oxford: Oxford University Press,
2002.

Arata, Luigi. "The Definition of Metonymy in Ancient Greece." *Style.*
Vol. 39, No. 1, pp. 55–70. University Park, PA: Penn State University
Press, 2005.

Aristotle. *Poetics.* Translated by Malcolm Heath. New York: Penguin
Classics, 1997.

Auerbach, Erich. *Mimesis: The Representation of Reality in Western
Literature.* Translated by Willard R. Trask. Princeton, NJ: Princeton
University Press, 1953.

Bachelier, Louis. *Louis Bachelier's Theory of Speculation: The Origins of
Modern Finance.* Translated by Mark Davis. Princeton, NJ: Princeton
University Press, 2006.

Bagehot, Walter. *Lombard Street: A Description of the Money Market.*
Homewood, IL. Richard D. Irwin, 1962.

Bailyn, Bernard. *The Ideological Origins of the American Revolution.*
Cambridge, MA: Belknap Press, 2017.

Barbon, Nicholas. *A Discourse of Trade.* London: The Melbourne, 1690.

Barkay, Rachel. "The Byzantine Period Wishing Spring of Ein Tur
in the Holy Land." *XII Internationaler Numismatischer Congress,
Proceedings II* (1997).

Barton, Bruce. *The Man Nobody Knows.* Boca Raton, FL: Lewis Press, 2011.

Baudrillard, Jean. *The Mirror of Production.* Translated by Mark Poster.
St. Louis: Telos Press, 1975.

———. *Simulacra and Simulation.* Translated by Sheila Faria Glaser. Ann
Arbor: The University of Michigan Press, 1994.

Beer, Gillian. *Open Fields: Science in Cultural Encounter.* Oxford: Oxford
University Press, 1996.

Berle, Adolf; and Means, Gardiner. *The Modern Corporation And Private
Property.* New York: Routledge, 1968.

Bet-Mansour, Eunice. Personal interview. November 14, 2013.

Bhattacharya, Rahul. *The Book of Greeks.* Hong Kong: Risk Latte Company Limited, 2011.

Bibb, Henry. *The Life and Adventures of Henry Bibb: An American Slave.* Madison, WI: University of Wisconsin Press, 2000.

Bijovsky, Gabriela. *The Currency of the Fifth Century CE in Palestine — Some Reflections in Light of the Numismatic Evidence.* Israel Antiquities Authority. Academia.edu.

———. *Gold Coin and Small Change: Monetary Circulation in Fifth–Seventh Century Byzantine Palestine.* Trieste: EUT Edizione Universita di Trieste, 2012.

Black, Fischer; and Scholes, Myron. "The Pricing of Options and Corporate Liabilities." In *The Journal of Political Economy.* Vol. 81, No. 3 (1973): 637–654.

Boas, Franz. "The Social Organization of the Kwakiutl." *American Anthropologist.* Vol. 22, No. 2 (1920): 111–126.

Boone, Daniel; and Hawkes, Francis Lister. *Daniel Boone's Own Story and The Adventures of Daniel Boone.* New York: Dover Publications, 2010.

Bordo, Michael: "The Imbalances of the Bretton Woods System 1965 to 1973: U.S. Inflation, the Elephant in the Room." *Hoover Institution Economic Working Papers.* Economic Working Paper 18115. Stanford: Hoover Institution, 2018.

Bremmer, Robert P. *Chairman of the Fed: William McChesney Martin Jr. and the Creation of the American Financial System.* New Haven and London: Yale University Press, 2004.

Brown, Charles Brockden. *Three Gothic Novels: Wieland, Arthur Mervyn, Edgar Huntley.* New York: Library of America, 1998.

Brown, Henry Box. *Narrative of the Life of Henry Box Brown.* New York: Dover Thrift Editions, 2015

Brown, Wendy. *Undoing the Demos: Neoliberalism's Stealth Revolution.* New York: Zone Books, 2015.

Bryan, William Jennings. *The Cross of Gold*. Lincoln: University of Nebraska Press, 1996.

Bullfinch, Thomas: *The Age of Fable, or Beauties of Mythology*. New York: Tudor Publishing Company, 1936.

Bunyan, John. *The Pilgrim's Progress*. New York: W. W. Norton and Company, 2008.

Burke, Kenneth. *A Grammar of Motives: The Problems of Meaning in Dramatic Perspective*. New York: Prentice-Hall, Inc., 1952.

Burrough, Bryan; and Helyar, John. *Barbarians at the Gate: The Fall of RJR Nabisco*. New York: Harper Business, 2009.

Butcher, Kevin, ed. *Debasement: Manipulation of Coin Standards in Pre-Modern Monetary Systems*. Oxford and Philadelphia: Oxbow Books, 2020.

Campbell, Brian. *Rivers and the Power of Ancient Rome*. Chapel Hill: The University of North Carolina Press, 2012.

Campbell, Joseph. *The Hero with a Thousand Faces*. Princeton, NJ: Princeton University Press, 1968.

Carla-Uhink, Filippo. "The End of Roman Gold Coinage and the Disintegration of a Monetary Area." PDF download from Academia.edu

Caro, Robert. *Means of Ascent*. New York: Vintage, 1991.

Casanova, Giacomo. *The Story of My Life*. New York: Penguin Classics, 2001.

Cassian, John. *The Institutes*. Translated by Boniface Ramsey. Mahwah, NJ: Newman Press of the Palest Press, 2000.

Castillo, Bernal Díaz Del. *The Conquest of New Spain*. Translated by John M. Cohen. New York: Penguin Classics, 1963.

Cavell, Stanley. *The Senses of Walden*. Chicago: The University of Chicago Press, 1992.

Cervantes Saavedra, Miguel de. *Don Quixote*. New York: Penguin Classics, 2003.

Chernow, Ron. *Alexander Hamilton*. New York: Penguin Books, 2004.

Cicero. *Rhetorica ad Herennium*. Translated by Harry Caplan. Cambridge: Harvard University Press, 1954.

Cohan, William D. *Why Wall Street Matters*. New York: Random House, 2017.

Coinage Act of 1792. Accessed from https://www.usmint.gov/learn/history/historical-documents/coinage-act-of-april-2-1792

Coinage Act of 1873. Accessed from https://fraser.stlouisfed.org/title/1095

Connally, John; and Agronsky, Martin. Interview accessed from https://www.youtube.com/watch?v=SsIGlSFB7E4

Connally, John. With Mickey Herskowitz. *In History's Shadow: An American Odyssey*. New York: Hyperion, 1993.

Connelly, Julie. "The CEO's Second Wife." *Fortune*, August 28, 1989.

Cotrugli, Benedetto. *The Book of the Art of Trade*. New York: Palgrave Macmillan, 2016.

Cribb, Joe. "The President's Address: Money as Metaphor 4." *The Numismatic Chronicle*, Vol. 169 (2009): 461–529.

Cronon, William. *Nature's Metropolis: Chicago and the Great West*. New York: W. W. Norton and Company, 1991.

Crosby, Alfred W. *The Measure of Reality: Quantification and Western Society, 1250–1600*. Cambridge: Cambridge University Press, 1997.

De Roover, Raymond. *San Bernardino of Siena and Sant'Antonino of Florence: The Two Great Economic Thinkers of the Middle Ages*. Boston: Harvard Graduate School of Business Administration, 1967.

Deane, Marjorie; and Pringle, Robert. *The Central Banks*. New York: Viking Penguin, 1994.

Del Mar, Alexander, *A History of the Precious Metals from Earliest Times to the Present*. New York: Cambridge Encyclopedia Company, 1902.

Derby, Elias. *The History of Paper Money in the Province of Massachusetts Before the Revolution, with an Account of the Land Bank and the Silver Bank*. Ann Arbor: University of Michigan Library, 2011.

Derounian-Stodola, ed. *Women's Indian Captivity Narratives*. New York: Penguin Classics, 1998.

Diamond, Jared. *Guns, Germs, and Steel: The Fates of Human Societies*. New York: Norton, 1999.

Douglass, Frederick. *Autobiographies: Narrative of the Life of Frederick Douglass, an American Slave*. New York: Library of America, 1994.

Douthwaite, Richard. *The Ecology of Money*. Google Books, 1999.

Duby, Georges. *The Early Growth of the European Economy*. Ithaca, NY: Cornell University Press, 1974.

Ehrlichman, John. *The Company*. New York: Pocket Books, 1976.

Ehrlichman, John. *Witness to Power: The Nixon Years*. New York: Simon and Schuster, 1982.

Einaudi, Luigi. *Selected Economic Essays*. New York: Palgrave Macmillan, 2006.

Ellis, Bret Easton. *American Psycho*. New York: Vintage, 1991.

Engels, Friedrich. *Origin of the Family, Private Property and the State*. New York: International Publishers Co., Inc., 1942.

———. *The Peasant War in Germany*. Translated by Moissays J. Olgin. New York: International Publishers, 1934.

Farley, Jack. "Questioning the 'Win-Win' Consensus on the Second Bank of the United States." Unpublished paper.

Fletcher, Angus. *Allegory: The Theory of a Symbolic Mode*. Ithaca, NY: Cornell University Press, 1964.

Foreign Exchange Training Manual, Lehman Brothers. Confidential document prepared for Barclays, undated.

Foucault, Michel. *Discipline and Punish: The Birth of the Prison*. Translated by Alan Sheridan. New York: Vintage, 1995.

———. *History of Sexuality, Vol. 1*. Translated by Robert Hurley. New York: Vintage, 1990.

———. *The Order of Things: An Archaeology of the Human Sciences*. New York: Vintage Books, 1994.

Franklin, Benjamin. *The Autobiography of Benjamin Franklin*. New York: Dover Thrift Editions, 2016.

———. *The Way to Wealth*. Carlisle, MA: Applewood Books, 1986.

Frazer, Sir James. *The Golden Bough: A Study in Magic and Religion*. New York: The Macmillan Company, 1940.

Freidenberg, Olga. *Image and Concept: Mythopoetic Roots of Literature*. Amsterdam: Harwood Academic Publishers, 1997.

Frost, Robert. "The Road Not Taken," in *Robert Frost: Collected Poems, Prose, and Plays*. New York: Library of America, 1995.

Gagain, John R. *Visions for the Global Economy*. Bloomington: iUniverse, 2012.

Gandila, Andrei. "The Mint of Thessalonica and the Mediterranean Economy in the 6th-7th c." *Revue Belge de Numismatique et de Sigillographie*. CLXIV (2018): 426-495.

Geisst, Charles. *Wheels of Fortune: The History of Speculation from Scandal to Respectability*. New York: John Wiley & Sons, Inc., 2002.

General Mining Act of 1872. Accessed from https://web.archive. org/web/20160519051800/http://www.usminer.com/ the-general-mining-act-of-1872/

Ghose, Zulfikar. *Hamlet, Prufrock and Language*. New York: Macmillan, 1978.

Gilchrist, J. *The Church and Economic Activity in the Middle Ages*. New York: St. Martin's Press, 1969.

Gilder, George. *Life After Google: The Fall of Big Data and the Rise of the Blockchain Economy*. Washington, DC: Regnery Gateway Publishing, 2018.

Goodman, Philip, ed. *The Passover Anthology*. Philadelphia: The Jewish Publication Society, 1961.

Goody, Jack. *Death, Property, and the Ancestors*. London: Routledge, 1962.

———. *The Domestication of the Savage Mind*. Cambridge: Cambridge University Press, 1977.

Goody, Jack; and Tambiah, S. J. *Bridewealth and Dowry*. Cambridge, MA: Cambridge University Press, 1973.

Gouge, William. *The Fiscal History of Texas*. Philadelphia: Lippincott, Grambo, and Co., 1852.

Goux, Jean-Joseph. *The Coiners of Language*. Translated by Jennifer Curtiss Gage. Norman and London: University of Oklahoma Press, 1994.

Gower, John. *Confessio Amantis*. London: Bell and Daldy Fletet Street, 1857.

Graeber, David. *Debt: The First 5,000 Years*. Brooklyn and London: Melville House, 2011.

Graham, Philip. *The Life and Poems of Mirabeau B. Lamar*. Chapel Hill: University of North Carolina Press, 1938.

Graves, Robert. *The Greek Myths, Volumes One and Two*. New York: Penguin Books, 1957.

Greenblatt, Stephen. *The Swerve: How the World Became Modern*. New York and London: W. W. Norton and Company, 2011.

Gregory of Tours. *A History of the Franks*. New York: Penguin Classics, 1976.

Haldeman, H. R. *The Haldeman Diaries: Inside the Nixon White House*. New York: G.P. Putnam's Sons, 1994.

Hall, James. "The Adventures of a One Dollar Note." *The Port Folio*, January 1817. Philadelphia: Harrison Hall, 1817: 242–247.

Hamann, Johann. *Writings on Philosophy and Language*. Translated by Kenneth Haynes. Cambridge: Cambridge University Press, 2007.

Hamilton, Alexander. "The Utility of the Union in Respect to Revenue from the New York Packet." Federalist 12.

Hamilton, Edith. *Mythology: Timeless Tales of Gods and Heroes*. New York: Little, Brown and Company, 1942.

Harari, Yuval Noah. *Sapiens: A Brief History of Humankind*. New York: Harper Perennial, 2015.

Harl, Kenneth W. *Coinage in the Roman Economy, 300 B.C. to A.D. 700.* Baltimore and London: The Johns Hopkins University Press, 1996.

Harris, George Washington. *Sut Lovingood's Yarns.* Edited by M. Thomas Inge. College and University Press Services, 1966.

Hasselbach-Andee, Rebecca, ed. *A Companion to Ancient Near Eastern Languages.* Hoboken, NJ: Wiley Blackwell, 2020.

Hautcoeur, Pierre-Cyrille; Rezaee, Amir; and Riva, Angelo. "Stock exchange industry regulation The Paris Bourse, 1893–1998." http://eh.net/eha/wp-content/uploads/2013/11/Hautcoeurb.pdf

Hawthorne, Nathaniel. *The Scarlet Letter.* New York: W. W. Norton and Company, 1988.

Henriques, Diana B. *A First-Class Catastrophe: The Road to Black Monday, The Worst Day in Wall Street History.* New York: Henry Holt and Company, 2017.

Herbert, Frank. *Dune.* New York: Ace, 1990.

Hesiod. *Works and Days.* Translated by A. E. Stallings. New York: Penguin Classics, 2018.

Hetzel, Robert; and Leach, Ralph. "The Treasury-Fed Accord: A New Narrative Account." *Economic Quarterly,* Vol. 87/1. Richmond: Federal Reserve Bank of Richmond, Winter 2001.

Holmes, Douglas R. *Economy of Words: Communicative Imperatives in Central Banks.* Chicago and London: The University of Chicago Press, 2014.

Homer. *The Odyssey.* Translated by Robert Fitzgerald. Garden City, NY: Anchor Books, 1963.

———. *The Iliad.* Translated by Robert Fitzgerald. Garden City, NY: Anchor Books, 1963.

Horkheimer, Max; and Adorno, Theodore. *Dialectic of Enlightenment: Philosophical Fragments.* Translated by Edmund Jephcott. Stanford: Stanford University Press, 2002.

Hume, David. *Of Money, and Other Economic Essays.* http://davidhume
.org/texts/etv1.html

Hummel, Jeffrey. "The Jacksonians, Banking, and Economic Theory:
A Reinterpretation." *Journal of Libertarian Studies,* Vol. 2, No. 2
(1978): 151–165.

Jacobs, Harriet. *Incidents in the Life of a Slave Girl.* New York: Signet
Classics, 2010.

James, William. *The Varieties of Religious Experience: A Study in Human
Nature.* New York: Penguin American Library, 1982.

Kapur, Away; Macleod, Niall; and Singh, Narendra. "Plutonomy: Buying
Luxury, Explaining Global Imbalances." http://www.lust-for-life
.org/Lust-ForLife/CitigroupImbalances_October2009/Citigroup
Imbalances_October2009.pdf

Kaufman, Frederick. *Bet the Farm: How Food Stopped Being Food.* New
York: Wiley, 2012.

Kaufman, Millard. *Plots and Characters: A Screenwriter on Screenwriting.*
Los Angeles: Really Great Books, 1999.

Kermode, Frank. *The Sense of an Ending: Studies in the Theory of Fictions.*
Oxford: Oxford University Press, 2000.

Kessler, Steven. Personal interview, November 11, 2013.

Keynes, John Maynard. *The General Theory of Employment, Interest, and
Money.* http://etext.library.adelaide.edu.au/k/k44g/k44g/html

———. *A Tract on Monetary Reform.* London: MacMillan and Co., 1924.

Khan, Lina. "Amazon's Antitrust Paradox." *Yale Law Journal,* Vol. 126,
No. 3 (January 2017).

Klein, Naomi. *No Logo.* New York: Picador, 2000.

Knapp, Georg Friedrich. *The State Theory of Money.* Translated by H. M.
Lucas and J. Bonar. Mansfield Centre, CT: Martino Publishing, 2013.

Kornbluh, Anna. *Realizing Capital: Financial and Psychic Economies in
Victorian Form.* New York: Fordham University Press, 2014.

Kroeber, A. L. *Handbook of the Indians of California*. New York: Dover Publications, Inc., 1976.

La Barge, Leigh Claire. *Scandals and Abstractions: Financial Fiction of the Long 1980s*. Oxford: Oxford University Press, 2015.

Langland, William. *Piers Plowman*. New York: W. W. Norton and Company, 2006.

Lanstein, Ronald J.; and William W. Jahnke. "Applying Capital Market Theory to Investing." *Interfaces* 9, No. 2 (1979): 23–38. Accessed April 10, 2020. www.jstor.org/stable/25059753

Levi-Strauss, Claude. *Myth and Meaning*. New York: Schocken Books, 1979.

Lewis, Michael. *Liar's Poker*. New York: W. W. Norton and Co., 1989.

Livingston, James. *No More Work. Why Full Employment Is a Bad Idea*. Chapel Hill: The University of North Carolina Press, 2016.

Lockheed Hearings. *Congressional Record*, September 16, 1971, pp. 32143–32217.

Lopez, Robert S. *The Commercial Revolution of the Middle Ages, 950–1350*. Cambridge: Cambridge University Press, 1976.

Lopez, Robert S.; and Raymond, Irving W., editors and translators. *Medieval Trade in the Mediterranean World: Illustrative Documents*. New York: Columbia University Press, 2001.

Lorris, Guillaume de. *The Romance of the Rose*. Translated by Frances Horgan. Oxford: Oxford University Press, 2009.

Luckett, Thomas. "Imaginary Currency and Real Guillotines: The Intellectual Origins of the Financial Terror in France." *Historical Reflections*, Vol. 31, No. 1 (2005): 117–139.

Lucretius. *On the Nature of Things*. Translated by Robert Allison. London: Arthur L. Humphreys, 1919.

Lyotard, Jean-Francois. *Libidinal Economy*. Translated by Ian Hamilton Grant. Bloomington and Indianapolis: Indiana University Press, 1993.

Magens, Nicholas. *An Essay on Insurances*. London: J. Haberkorn, 1755.

Malinowski, Bronisław. *Argonauts of the Western Pacific: An Account of Native Enterprise and Adventure in the Archipelagoes of Melanesian New Guinea*. London: Routledge and Kegan Paul Ltd., 1966.

———. *Magic, Science and Religion and Other Essays*. New York: Doubleday Anchor Books, 1954.

Malkiel, Burton. *A Random Walk Down Wall Street: The Time-Tested Strategy for Successful Investing*. New York: W. W. Norton and Company, 2016.

Manu. *The Laws of Manu*. Translated by Wendy Doniger. New York: Penguin Books, 1991.

Martin, Felix. *Money: The Unauthorized Biography*. New York: Alfred A. Knopf, 2014.

Martin, Wendy, ed. *Colonial American Travel Narratives*. New York: Penguin Classics, 1994.

Martineau, Harriet. *Illustrations of Political Economy*. London: Charles Fox, 1832.

Marx, Karl. *Capital: A Critique of Political Economy*. New York: The Modern Library, 1906.

———. *Grundrisse*. New York: Penguin Books in association with New Left Review, 1973.

Mauss, Marcel. *A General Theory of Magic*. Translated by Robert Brain. London: Routledge, 1972.

McCann, James C. *People of the Plow: An Agricultural History of Ethiopia, 1800–1990*. Madison: The University of Wisconsin Press, 1995.

McCloskey, Deirdre N. *The Rhetoric of Economics*. Madison: The University of Wisconsin Press, 1998.

McCool, Daniel. *River Republic: The Fall and Rise of America's Rivers*. New York: Columbia University Press, 2012.

McCullough, David. *John Adams*. New York: Simon and Schuster, 2001.

McLuhan, Marshall. "Myth and Mass Media." In *Myth and Mythmaking*, ed. Henry A. Murray. New York: George Braziller, Inc., 1960.

———. *Understanding Media: The Extensions of Man*. New York: Signet Books, 1964.

Melville, Herman. *Redburn, White-Jacket, Moby-Dick*. New York: Library of America, 1983.

Metclaf, David. "The Mint of Thessalonica in the Early Byzantine Period." In *Villes et peuplement dans l'Illyricum protobyzantin*, pp. 111–129. Rome: l'École Française de Rome, 1984.

Michaels, Walter Benn. *The Gold Standard and the Logic of Naturalism*. Berkeley: University of California Press, 1987.

Morrison, Cécile. "Byzantine Money: Its Production and Circulation." In *The Economic History of Byzantium: From the Seventh through the Fifteenth Century*. Angeliki E. Laiou, editor in chief. Washington, DC: Dumbarton Oaks Research Library and Collection, 2002.

Morrison, Cécile; and Schwartz, James. "Vandal Silver Coinage in the Name of Honorius." *Museum Notes (American Numismatic Society)*: Vol. 27, pp. 149–179, 1982.

Mortimer, Thomas. *A General Dictionary of Commerce, Trade, and Manufactures*. London: Richard Phillips, 1810.

Natenberg, Sheldon. *Option Volatility and Pricing: Advanced Trading Strategies and Techniques*. New York: McGraw-Hill, 1994.

Needler, George Henry, trans. *The Nibelungenlied*. New York: Henry Holt and Company, 1904.

Niebuhr, Richard H. *Christ and Culture*. New York: Harper and Row, 1951.

Nietzsche, Friedrich. *The Birth of Tragedy and The Case of Wagner*. Translated by Walter Kaufmann. New York: Vintage Books, 1967.

Nixon, Richard. "The Challenge of Peace." Speech accessed from https://www.youtube.com/watch?v=ye4uRvkAPhA

———. *In the Arena: A Memoir of Victory, Defeat and Renewal*. New York: Pocket Books, 1990.

———. *The Memoirs of Richard Nixon*. New York: Grosset and Dunlap, 1978.

———. *Six Crises*. New York: Doubleday and Company, Inc., 1962.

NixonTapes.org. http://nixontapes.org/pdd/1971-08-01_31.pdf Accessed March 10, 2020.

Nolte, Ingmar; Salmon, Mark; and Adcock, Chris, editors. *High Frequency Trading and Limit Order Book Dynamics*. London and New York: Routledge, 2015.

Norris, Frank. *The Pit — A Story of Chicago (The Epic of the Wheat)*. New York: Penguin Classics, 1994.

O'Hagan, Andrew. "The Satoshi Affair." *London Review of Books*, Vol. 38, No. 13. June 30, 2016.

Oliphant, Laurence. "The Autobiography of a Joint Stock Company (Limited)." In *The Financial System of Nineteenth-Century Britain*, ed. by Mary Poovey. Oxford: Oxford University Press, 2003.

Ovid. *Metamorphoses*. Translated by Mary M. Innes. New York: Penguin Classics, 1988.

Papaconstantinou, George. *Game Over: The Inside Story of the Greek Crisis*. Athens: Kyriakos Papadopoulos Publishing, 2016.

Patel, Raj. *The Value of Nothing*. New York: Picador, 2009.

Pearson, Karl. "The Problem of the Random Walk." *Nature*. 72, 294 (1905).

Penna, Vasiliki. "Reassessing the Gold Coinage of Basil I: The Testimony of an Unknown Byzantine 'Pattern' Coin." In *Travaux et mémoires 16: Mélanges*, edited by Cécile Morrisson. Paris: Association des Amis du Centre d'Histoire et Civilisation de Byzance, 2010.

Pickens, Boone. *Boone*. Boston: Houghton Mifflin Company, 1987.

Piketty, Thomas. *Capital in the Twenty-First Century*. Translated by Arthur Goldhammer. Cambridge, MA, and London: The Belknap Press of Harvard University Press, 2014.

Pinnell, Owen, and Jess Kelly. "Slave markets found on Instagram and other apps." *BBC News Arabic*, October 31, 2019. https://www.bbc.com/news/technology-50228549. Accessed 3/28/2020.

Polanyi, Karl. *The Great Transformation: The Political and Economic Origins of Our Time*. Boston: Beacon Press, 2001.

Polanyi, Karl; Arensberg, Conrad; and Pearson, Harry, editors. *Trade and Market in the Early Empires*. Glencoe, IL: The Free Press, 1957.

Polo, Marco. *The Travels of Marco Polo*. Translated by Manuel Komroff. New York: The Modern Library, 1953.

Poovey, Mary. *Genres of the Credit Economy: Mediating Value in Eighteenth- and Nineteenth-Century Britain*. Chicago and London: University of Chicago Press, 2008.

Prince, Gerald. *A Dictionary of Narratology*. Lincoln and London: University of Nebraska Press, 2003.

Principe, Lawrence M. *The Secrets of Alchemy*. Chicago and London: The University of Chicago Press, 2013.

Propp, Vladimir. *Morphology of the Folktale*. Translated by Laurence Scott. Austin: University of Texas Press, 1968.

Prudentius. *The Psychomachia of Prudentius*. Translated by Aaron Pelttari. Norman: University of Oklahoma Press, 2019.

Quiggin, A. Hingston. *A Survey of Primitive Money: The Beginnings of Currency*. London and New York: Routledge, 2018.

Quintilian. *Institutes of Oratory; or, Education of an Orator*. Translated by Rev. John Selby Watson. London: George Bell and Sons, 1907.

Randall, Randolph C. "Authors of the *Port Folio* Revealed by the Hall Files." *American Literature* 11, No. 4 (1940): 379–416. Accessed April 9, 2020. doi:10.2307/2920854

Rescher, Nicholas. *Aporetics: Rational Deliberation in the Face of Inconsistency*. Pittsburgh: University of Pittsburgh Press, 2009.

Reston, Jr., James. *The Lone Star: The Life of John Connally*. New York: Harper and Row, 1989.

Robertson, Adriana. "Passive in Name Only: Delegated Management and 'Index' Investing." *36 Yale Journal on Regulation 795.* 2019. Available at SSRN: https://ssrn.com/abstract=3244991

Rogers, John. *The Matter of Revolution: Science, Poetry, and Politics in the Age of Milton.* Ithaca, NY: Cornell University Press, 1998.

Rorty, Richard. *Philosophy and the Mirror of Nature.* Princeton, NJ: Princeton University Press, 1979.

Rycroft, Chris H.; and Martin Z. Bazant. "Lecture 1: Introduction to Random Walks and Diffusion," Department of Mathematics, Massachusetts Institute of Technology, February 1, 2005. https://ocw.mit.edu/courses/mathematics/18-366-random-walks-and-diffusion-fall-2006/lecture-notes/lec01.pdf

Safire, William. *Before the Fall: An Inside View of the Pre-Watergate White House.* New York: Belmont Tower Books, 1975.

Sahlins, Marshall. *Stone Age Economics.* New York: Aldine Publishing Company, 1972.

Saussure, Ferdinand de. *Course in General Linguistics.* Translated by Wade Baskin. New York: Philosophical Library, 1959.

Sayre, Gordon, ed. *American Captivity Narratives: Olaudah Equiano, Mary Rowlandson, and Others.* Boston, New York: Houghton Mifflin Co., 2000.

Schmandt-Besserat, Denise. "The Evolution of Writing." https://sites.utexas.edu/dsb/tokens/the-evolution-of-writing/

Seaford, Richard. *Money and the Early Greek Mind: Homer, Philosophy, Tragedy.* Cambridge: Cambridge University Press, 2004.

The Second Bank of the United States: A Chapter in the History of Central Banking. Philadelphia: Federal Reserve Bank of Philadelphia, 2010.

Seemann, O. *The Mythology of Greece and Rome with Special Reference to Its Use in Art.* New York: Harper and Brothers, Publishers, 1877.

Seltman, Charles. *A Book of Greek Coins.* London: Penguin Books, 1952.

Shakespeare, William. *Macbeth.* New York: Signet Classics, 1998.

Shaw, George Bernard. *The Perfect Wagnerite: A Commentary on the Niblung's Ring.* New York: Brentano's, 1909.

Shell, Marc. *Money, Language, and Thought: Literary and Philosophic Economies from the Medieval to the Modern Era.* Baltimore and London: Johns Hopkins University Press, 1982.

Shultz, George P.; and Dam, Kenneth W. *Economic Policy Beyond the Headlines.* Stanford: Stanford Alumni Association, 1977.

Simmel, Georg. *The Philosophy of Money.* Translated by David Frisby. London and New York: Routledge, 1978.

Smith, Adam. *An Inquiry into the Nature and Causes of the Wealth of Nations.* New York: The Modern Library, 1937.

Smith, Bryant. "Legal Personality." digitalcommons.law.yale.edu/ylj/vol37/iss3/1

Spengler, Oswald. *The Decline of the West.* Translated by Charles Francis Atkinson. Oxford: Oxford University Press, 1991.

Spenser, Edmund. *The Faerie Queene.* New York: Penguin Classics, 1979.

Stevens, Wallace. *The Palm at the End of the Mind: Selected Poems and Play.* New York: Vintage, 1990.

Sypher, Wylie. *Comedy, Including an Essay on Comedy by George Meredith; Laughter by Henri Bergson; "The Meanings of Comedy" by Wylie Sypher.* New York: Doubleday Anchor, 1956.

Tawney, Richard. "Puritanism and Capitalism." *The New Republic*, May 12, 1926.

Temin, Peter. *The Economic Consequences of the Bank War: An Analysis of the Inflation of the 1830s.* Working paper, Alfred P. Sloan School of Management. Boston: Massachusetts Institute of Technology, 1967.

Thoreau, Henry David. *Walden and Other Writings.* New York: Modern Library, 1992.

Thunder, Ailbhe. "Fictions of Finance: Economic Narrative in Contemporary Culture." PhD diss., Cardiff University, 2006.

Todd, Tim. *The Balance of Power: The Political Fight for an Independent Central Bank, 1790–Present.* Kansas City, MO: Public Affairs Department of The Federal Reserve Bank of Kansas City, 2012.

Todorov, Tzvetan; and Arnold Weinstein. "Structural Analysis of Narrative." *NOVEL: A Forum on Fiction* 3, No. 1 (1969): 70–76. Accessed April 11, 2020. doi:10.2307/1345003

Torre, Jose. *The Political Economy of Sentiment.* London: Pickering & Chatto, 2007.

Triffin, Robert. *Gold and the Dollar Crisis.* New Haven, CT: Yale University Press, 1960.

———. "Gold and the Dollar Crisis: Yesterday and Tomorrow." *Essays in International Finance,* No. 132. Princeton, NJ: Princeton University Department of Economics, 1979.

Trump, Donald; and Schwartz, Tony. *Trump: The Art of the Deal.* New York: Ballantine Books, 2015.

Turgot, Anne Robert Jacques. *The Economics of A. R. J. Turgot.* Translated by P. D. Groenewegen. The Hague: Martinus Nijhoff, 1977.

Updike, John. *Rabbit Is Rich.* New York: Random House, 1981.

Vaihinger, Hans. *The Philosophy of As If: A System of the Theoretical, Practical and Religious Fictions of Mankind.* Translated by C. K. Ogden. New York: Harcourt, Brace and Company, 1925.

Varenius, Björn. "The Hedeby Coinage." http://www.arkeologiskasa fundet.se/csa/Dokument/Volumes/csa_vol_2_1994/csa_vol_2_1994_ s185-193_varenius.pdf

Wagner, Richard. *Das Rheingold in Full Score.* New York: Dover, 1985.

Warburton, Christopher. *The Development of International Monetary Policy.* New York: Routledge, 2018.

Weinberger, Caspar W. with Gretchen Roberts. *In the Arena: A Memoir of the 20th Century.* Washington, DC: Regnery Publishing, Inc., 2001.

Weinel, Heinrich. "Richard Wagner and Christianity." *The American Journal of Theology,* Vol. 7, No. 4 (October 1903): 609–634.

Whitehead, Frank. "Roland Barthes's Narratology." *The Cambridge Quarterly* 21, No. 1 (1992): 41–64. Accessed April 11, 2020. www.jstor.org/stable/42971737

Williams, Steven. Personal interview, July 6, 2017.

Wolfe, Tom. *Bonfire of the Vanities.* New York: Picador, 1987.

Woodmansee, Martha; and Osteen, Mark, editors. *The New Economic Criticism: Studies at the Intersection of Literature and Economics.* London and New York: Routledge, 1999.

Zoeller, Christoffer; and Bendelj, Nina. "Crisis as Opportunity: Nixon's Announcement to Close the Gold Window." *Socius: Sociological Research for A Dynamic World*, Vol. 5 (2019): 1–14.

Zuckerman, Gregory. *The Greatest Trade Ever.* New York: Crown Books, 2009.

image credits

FREDERICK KAUFMAN, an English professor by training and profession, has for the past decade focused his attention on the fiction that is money. His unorthodox insights into the ways of Wall Street have resulted in numerous magazine articles for publications ranging from *Scientific American* to *Wired* to *Foreign Policy* to *Harper's*, as well as television appearances on NBC, Bloomberg, Fox Business Network, and *Democracy Now!*, and invitations to lecture in both the United States and Europe, including an address to the General Assembly of the United Nations. This is his fourth book.